The Bitter End

'There must be no thought of saving the troops or sparing the population. The battle must be fought to the bitter end at all costs . . . Commanders and senior officers should die with their troops . . .'

from Winston Churchill's
signal to General Sir Archibald Wavell,
10 February 1942.

The Bitter End

Richard Holmes

AND

Anthony Kemp

ANTONY BIRD PUBLICATIONS

First published 1982 by

ANTONY BIRD PUBLICATIONS LTD
Strettington House, Strettington, Chichester

British Library Cataloguing in Publication Data

Holmes, Richard
    The bitter end: the fall of Singapore
    1941–1942.
    1. World War, 1939–1945 – Campaigns – Malay
    Peninsular
    2. Singapore – Siege, 1942.
    I. Title II. Kemp, Anthony
    940.54'25   D767.55

ISBN 0 907319 03 3

Designed by John Mitchell
Printed in Great Britain by
Clarke, Doble and Brendon
at Plymouth

CONTENTS

LIST OF PLATES

Between pages 76 and 77

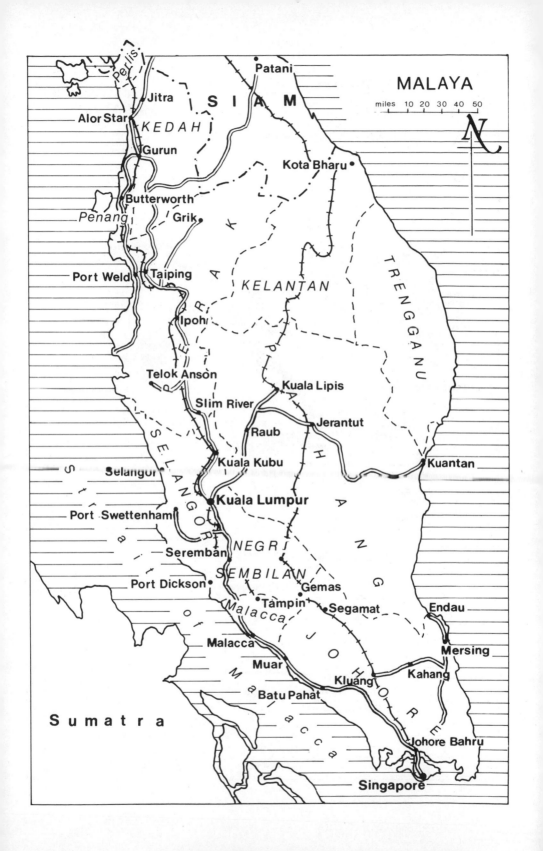

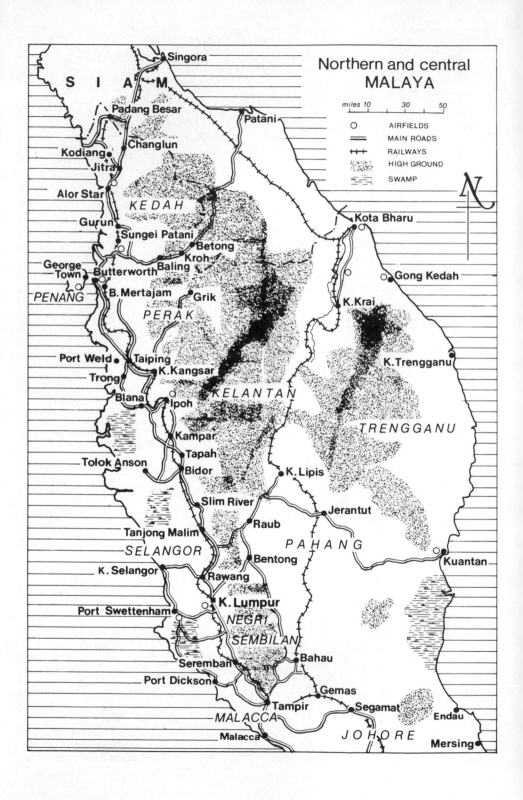

Northern and central
MALAYA

miles 10   30   50

○ AIRFIELDS
— MAIN ROADS
+++ RAILWAYS
HIGH GROUND
SWAMP

S I A M

Singora
Padang Besar
Patani
Changlun
Kodiang
Jitra
Alor Star
KEDAH
Gurun
Kota Bharu
Sungei Patani
Betong
Kroh
Gong Kedah
George Town
Butterworth
Baling
PENANG
B. Mertajam
Grik
K.Krai
PERAK
Port Weld
Taiping
K.Kangsar
K.Trengganu
Trong
Blana
Ipoh
KELANTAN
TRENGGANU
Kampar
Tapah
Tolok Anson
Bidor
K. Lipis
Slim River
Jerantut
Raub
Tanjong Malim
PAHANG
SELANGOR
Bentong
Kuantan
K. Selangor
Rawang
Port Swettenham
K. Lumpur
NEGRI
SEMBILAN
Seremban
Bahau
Port Dickson
Gemas
Tampir
Segamat
Endau
MALACCA
JOHORE
Malacca
Mersing

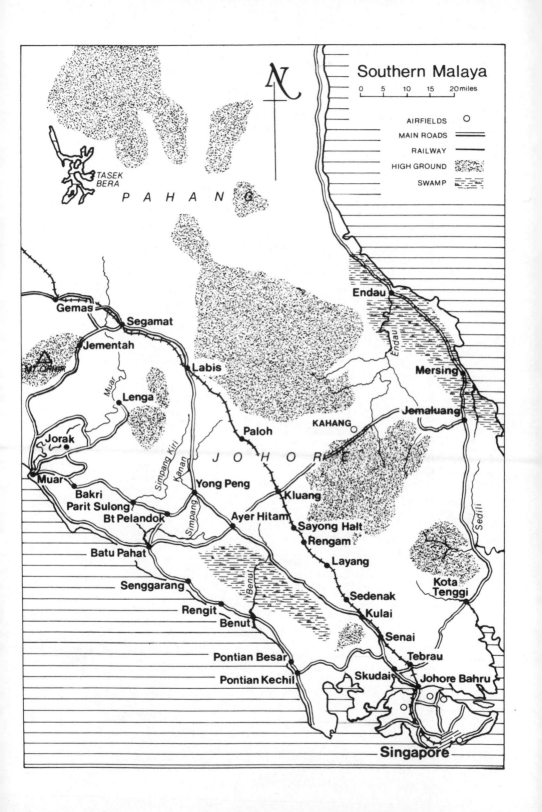

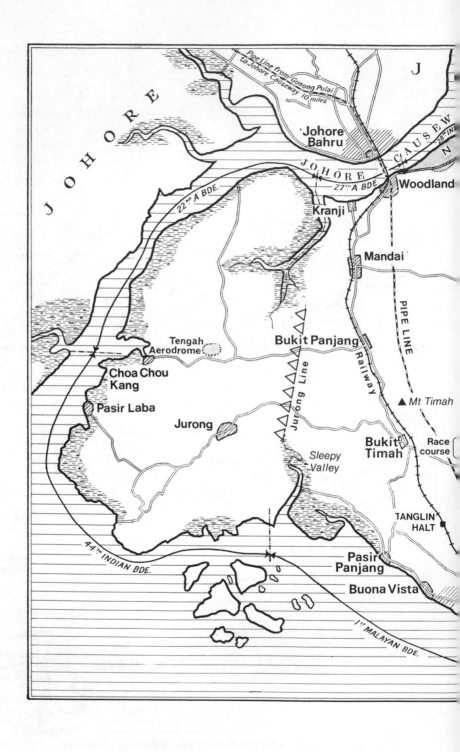

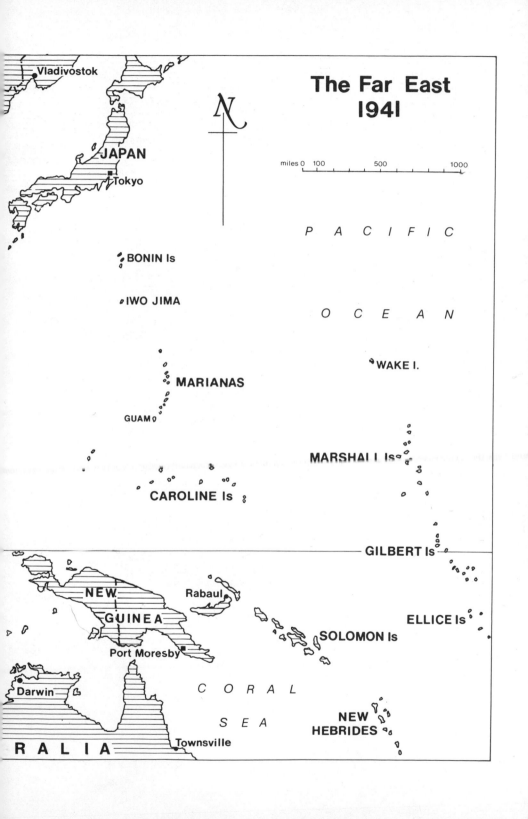

The Far East 1941

miles 0   100   500   1000

Vladivostok

JAPAN

Tokyo

BONIN Is

IWO JIMA

P A C I F I C

O C E A N

MARIANAS

GUAM

WAKE I.

MARSHALL Is

CAROLINE Is

GILBERT Is

NEW

GUINEA

Rabaul

Port Moresby

SOLOMON Is

ELLICE Is

Darwin

C O R A L

S E A

NEW
HEBRIDES

RALIA

Townsville

1

FORTY YEARS ON

'THIS country really dropped us in the shit, didn't it?' said Geoffrey
Adams, once a subaltern in the ill-fated 18th Division, when asked what
his feelings were at the moment of surrender at Singapore. That
capitulation, forty years ago on 15 February 1942, was described by
Winston Churchill as 'the worst disaster and largest capitulation in
British military history.' Commander Stephen King-Hall, speaking in
the House of Commons, was equally blunt, calling it 'the greatest
surrender in numbers of troops in the whole history of the British army.'
Hard words were used at the time, and retrospect has done little to
soften them: even today, the bitterness and resentment linger on.

It is an odd quirk of national character that the British are often
able to delude themselves that their defeats were, in fact, glorious
victories. The 'spirit of Dunkirk' is summoned up with remarkable
frequency; schoolboys learn of the death of Sir John Moore at Corunna,
though their masters sometimes omit to tell them that Sir John died as
his army was being booted neck and crop out of Spain after a fruitless
campaign; and speak to an Englishman of the Crimean War, and he will
undoubtedly call to mind the Charge of the Light Brigade, the very
epitome of the heroic disaster. Lord Strabolgi, in a book published
shortly after the Malaya campaign, wrote:

This over-caution, this over-emphasis on defensive tactics, this eulogising of
successful evacuations of fighting armies after defeat in the field, is another form
of defeatism. It is the British manifestation of the disease which struck down
France. . . . Probably the worst and most spectacular symptom of the evil was
the campaign in Malaya and the surrender of Singapore Island.

The surrender itself was a somewhat low-key event, coming at the
end of a campaign that had lasted only seventy days. The Japanese
photograph of the surrender party, showing a dismal-looking group of
British officers with flapping shorts and rather incongruous tin hats,
carrying a limp Union Jack, has become the classic popular image of the

disaster. But, as historians and veterans alike have been swift to point out, that limp flag signified a good deal more than merely a military defeat.

It was the end of an era in Asia: a major colonial power had been publicly humiliated by a native race. As Ken Harrison, who fought in the campaign as a sergeant in 8th Australian Division put it:

After Singapore, Asia changed. For the British it could never be the same again.

The historian James Leasor made the same point in his book *Singapore: The Battle that Changed the World:*

the surrender marked the end of the white man's inherent supremacy over the coloured man – the Western rulers, the Eastern ruled – a legend virtually unchallenged before.

At the time, however, it was the immediate military consequences of the surrender that attracted attention. The news whipped up a storm of rhetoric in Parliament, the newspapers were deluged with letters, and a number of books were written in the immediate aftermath. The people of Britain were hungry for scapegoats and the Government was driven onto the defensive. Some saw the defeat as more than merely the consequence of poor generalship or indifferent strategy, and mounted an attack upon the capitalist system which had, in their eyes, drawn up the blueprint for catastrophe. Mr Sloane, MP for South Ayrshire, attacked the supposed rapacity of expatriate businessmen in the Far East. He complained bitterly that:

these ornaments of British capitalism have done more to degrade Britain in the eyes of the East than any scoundrels since our depredations in Africa. These tin, rubber and oil companies have exploited the bodies and souls of the natives of the Far East. Those natives have lived in poverty and misery, and the only crime they have committed is to be born in the richest country in the world.

He went on to refer to Malaya as 'the greatest sink of corruption in the world,' and described the business community as 'a swindling gang of sharks.'

Churchill was forced to promise an official enquiry, but this never took place. The war against Hitler went on, and events in the Far East assumed a lesser significance. Indeed, it seemed almost as if this theatre of war was deliberately played down: not for nothing did 'Bill' Slim's 14th Army in Burma call itself 'The Forgotten Army.' But if politicians became preoccupied with other issues, ordinary people still had their own opinions to voice. A series of radio plays about the life of Christ had been broadcast in December 1941, inspired someone to write sternly to the *Radio Times:*

Sir. The fall of Singapore to the Japanese is surely God's judgement upon the British people for allowing the BBC to disseminate this blasphemous outrage.

Just what was the extent of the disaster that provoked so much bitter comment? Approximately 140,000 British and Commonwealth troops were involved in the campaign. Of these, some 9,000 were killed, a few managed to get away, and about 130,000 were taken prisoner. These figures do not include European civilians who were interned, or the large numbers of natives killed by bombing and shelling or otherwise disposed of by the conquerors. As far as the Japanese were concerned, they used three divisions totalling some 55,000 men to achieve their victory, and lost only 3,500 killed in the eight weeks of the campaign. As their reward, they captured vast quantities of much-needed raw materials and military stores, and struck a fatal blow against western prestige in the Far East.

The sheer scale of the catastrophe is stunning even today. Not only did it involve the defeat and capture of a large British army, but it also brought about the destruction of a well-established way of life. Nor was the defeat confined to the land. The RAF, so recently fêted for its victory over the *Luftwaffe,* was swept from the skies above Malaya by an air force which had hitherto been regarded as a joke in rather questionable taste. The navy did not escape scot-free. The loss of *Prince of Wales* and *Repulse* was particularly hard to bear. Britannia no longer ruled the waves: she had surrendered her trident to a bunch of anonymous men who flew torpedo-bombers.

It is extremely difficult, even after forty years, to write a balanced account of events in Malaya and Singapore: the wounds are still deep. Even today, speaking to survivors, one becomes aware of the need to apportion blame, and to defend long-cherished opinions to which the passage of time has given the status of fact. Major-General Woodburn Kirby, Official Historian of the campaign, wrote *Singapore: The Chain of Disaster,* in which he gave vent to far harsher judgements than those contained in the Official History. 'One can sum up,' he wrote.

by saying that those responsible for the conduct of the land campaign in Malaya committed every conceivable blunder.

Participants in the campaign were even more outspoken. A former Australian warrant officer spoke of the 'pathos, cowardice and high-level deception' which characterised the defeat, while another Australian complained, with typically antipodean directness, that: 'The High Command was too bloody old, full of ancient Indian Army colonels.'

In his book *Singapore Story,* Kenneth Attiwill, himself a veteran of

3

the campaign, described the search for scapegoats. 'During and after the fighting,' he wrote,

we felt resentful. In the prison camps we always swore there would be a big showdown when we came home and told our story. We were not to blame. We blamed those in authority, the British Government, the generals. Some people blamed the Australians, the Chinese, the Malays, the civilians; others blamed the Navy, the Army, the Air Force.

Soldiers accused civilians of obstructivness and greed, and civilians reciprocated by lambasting the blimpishness and inefficiency of the armed forces.

The leading actors in the tragedy have inevitably come in for more than a little criticism. At the very top of the pyramid was the Governor and nominal Commander-in-Chief, Sir Miles Shenton Thomas, upon whose shoulders much of the blame for the defeat has been heaped. Portrayed by many as a blunderer and a fool, he never publicly answered his critics, although a series of notes in his private papers, refuting the charges made against him in the Official History, demonstrate a high degree of common sense. All those who knew him regarded him as being affable and approachable, a man who got on well with the European and Asian communities. He was not an intellectual or a particularly dynamic personality: indeed, if had been, he might have been suspect to his masters at the Colonial Office. In many ways he typifies generations of worthy colonial administrators and, but for the accident of war, he would have returned home to a well-deserved peerage and a comfortable retirement.

Ian Morrison, the *Times* correspondent in Singapore, described Sir Shenton as being:

a good solid official who had spent much of his life administering our African colonies. He took his responsibilities to the native population seriously and the Chinese leaders knew that he would not let them down. He had that stolid British doggedness. But he was not a realistic thinker or even a very clear-headed one. He was sanguine to the verge of complacency. He had risen to his position, not by virtue of any outstanding ability, but by dint of long years of steady conscientious work. There was no colour or forcefulness about him nor much decisiveness. . . . The Governor was the last man to rally people in a crisis and inspire them to suffering, sacrifice and heroism.

But there is another side to the Governor's character. His very doggedness caused him to stay on to the end, despite suggestions that he should be evacuated. His wife, Lady Thomas, busy to the last with war work, fell ill and spent three and a half years in captivity, separated from her husband. When the end came, Sir Shenton, dressed in open-necked shirt and shorts, joined the rest of the civilians on the cricket field and walked with them to captivity. He must have been tough to survive imprisonment, which included spells of solitary confinement for non-cooperation with the Japanese.

Another attractive target for the critics is Air Chief Marshal Sir Robert Brooke-Popham, recalled from retirement on the outbreak of war and appointed Commander-in-Chief in the Far East in October 1940, at the age of 62. In this capacity he served until replaced at the end of December 1941 – in the middle of the battle. Major-General Woodburn Kirby wrote of him:

He was . . . very dependent on his staff, for he had developed the habit of falling asleep at any time of day and often in the middle of a conference at which he presided, therefore often missing much of the subject under discussion. Although a man of great charm, he had clearly passed his prime and was not a forceful enough personality to deal with this complicated and difficult situation.

The above, however, tells only part of the story. Brooke-Popham was not a fool, but his hands were tied. His authority as Commander-in-Chief was narrowly circumscribed. He pressed time and time again for adequate reinforcement of modern aircraft, but the Far East had a low priority. On the one hand he was ordered not to provoke the Japanese, but on the other he was required to maintain an adequate state of preparations for war. Many greater men would also have come to grief.

Perhaps the most familiar character in the drama is Lieutenant-General A. E. Percival, who was appointed GOC Malaya in April 1941. Sent out to do what many regarded as an impossible job, this unfortunate general has since been heaped with reproaches, and in the eyes of many he is still the buck-toothed incompetent who lost the campaign. An obvious candidate for the unattractive post of scapegoat, Percival was no 'character' who went down in a last stand yelling defiance at his enemy. Rather, he was a sober staff officer who weighed up the situation and decided to surrender rather than cause appalling – and probably pointless – suffering, especially to the Asian citizens of Singapore.

This decision was typical of a man who most would agree was both considerate and honourable. He refused the chance to escape and joined his men in captivity – a path not all senior officers followed. But Morrison summed up his character as being 'completely negative, with no vigour, no colour, and no conviction.' Admittedly the odds against his success were enormous, but had he shown more drive and less blandness, the verdict of history might well have been different.

Myths and misconceptions cluster around the story of Singapore like vultures round a corpse. It is often asserted that the place was a fortress whose guns pointed the wrong way. But Singapore was never a fortress in the proper sense of the word, designed to withstand attack from any direction. A naval base was built on the North coast of Singapore Island and, under the assumption that the only possible attack could come from the sea, large coastal guns were installed to fire seawards. When the Japanese actually attacked from the North, most of the guns were traversed to fire inland. The problem was that they had mostly the wrong kind of ammunition – armour-piercing rounds to deal with the armoured hulls of warships rather than the high-explosive needed for effective use against land targets. Had they had the right ammuniton, the guns would only have been able to delay, rather than avert, the final outcome. There was more than a little truth in General Sir Ian Hamilton's 1925 comment: 'We have built a half-fortress and are proposing to half-garrison it.'

Another oft-stated accusation is that the troops fought badly, which naturally wounds those who took part in a number of bitter struggles. There were, of course, villains as well as heroes. We shall see some ugly scenes at the quayside where armed parties of deserters stormed onto some of the last ships to leave the beleaguered island. That some of the guilty ones were Australians received wide publicity, as did the precipitate flight of RAF ground crews from some of the up-country airfields. There was no glory to be had in being captured at Singapore. Those who staggered back from Dunkirk – where there were some scenes reminiscent of the worst moments at Sinagpore – were welcomed as heroes, and bought pints in pubs all over England. What would have happened to them if there had been no little ships to pick them up, sheltering under the protective cloud of Spitfires and Hurricanes? Would the reputations of men like Alanbrooke, Alexander and Montgomery have survived intact?

The truth is that many of the defenders of Malaya did well when one considers the handicaps under which they were operating: a school second eleven thrown into a match against a First Division club. Lieutenant-Colonel Dennis Russell-Roberts wrote:

It is perhaps difficult for most people to realise the immensity of that retreat. It was far longer and of greater duration than either the Retreat from Mons or to Dunkirk. It was carried out in far worse climatic conditions, without any armour, almost completely without air support and without a Navy, perhaps the most vital consideration of the lot in the defence of a long peninsula.

The performance of British and Indian troops was sometimes patchy, but it is hard to fault the sustained fortitude of Lieutenant-Colonel Stewart's 2nd Argyll and Sutherland Highlanders, or the desperate

6

valour of Captain Graham's Sikhs and Gujars of 1/8th Punjab at Kampar.

Another hoary old legend is that of the whisky-swilling planter, fostered by the tales of Somerset Maugham. A few there certainly were, but probably neither more nor less than in any expatriate British community then or now. The bulk of the Europeans in Malaya worked hard in an enervating climate. Drinking was a normal social occupation, and in the extreme heat and humidity vast quantities of *stengahs* and Tiger beer were consumed, without apparent ill effects. After the outbreak of war in Europe Malaya was known as the 'dollar arsenal', and a considerable part of Britain's war effort in the early years was financed by Malaya's exports of tin and rubber.

This was the prime purpose of the white community – to produce the goods. In addition, however, all Europeans were involved in some sort of war work. After a long day the men turned out for training in the volunteers or the civil defence organisations, and the women busied themselves with fund-raising. Malaya and Singapore produced large sums of money to help finance the war effort. Patriotism was the order of the day after September 1939. Charity games were a favourite method of fund-raising, and 'rasketball' proved extremely popular. This was a free-for-all played with a team of ten men versus fifteen women. The rules stipulated that you could do anything to the ball, 'even positively hate it', as long as you did not 'sit on it, lie with it, cuddle it, puncture it or burst it.'

All this good clean fun typified the attitude of a group of people who lived together, in an often hostile environment, far away from home. When the crisis came a few slunk away, but the vast majority did their best under trying circumstances, and it is only fair to state that most of them lost everything they owned. While the families of military prisoners were looked after, the evacuated wives of many employees of commercial firms ended up in Britain penniless. Mrs Vera Magnay, for example, was married to a temporary employee of the Admiralty, who volunteered to stay behind in Singapore while she was evacuated to Ceylon. She arrived there with no money and with only one suitcase, and was forced to find a job. Discovering that she was pregnant, she managed to get back to England. 'All I got from their gracious Lords Commissioners of the Admiralty,' she recalled, 'was £11 per month to keep myself and the baby:' Her husband returned home after the war:

a very sick man. All he came home to was three hundred pounds. He was so utterly disgusted with his treatment from the Admiralty, and my treatment.

Businessman Montague Selfe returned from captivity having had no pay at all from his firm. 'I didn't get a damn thing,' he remarked with understandable asperity. All he did receive was £60.00 from the Government as compensation for a finger that was amputated in Changi prison. One could quote a number of similar cases, and it is hard to resist the conclusion that a number of commercial concerns based in Britain behaved disgracefully towards their expatriate staff.

The military prisoners of war and civilian internees emerged long after the 'real' war in Europe was finished, after three and a half years of incarceration under conditions of the most appalling degradation and deprivation. Many of them were broken physically, owing either to the brutality of their guards or the ravages of tropical diseases which raged in the prison camps. Others were never to recover from the psychological impact of the horror which had surrounded them. Their return to England was not always a matter of wine and roses. One of the prisoners wrote of his return in 1945:

I was getting off a bus in my home town when a person I knew very well got off, dressed in the uniform of the Home Guard, flashes up. His first words after a greeting were not of welcome, but: 'this is the uniform you should have been wearing. We defended our country while you were sitting on your backside in a prisoner of war camp in Singapore.'

Ours is by no means the first attempt to tell the dismal story of the fall of Singapore. Of the more academic studies, Raymond Callahan's *The Worst Disaster,* Louis Allen's *Singapore 1941–1942,* and Woodburn Kirby's *Singapore: The Chain of Disaster,* deserve honourable mention. There are also a number of accounts based either upon personal experience, like Kenneth Harrison's *The Brave Japanese* and Betty Jeffrey's *White Coolies,* or upon collected eye witness accounts, like Kenneth Attiwill's *Singapore Story.* We have attempted to strike a useful balance between sober military history and the vivid accounts of survivors. During our research we have been fortunate in gaining access to a considerable amount of previously unpublished testimony, and have conducted a large number of interviews with survivors: where possible, we allow the participants to speak for themselves. We make no claim to expunge all the question marks hanging over the campaign, but hope to be able to shed some light upon the mournful episode.

History is, above all, about people, and we can do no better than to follow the example of Ian Morrison, who dedicated his book, *Malayan Postscript,* to:

Tens of thousands of men, of many races, (who) fought and bled and died in the Malayan jungle in an effort that was to prove, through no fault of their own, vain.

2

AN EMPIRE TO DEFEND

Singapore . . . is one of the most important strategic positions in the world, and certainly the most important in the whole of Asia. A naval Power securely established at Singapore commands the Straits of Malacca. Through these straits pass the shipping sailing between the Indian and Pacific Oceans, and through these straits passes the direct trade route between the Dutch East Indies, Australasia and Europe via the Suez Canal. In a war between the British Empire and Japan . . . the importance of Singapore as a naval and air base cannot be exaggerated. Yet no naval and air Power can be secure at Singapore unless Malaya is firmly held. . . .

The above was written by Lord Strabolgi at the time of the loss of Malaya and Singapore, and to a certain extent it is still true in the strategic sense even today. Before the Second World War, British planners were very much aware of the importance of Singapore, but this was considered in the Imperial sense rather than as a problem for local defence. The true significance of Malaya as the 'dollar arsenal', producing vital strategic goods, did not really sink in until war with Germany broke out. The great naval base was built to protect the trade routes and British colonies in the East in the broadest sense, and not for the specific defence of the colony.

However, in order to be able to place the events of 1941-2 in their true perspective, it is necessary to understand how Malaya and Singapore became British possessions in the first place, and the steps taken to defend them.

The first colonisers in the area were the Portuguese who arrived with cannon and Christianity, in search of converts and spices. An advance party made a reconnaissance to Malacca in 1509, but was beaten off by the natives. Two years later a large fleet commanded by d'Albuquerque returned to the scene, and after a bitter battle and subsequent butchery of the inhabitants, the town was captured. The new masters then proceeded to fortify their prize and to construct churches by the dozen. One of the early visitors was Francis Xavier, founder of the Jesuit order, who was based in Malacca from 1546 to 1551. When he finally left on a mission to China, he was so horrified at the settlers' morals that he shook the dust of the place from his feet.

Although in those early days, vast trading fortunes were made, this could not disguise the fact that the Portuguese empire was in decline. At the beginning of the 17th century, new and covetous rivals began to appear on the scene in ever increasing numbers – the Dutch and the English. At first they restricted themselves to piracy by capturing Portuguese shipping on the high seas, but they soon cast envious eyes upon the source of all this wealth and contemplated the breaking of the monopoly.

Early attempts at settlement by the English proved abortive, and after the massacre of their garrison at Amboyna by the Dutch in 1623, they contented themselves with the exploitation of India. The Dutch then passed over to the attack, and after a lengthy siege, captured Malacca in 1641. The Portuguese were unable to effect its relief by sending a fleet from European waters – shades of 1942. The Dutch then proceeded to erect a new monopoly in their own favour, and during the following century, engaged in numerous petty wars with the native states in the Malay peninsula.

Holland, however, was itself waning as a power and its officials in the East grew fat on corruption. The British East India Company began once again to turn its attention to the spice trade of the East Indies and to look for a suitable naval base from which to conduct its wars against the French. Here again we have an example of the wider strategic implications of the area.

In 1772, a certain Captain Light arrived in Kedah, and from the local Sultan he received the offer of the island of Penang in return for the Company's protection. The latter was initially unimpressed and it was not until 1786 that the East India Company formally took possession of the small swampy island. It was originally called Prince of Wales Island in honour of the future George IV, but this name soon fell into disuse, and the native name Penang (which literally means Betel Nut) was substituted.

For years, the fate of the Penang settlement hung in the balance. The East India Company was unsure of its value, but both population and the volume of trade increased steadily. In 1805 it was upgraded into a Presidency, and the post of Assistant Secretary was offered to one Thomas Stamford Raffles.

Raffles prospered in the Company's service and in 1817 he became the Lieutenant-Governor of Bencoolen. It was at this stage in his career that he turned his attention to finding a base that was better placed strategically than Penang, and his eye lighted upon the uninhabited swampy island known to the natives as Singapore – the Lion Gate. Acting more or less on his own initiative, Raffles did a deal with the Sultan of Johore, leasing the place in return for an annual payment. In 1819 he wrote:

Singapore is everything we could desire, it will soon rise in importance. It possesses an excellent harbour and everything that can be desired for a British port. . . . We have commanded an intercourse with all the ships passing through the Straits of Singapore. We are within a week's sail of China, close to Siam, and in the very seat of the Malayan Empire.

Expansion of the trading post was rapid, and in spite of Dutch protests, the Company was forced to accept responsibility for the new acquisition.

The foregoing paragraphs of background history have not been concerned with the blossoming of the British Empire in the Far East, but rather with the purely trading concerns of the East India Company – which maintained its own armed forces to defend its legitimate interests. Penang and Singapore were trading posts and it was Company policy not to get involved in the interior, where the native states existed in a state of near-anarchy throughout most of the 19th century. When the Company ceased to exist in 1858, the Government of India took over British interests in Malaya, and in 1867, responsibility passed to the Colonial Office in London.

In the long run, however, it proved impossible to remain aloof, and step by step, the British government became involved in the interior, for a peaceful hinterland was a necessary adjunct to prosperous commerce. Various treaties had to be made with native rulers, but it was not until 1873 that intervention became active. The chiefs in Perak were forced to accept a British Resident, and one by one the other states followed suit. By 1909, the area which we refer to as Malaya was entirely under British protection.

Singapore had been defended from the very beginning, and in Raffles' time an earthen battery had been constructed on the shoreline by the harbour. The first of the permanent forts was Fort Fullerton, started in 1829 on the site of what is now the Fullerton Building. This work proved unpopular with the merchant community as it was sited near the city warehouses and 'it was feared that it might well draw fire onto the area if the city was attacked from the sea'. This is an early instance of the business community tending to put profit before the general interests of defence.

Throughout the 19th century, forts and batteries were built, with the main emphasis being placed on the defence of the harbour area from a seaward attack. Fort Canning, for many years the garrison headquarters, was started in 1859 and took two years to build. In 1854 the first volunteer unit was formed from the European community, designed to act in case of civil commotion. This was the forerunner of various self-defence forces which tended to function as rather exlusive clubs for the white male residents, until general mobilisation was decreed in 1940.

By the 1930's the political set-up was somewhat complicated. The Straits Settlements, comprising Singapore, the territory of Malacca, Penang Island and a strip of land on the mainland opposite known as Province Wellesley, were a Crown Colony ruled by a governor responsible to the Colonial Office. That same governor was the High Commissioner for the Malay States – the Federated States (Perak, Selangor, Negri Sembilan and Pahang) and the Unfederated States (Kedah, Perlis, Kelantan, Trengganu and Johore). Each of these was nominally under its native ruler with a British Resident or British Adviser, answerable through the Governor/High Commissioner to the Foreign Office.

Malaya is shaped like an elongated lozenge with an area slightly larger than England and Wales combined. To the North, it is attached to Thailand by a narrow neck of land, Singapore, the island at the southernmost tip, is similar to the Isle of Wight in size and shape. Three quarters of the land mass is covered with tropical rain forest – vast areas of stiflingly humid jungle spread over a mountainous spine. The coastal plains are fertile but often swampy and the actual coast is a mixture of sandy beaches and tangled mangrove thickets. The east coast is the least hospitable, and as a result, most development in terms of roads, railways and population has tended to be concentrated in the West. The main industries (and exports) were rubber and tin.

In 1940, the population amounted to some five and a half million, mostly Chinese and Malays each with some two and a quarter million. The third largest racial group were the Tamil Indians (750,000) and right on top of the pyramid there were 31,000 Europeans.

Singapore was the heart of this polyglot community, a teeming city with extremes of poverty, degradation and squalor, contrasting with the vast wealth of a small section of society. The Island is joined to neighbouring Johore by a casuseway carrying a road and rail link. The commercial harbour in the South was crowded with sampans, and from the godowns (warehouses) on the shore, the commerce of the orient flowed out all over the world. The reeking overcrowded native quarters seething in the oppressive heat provided a contract to the calm beauty of the European residential areas where the *tuans* lived.

Who were these *tuans*? The majority were British expatriates who had gone there either to administer or to make money. Based in the towns were the government officials, the bankers, the merchants and their employees. Up-country were the rubber planters, mine overseers and district officials scattered over vast areas. Like their compatriots in other colonies they created a life for themselves that was completely separate from that of the indigenous inhabitants. Snobbishness naturally played a part, but in reality there was no community of interest between Europeans and Orientals – many of whom were extremely rich in their own right.

European life in Malaya and Singapore revolved around the clubs, the main hotels and the department stores – microcosms of middle class life in Britain in the 1930's. Singapore boasted an Anglican cathedral and the other denominations were naturally represented in force. The ladies went shopping at Robinsons and the Cold Stores, and drank their morning coffee there, meeting their friends. Raffles Hotel was an oasis of slightly dowdy palm court splendour, and any impudent soldier who ventured there would be firmly removed.

Gunner Russell Braddon went to Raffles armed with a letter of introduction to a family friend. He entered, ignoring the Out of Bounds sign and sat waiting. A woman entered and noticed this Australian soldier:

'Boy,' she called. The drinks waiter came running. 'Tell that soldier,' she said in the clear, ringing tones of the very rich when talking about the very poor whom they fondly imagine to be deaf, 'that he's out of bounds in here and ask him to leave'.

On Singapore Island, the Tanglin Club, the Cricket Club and the Swimming Club where all popular. Nothing as vulgar as money changed hands. One signed a chit for everything and the worst insult was for a white man to be regarded as 'pencil shy' – being unwilling to stand his round. There was seldom any need for this, however, as money was fairly plentiful and life was not unduly expensive.

At this time and age, it is easy to sneer at the petty prejudices of the expatriate community, but the fact remains that they were pioneers and the Empire they created, although often narrow-minded was not a vicious one. Anne Kennaway (now Mrs. Anne Scott) went back to Malaya in 1940 after schooling in England, to rejoin her father, who she described in an unpublished manuscript:

Escot (the family rubber estate) was a patriarchal kingdom. My father ruled the welfare of everyone in it. He provided homes for his labourers and was responsible for their health and schools for their children. He adjudicated in their family quarrels, rescued Cookie from his gambling debts and was the final arbitrator in any disagreement. He was trusted absolutely and his word was law.

Many of the settlers were expatriates in the true sense of the word, whose only homes were in Malaya and whose ties with 'home' were nebulous. The climate was suitable for white women, many of whom accompanied their husbands, but it was difficult for children. White children grew up pale and sickly, and were thus sent back to boarding schools in England to complete their education. Often they were accompanied by their mothers, and thus many men lived lonely lives out on the plantations or in the city clubs.

One attempt to alleviate the problems of climate was the establishment of a hill station in the Cameron Highlands, which boasted a hotel, golf course and an Inn. Several Europeans built retirement bungalows there and there were two schools – where the children were dressed in uniforms more redolent of Surrey than the tropics.

Anne Kennaway took a job as receptionist at the Smoke House Inn in the Cameron Highlands:

It seemed to create the atmosphere of an English country pub, built with mock oak beams and lattice windows. Inside, the bar was decorated with horse brasses, poker work and other reminders of English rural life. In spite of these attempts it did not succeed. Somehow the effect was too contrived.

At the top of the European tree were the senior administrators, headed by the august and splendid personage of the Governor, and the members of the great commercial dynasties whose fortunes had been founded in the 19th century. Below them were the lesser independent merchants and the middle rank civil servants, including officers of the armed forces and police. Then came the white employees, clerks, railway officials etc., and at the bottom of the pile, the common soldiery.

John Burnham was an employee of a commercial concern and acted as their shipping agent in Malacca before the war. He described his daily life:

The ships used to anchor three miles off the coast, so up at 5.30 in the morning, go out to meet them, discuss the cargo with the captain and arrange for the lighters to be towed up through the river . . . my job was to collect cargoes of rubber and tin, pepper and general goods, take it out to the ship, load it and send her on her way . . . breakfast on board which was a stable hot curry with large quantities of beer and gin. The fact that we drank beer and gin was quite incidental – it seemed to go with the curry rather than the time of day . . . the day would finish at about half past five. Back to my bungalow on the hill a mile away from the office, have a shower and usually go down and play a game of tennis at the local club, or perhaps a game of rugger depending on the day of the week.

It was only the British who could even dream of playing Rugby in such a climate, and no wonder foreigners thought that they were all mad. All accounts of life in pre-war Malaya stress the playing of games. Anne Kennaway remembered:

By midday the heat was intense and we lay in a soporific state on our beds all afternoon. After tea when it was cooler we collected tennis raquets and drove to the Tanjong Malim Club. . . . Spectators sat around the courts in rattan chairs sipping drinks. In the club house was a large room containing a billiard table, a well-thumped piano and the bar. Upstairs was a lounge, bridge tables stacked in one corner and more rattan chairs whose cushions were covered in faded chintz.

Those were the residents who lived their gentle lives against the violently coloured backdrop of Malaya and whose activities impinged little upon the native population.

THE DILEMMAS OF DEFENCE

Neither Singapore nor Malaya as a whole had been taken by force of arms and the local inhabitants were quiescent. Between the wars a small British-officered police force kept the peace, backed up by a small garrison of troops largely based in Singapore. The Royal Navy still ruled the waves, at least in theory, and the Union Jack waved over Fort Canning, the 'citadel' of Singapore which was totally outdated as a defensive work.

The First World War did not really affect Malaya, but it was to cause a radical reappraisal of the defence of Britain's Far Eastern possessions. Japanese aggression in China caused a flutter in Whitehall, but the underlying reason was that the balance of power had tilted against Britain. In the days of Russian supremacy in the Far East, a British alliance with Japan – described in more detail in the following chapter – made good sense. However, while Britain and the other major European powers were locked in their deadly struggle in the West, the Japanese had made good use of the political vacuum to gobble up the ex-German colonies. With the descent of Russia into anarchy and civil war, the advent of peace caused Britain and the USA to look again at the Pacific. What was plainly apparent was that Japan could pose a threat to British commerce in the East at some future date. Her eyes were cast covetously upon China and that unfortunate country was to be the catalyst for a realignment of allegiances.

The United States had long favoured an 'open door' policy there and was resisting attempts by other powers to establish colonies in that vast creaking empire, but Japan already had a toehold in Manchuria and the Shantung Peninsula. The First World War had witnessed a vast increase in both the American and the Japanese navies, and the former was in a position to outbuild Britain if she so wished.

In 1919, Admiral Jellicoe visited Singapore and recommended the construction of a modern base there in order to secure sea communications, and at the same time, the British government realised that a fleet ought to be stationed there. This, however, was an impossibility, as a base would first have to be created, and, in any case, the official doctrine was that a war would not occur for at least ten years. Britain's only other outpost in the area was Hong Kong, the dockyard of which was totally inadequate for large warships, and it was realised that the colony was too far isolated to be successfully defended.

In 1921, the Committee of Imperial Defence was asked to consider the vital question of sea communications on the routes to the East of Ceylon. Most traffic steamed from there through the Straits of Malacca to Singapore and then spread out to the East Indies, Hong Kong, Indo-China and Shanghai, while the other main route led south-east to Australia and New Zealand.

The proposed base had to fulfil certain criteria. It had to be close enough to the supposed area of operations, close enough to a source of oil fuel, it had to be defensible in the absence of the fleet and have a source of labour both skilled and unskilled. The Committee came up with two possibilities – Singapore and Sydney, and ultimately, after mature reflection, decided upon the former.

A decision was easier to make than to implement, and from then on, the Singapore base was to be the subject of a lengthy game of political musical chairs, interspersed with bouts of inter-service rivalry. First, however, came the series of treaties that was to sow the seed of future conflict and was to determine the alignment of forces in the Pacific.

In 1921 the Washington Naval Conference convened to lay down future naval building programmes in view of the desire for general disarmament, and the following year a treaty was signed limiting capital ship tonnage between Britain, the United States, Japan, France and Italy. A ratio for America, Britain and Japan was agreed as 5:5:3 which at the time appeared to satisfy those concerned. An additional article determined that no new fortifications and naval bases would be constructed in certain areas of the Pacific, but this did not apply to Singapore.

This left outstanding the problem of the Anglo-Japanese alliance, which was opposed by Washington in view of Japan's aggressive intentions in China. Retention of the treaty would be harmful to Anglo-American relations. It had, however, to be replaced by something acceptable to Japan which would not involve 'loss of face'. The result was the Four-Power Treaty between Britain, France, America and Japan which concerned their respective possessions in the Pacific, and the wider Nine-Power Treaty confirming the territorial integrity of China. But it was clear that Japanese feelings were deeply wounded. 'You had an alliance with us on Sunday, you broke it on Monday and started a base on Tuesday. Surely the inference is that you no longer trust us', was the terse comment of a Japanese general to the British military attaché in Tokyo.

But things did not move so swiftly in Britain, impoverished by the war and convinced that the age of universal peace and disarmament had dawned. After all, if there would not be a war for at least ten years, there was no need to hurry. Firstly, the site for the new base had to be determined. The choice was between the exisiting Keppel Harbour on the South of the island, and a new site to the North on the Johore Strait. On Admiralty recommendation the latter was decided on and approved by the Cabinet in February 1923. Naturally, Australia and New Zealand pressed for construction to start, but politics intervened. In 1924 the first Labour government came to power and promptly decided to abandon the Singapore project in spite of Commonwealth protests. Later in the same year the Conservatives were returned to power and just as promptly reinstated the scheme, but three years had passed since the original approval and nothing had been done.

It is one thing to construct a naval base, and quite another to defend it, and throughout its period of building, there were bitter controversies between the Services. It was the view of the Army at the time that an advance down Malaya was impossible and that the tactics employed by the Japanese against Port Arthur in 1904, where they landed troops and took the base from the land side, could not be used against Singapore. They predicted, therefore, that any attack would come from the sea, and to defend against this the traditional heavy guns should be emplaced.

In fairness it should be borne in mind that in 1924, aircraft were still a comparatively primitive weapon with a short range and limited capacity for carrying bombs. The problem was that once the concept of defending Singapore primarily by heavy guns was accepted, there was little chance of changing it, given the innate conservatism of the professional military mind. Exactly the same thing was happening at exactly the same time in France. The advances made by tanks and aircraft were conveniently ignored as successive committees wrestled with the problems of building inanimate fortifications.

It was the junior service that saw the writing on the wall, but its senior officers protested in vain. The Air Ministry did point out that aircraft, especially torpedo-carrying bombers, would provide a useful supplement to the fixed defences, for they could attack a potential enemy at far greater range than guns. The army and the navy disagreed, as guns had usually in the past proved to be an adequate deterrent against warships.

The Committee of Imperial Defence deliberated on, and it was not until 1926 that it made its recommendations. It was agreed that a new airfield should be constructed at Seletar, but that the first stage should be the installation of a number of medium guns plus a battery of three 15-inch, the most powerful guns ever mounted by Britain for land service. The idea of substituting aircraft for further guns was put off for later discussion, but it was proposed to extend the line of strategic airfields from Calcutta where it terminated, to run down the Malay peninsula to Singapore.

No sooner had one committee ended its deliberations than another was set up, in 1927, to make recommendations about siting the guns and the size of the garrison required. It immediately ran into opposition from the government in Singapore, which was unwilling to make land available for military purposes without being assured that they would not have to pay for it. This occasioned further delays and referral back to the Chiefs of Staff Committee in London. There, in 1928, it was decided that the first stage of construction should proceed and be completed in five years, and again it was emphasised that the nature of the country in Johore was such that enemy forces would be unable to move through it. At the same time, the official doctrine that war with any power would not occur for ten years was restated, with the proviso that this assumption should be reviewed annually. At this stage of course, Hitler was only a distant smudge on the horizon and Japan, although irritating, could not possibly pose an immediate threat.

The following year the second Labour Government was elected and again an element of indecision was introduced into the political arena. In November the Cabinet decided that pending the results of a proposed naval disarmament conference, work on the base should be slowed down: any work that could be suspended should be, and no new work should be undertaken.

This gesture of good faith proved to be in vain in the long run. True, the London Naval Treaty of 1930 ensured a further reduction in warship building by the three main naval powers and demonstrated to the government that its decision had been a valid one, but events were speeding towards a climax. In 1931, the liberal tradition of government in Japan, which had been dominant since the war, began to break up. In 1930, Japanese extremists staged an 'incident' in Manchuria and proceeded to occupy the whole of the country. China protested to the League of Nations which called upon the Japanese to withdraw, only to be ignored. In 1932 there was fighting in Shanghai between the Japanese and the Chinese, and in March 1933, the former withdrew from the League of Nations.

The following month, the Chiefs of Staff submitted a report on the situation in the Far East in which they made the point that Japan was in a position to strike without warning against British interests there. They also made a plea that the 'ten years rule' should be abandoned, and this was accepted by the Cabinet in principle so long as no increased expenditure was involved. Later in the year, the Chiefs of Staff returned to the attack, stating in their report that:

the accumulation of deficiencies resulting from the long continuance of the ten years rule is very heavy, and if we are to be ready for . . . grave emergencies . . . a steady increase in certain of our estimates over a number of years is essential.

In the same year Germany withdrew from the League of Nations, and in 1934 she repudiated the Treaty of Versailles. With this threat, and with Japan on the rampage in the Far East, Britain took the first steps on the road to rearmament. However, the aircraft versus guns controversy was still rumbling away in the corridors of Whitehall. In 1931 a committee under the chairmanship of Stanley Baldwin heard evidence from the three Services. Developments in aircraft design and performance had made great strides, and the Air Ministry, basing its claims on the mobility of aircraft, repeated its assertion that they could provide an adequate deterrent to attack by warships, at far less cost than fixed guns.

It was this very mobility that caused concern at both the War Office and the Admiralty. If a surprise attack occurred, would the aircraft be there? They preferred to rely on fixed guns which could not be removed for use elsewhere. In May 1932, the committee ended up with the inevitable compromise, recommending that the main emphasis should be placed on heavy guns but that aircraft should also play a part. This was accepted by the Government, which also decided to speed up work on the base and to build a second airfield.

This was all very well, but the carpet was about to be tugged away from under the assumptions upon which the deliberations of the 1920's were based. The various naval treaties had not considered Germany, as her navy had been scuttled at Scapa Flow and she was forbidden to construct capital ships. But by repudiating the Treaty of Versailles Hitler signified his intention to rearm. The appearance of a potential enemy navy in European waters completely altered the strategic balance as far as Britain was concerned. The London Naval Treaty of 1930 was due to expire in 1936, and Britain, faced with the opening of a Pandora's box, held preliminary talks with Germany in 1935. This resulted in an agreement that Germany could build up to 35 per cent of the surface tonnage of the British Navy, and meant in fact, that when the German building programme had been completed, a large proportion of Britain's warships would have to be retained in the Atlantic and the North Sea.

In the meantime, out in the East, work on the naval base at Singapore was in progress, and the first stage was due to be completed in early 1937: already, in 1935, the government had authorised the start on a second stage. This was to include a further heavy gun battery and two more airfields. The idea was that Singapore would be able to hold out until a relieving fleet had been sent from Europe. A time-scale of seventy days was assumed for this purpose. It was at this stage that the term 'fortress' began to be applied to Singapore by the press – which waxed eloquent about the 'Gibraltar of the East'.

Vast works indeed were in progress. A dry dock capable of taking the largest ships afloat was excavated from the coastal swamp and fitted out. Oil storage tanks were installed and bomb-proof magazines were built. Barracks, workshops and stores were constructed and a huge floating dock and a floating crane were towed out from England. Huge armies of coolies dug the pits in which the 15-inch and 9.2-inch guns were to be emplaced. Hordes of skilled Europeans were imported by the Admiralty to work on the Naval Base and the army sent out specialists to install the guns and their ancillary plotting and communications equipment.

By definition, a fortress is a location capable of being defended against attack from any direction, and although the word impregnable is popular with reference to a fortress, there is really no such thing as an impregnable fortress. Even if a locality can be made so strong that it cannot be stormed, it must inevitably succumb to starvation or treachery if the enemy is prepared to wait or to negotiate. Anyway, the classic fortress had been conceived in the days before aircraft were capable of flying over fixed defences and dropping their bombs in the interior. We have seen that attack from the land side was regarded as impossible and that no steps were taken to build defences there: it can therefore be stated, quite categorically, that Singapore was not in any sense of the word at any time, a 'fortress'.

The 'official' doctrine was that the only possible attack on Singapore would come from the sea, but numerous officers were already reconsidering this. Major-General B. W. Key, who was to command 11th Indian Division during the latter stages of the Malaya campaign, was at the Staff College at Quetta in India in 1930.

Our last exercise was that the Japanese had taken on Singapore. It lasted for about a fortnight and we had RAF and Naval officers there. . . . To my surprise I discovered that I was leading one of the syndicates. In our appreciation, all of the syndicates came to the same conclusion that the Japs would never attack Singapore from the sea. They would have to land somewhere in Malaya to get aerodromes before they could get to Singapore. Two or three years later the Staff College actually went to Singapore and carried out an exercise to see for themselves. The Air Officer Commanding (Babington) was asked to address them . . . and I was told what he said . . . 'I don't know what you chaps are doing here, you're just wasting your time. The defence of Malaya is an air force problem and the sooner you get back to your proper roles and jobs the better.'

The above quotation serves well to introduce the final phases of the defence controversy and the strange tug of war between the Air Force and the Army. While the naval base was under construction, the RAF established a chain of airfields up the West coast of the Malay peninsula and on through Burma, to complete the strategic chain from Britain via India. These were also used for the commercial air route. But the need for reconnaissance over the Gulf of Siam, and for offensive operations against an approaching fleet, led the air force to decide on the construction of further airfields on the East coast and in the extreme North on the Siamese border. These were sited at Kota Bharu, Kuantan and Kahang. It was an excellent idea to have forward bases in order to increase the range of reconnaissance, but unfortunately, there was no consultation with the army as to how they were to be defended. In fact, in the face of a hostile landing, their defence would prove to be virtually impossible.

However, as the nearest Japanese bases were hundreds of miles away it was not considered likely that there would be a landing, and therefore it would not be necessary to detach troops to guard the distant airfields. But it was beginning to dawn on those concerned that the defence of the naval base did in fact involve the defence of the whole of Malaya. In 1937, Major-General W. G. S. Dobbie, GOC Malaya, became aware of the threat posed by the large number of Japanese present in Malaya. They owned tin mines and rubber estates, often managed by retired officers. Japanese also had a virtual monopoly of barber shops, photographic dealerships and as such were in frequent contact with the troops. Japanese boats provided much of the fish eaten in Malaya and Singapore and thus they had an intimate knowledge of the coastline.

Mrs Vera Magnay remembered:

We had a Japanese dentist. All the Naval Base men had him I reckon. He was a very good dentist and he had a very very beautiful wife. She used to hold the hand of these men as he did their teeth. And now I'm absolutely convinced they were spies. All the women went to Japanese hairdressers because they were so good.

Mrs Terry Morris went up to the Cameron Highlands for a short holiday with some friends:

We took a lot of photographs when we were there and we put them in for developing, to a Japanese of course. We later heard that's how they got all their information – they were the developers and they took all the photographs of everybody. I presume they printed an extra copy for intelligence.

Dobbie's staff uncovered evidence of massive Japanese espionage and a general reappraisal of the situation was ordered. One of the reasons advanced for the security of the base was that it would be impossible for an enemy to make a landing during the period of the north-east monsoon. This blew from October to March, and the heavy winds coming in across the South China Sea, brought low cloud, heavy rain and high seas to the East Coast. Churchill later wrote:

I was repeatedly informed at the time of the Japanese landing that owing to the season of the year, the ground was so waterlogged that there could be no question of an advance southwards until the spring.

During the monsoon in 1936–7, exercises were held to test the possibility of landings on the East coast. They proved that it would be possible to land and that the consequent poor visibility would hamper air reconnaissance of any enemy force in the offing. In November, Dobbie sent a report to the War Office based on a study made by his Chief of Staff, a certain Colonel A. E. Percival. In this he prophesied exactly what would happen. The Japanese would secure advance air bases in Thailand and Indo-China, in order to cover landings at Singora and Patani in the South of Siam and at Kota Bharu on the East coast of Malaya. They would then advance down the road and rail network of the West coast and attack Singapore from the North. Dobbie concluded that to guard against this the defensive concept would have to be extended to include the whole of Malaya, and that a vastly increased garrison would be required.

The following year, Dobbie sent in another report warning of the dangers of a landing in Johore near Mersing, which could only be countered by having troops stationed in Johore itself. He asked for funds to construct a defensive position, not only on the North coast of Singapore Island, but also on the mainland. This would keep enemy artillery sufficiently far away to stop them shelling the naval base, and would protect vital reservoirs and water pumping stations on the mainland. In view of the fact that the term fortress was being widely used, it seems incredible that the main water supply came in over the causeway from the mainland. This provided two-fifths of the Island's daily requirement of water.

Dobbie was granted the somewhat paltry sum of £60,000 with which to realise his plans, which were for a line of pill-boxes fronted by wire obstacles and backed up by metalled roads. Part of this sum was actually spent and some pill-boxes were built in Johore. But when the time came to use them in January 1942, most had been overgrown by jungle and nobody knew exactly where they were.

It was thanks to Dobbie and Percival that the fact did finally sink in that the defence of Singapore rested upon the defence of the whole of the Malay peninsula including the far-flung airfields. But organising this defence, at a time of general shortage of manpower and aircraft, was not quite so simple. Where were the resources to come from?

One of the criticisms that has been raised is that the inhabitants of Malaya did nothing to help to defend themselves, and by this one has to mean the Europeans. They alone had the power and the means to do something, and many of the natives were understandably apathetic. After all, they had no real share in the running of the country. The Sultans had small bodyguards and some of them were extremely pro-British. The Sultan of Johore had paid for one of the 15-inch guns at Johore Battery and was permitted to ceremonially fire the first shot.

This brings us to the question of the volunteer movement and the attitude of the civilian government in general. The volunteers had been formed before the war as auxiliary units on a strictly limited basis and compulsory service was only introduced in 1940. The Royal Naval Volunteer Reserve was constituted in 1934, and in 1939, it had an approved strength of 100 European Officers and 300 Malay ratings in Singapore, and in Penang, 30 European Officers and 100 Malay ratings. There was a similar organisation in the Federated Malay States. When war with Germany broke out in September 1939, a number of specialists were called up, and some motor launches were employed on patrol duties.

The volunteer air force was started in 1936 with a few regular RAF officers and airmen as its backbone. Using the equipment of the various flying clubs, flying training was carried out, and in 1939, it became the Malayan Volunteer Air Force. In 1941 there were some 20 officers and 150 other ranks, many of whom were qualified pilots.

The volunteer land forces were also started before the war, largely inspired by the Ex-Service Association of Malaya. Various units were formed which were divided up on a racial basis. When war broke out in Europe, there were two infantry battalions, a light field battery, various engineer units, an armoured car section, signals and so on in Singapore. Penang and Province Wellesley also had two infantry battalions, and there was a small unit in Malacca. Small forces were organised in the Federated States and there was an engineer company in Johore.

As distinct from the volunteers, there was the single regular battalion of the Malay Regiment in the Federated States and a small regular force of Malays and Indians in Johore. In April 1941, it was decided to raise a second battalion of the Malay Regiment.

None of these units was particularly well equipped. After all, attack was considered extremely unlikely. Weapons were in short supply for the regular forces and the military authorities were by all accounts not particularly impressed by the volunteers – in spite of their smart turn-out at inspections. Certainly, at no time was there any effort made to mobilise the population for all-out war, and what efforts were made were largely a matter for the Europeans. The tragedy is that the Chinese were the natural enemies of Japan and there were large numbers of them itching to stick a bayonet into a Japanese.

Thus we come to the tangled web of command that existed before war broke out. As we have said, the nominal Commander-in-Chief was the Governor, but this was merely an empty title, and the power rested with the military commanders on the spot, of whom there were three, one for each service. Traditionally the General Officer Commanding Malaya had been responsible for the actual defence measures, working through a Defence Committee on which the other services and the civil administration were represented.

In August 1938, a civilian official, C. A. Vlieland, was asked to examine the provision of food supplies for Malaya should Britain become involved in a war. Realising that he had to have a working knowledge of the defence proposed, he asked for and got access to the plans, and saw to his surprise that they only included Singapore and southern Johore.

Vlieland came to the valid conclusion already propounded by Percival and Dobbie (who was still GOC) that the scheme should be extended to cover the whole of Malaya. He also felt that the administration and the other services should have more say in defence matters generally. He proposed to the Governor that a new form of

Defence Committee should be formed with the Governor as chairman and with a Secretary for Defence to represent the administration. This would then become the War Committee on the outbreak of hostilities.

Implicit in the work of British planners, was the belief that a fleet would eventually arrive to succour the defenders of Singapore but the whole question of a fleet for the Far East was fraught with problems. British representatives in Tokyo and Bangkok continued to press the government in London for assurance that ships would be sent. On 7 November 1938, Sir Josiah Crosbie wrote from his embassy in Bangkok to the Foreign Secretary:

What is wanted in my opinion is a very considerable manifestation of force in the shape of a squadron of battleships and cruisers as large and as numerous as can be spared from European waters.

Crosbie wanted this force to demonstrate to neutrals Britain's ability to react swiftly to any threat. He was backed up by his colleague in Tokyo:

From the point of view of maintenance of British influence in this country, a strengthening of our naval forces in the Far East is of vital importance. Japan at the present time is ruled by men who are influenced in the main by prevalent German ideas of 'power politics', and to such minds as these, the moving of a few capital ships represents a far more convincing argument than any number of protests or the most passionate advocacy of the sanctity of the treaties.

The Admiralty wriggled on the hook. While agreeing in principle that a fleet ought to be sent, it hedged its bets on account of the shortage of ships. In March 1939 the naval authorities stated:

The Admiralty must continue to rely on their present policy of keeping one principal fleet at Home and another in the Mediterranean. This policy in no way precludes a fleet being sent should the necessity arise. If the Japanese begin to encroach upon Malaya or the Dutch East Indies, the Admiralty would consider that these circumstances would demand the despatch of a fleet to the East. But until the position is far more serious than it is now, the Admiralty would hesitate to recommend such a step which would involve the withdrawal of the greater part of our fleet from the Mediterranean.

The Admiralty was also at pains to reassure the Australians. In March 1939, the First Sea Lord wrote to the Navy Board at Melbourne:

there has never been doubt that a force of capital ships would have to be sent to the East in the event of war with Japan. What is uncertain is the strength of this force. . . . I have repeatedly told you that 1939 is a very difficult year for us, but that position will improve a great deal after 1940 with completion of new ships.

In July 1939, the Chiefs of Staff were forced to raise the hypothetical 'period of relief to ninety days, and they then suggested that the Governor start stockpiling fuel for six months – no mean undertaking. At the same time, however, they realised that reinforcements of troops and aircraft would have to be sent. India was instructed to send an infantry brigade from the Imperial Reserve, and additional bomber squadrons were allocated – two from India and two from England, flown out along the strategic airfield chain.

One of the latter reinforcements was No. 62 Squadron flying the Blenheim Mk 1. They left Cranfield towards the end of August and flew out via Sidi Barrani, the Persian Gulf, India and Burma, finally landing at Alor Star, minus only one aircraft that had force-landed in neutral Siam. F. C. Griffiths was a pilot with the squadron and wrote in an unpublished account of the flight:

The next day (18 September) came the last stage to Tengah, a new airfield some 14 miles from Singapore City on the Western half of the Island. A short two hour flight in good weather and we arrived as a squadron in close formation. . . . Had there not been a war on, our flight might have made headlines for it was the first really long distance flight of a land-based squadron. . . . It is sad to recall that from this time onwards the squadron achieved virtually nothing; except the award of one V.C.

The war was far from Singapore yet flying had to be curtailed to preserve the aircraft for the conflict which was bound to come one day. Pilots were only to fly for three hours each month

Captain Dennis Russell-Roberts arrived in Singapore in August with his regiment as part of the reinforcements from India.

When . . . the infamous Russo-German treaty was signed in the last days of August 1939, the whole picture in the Far East changed overnight. The Japs became dismayed; their real enemy, Russia, appeared more formidable than ever.

And what a change that meant for everyone in Singapore. Instead of finding ourselves on a semi-war footing with all the restrictions which that imposed, we were able to carry on with normal peace-time living and training. The threat of war in the Far East had faded into the dim distance.

Singapore undoubtedly had its attractions. Chinese servants were plentiful, inexpensive and efficient. Drink and cigarettes for the Services could be bought cheaply. Every kind of sport flourished. The sun shone. When a large part of the world was floundering in the grip of war this was surely a little spot of paradise. Those in Singapore could scarcely be blamed for enjoying it.

In August and September 1939, the British ambassadors in Tokyo and Bangkok continued to press for a fleet to be sent out to Far Eastern waters, but their pleas fell on deaf ears. Vast sums of money had been spent on preparing the naval base and it was ready to receive a fleet. The heavy guns had been installed and were in full working order. Britain's allies the French would keep the Japanese out of Indo-China.

The outbreak of war in Europe was of course a terrible thing, and the citizens of Malaya were ready to do their bit – raising funds and producing vital goods. John Burnham remembered the prevailing attitude to the threat from Japan:

the great weakness that we had was this belief that all Japanese pilots were one eyed . . . we had this enormous fortress in Singapore and it was impossible, utterly impossible, for anyone to land on the north-east coast of Malaya and make any progress through this ghastly swamp of jungle . . . we were fed on this belief that we had this fantastic fortress – 'they can't land anywhere, and if they do they will be isolated and can be contained – they certainly won't be filtering around our positions, that's impossible in the jungle. . . .' That was the foundation of our great belief that we could withstand any attack from Japan.

3

THE CHERRY TREE BLOOMS
The Rise of Japan

MOST books about the loss of Malaya and Singapore have dealt in some detail with the planning of the Japanese attack. To understand the reasons for this onslaught, however, it is necessary to delve more deeply into the history of Japan and its explosion onto the world stage. Had those involved at the time looked more closely at their enemy, the catastrophe might well have been avoided or at least reduced in scope. During the 1930s there was a strong tendency in the West to regard the Japanese as an inferior Asiatic race not far removed from barbarism. Many of the views expressed at the time, seem, forty years on, to be literally incredible. In his book *Naked Island*, Russell Braddon repeated what the Australians were told by an intelligence officer:

Apparently the Japanese were very small and very myopic and thus totally unsuited either physically or optically to tropical warfare. Nor was that all. They had aeroplanes made from old kettles and kitchen utensils, guns salvaged from the war against Russia in 1905 and rifles of the kind used by civilised peoples only in films about the Red Indians. Also, they were frightened of the dark.

Lieutenant Terry Morris was a territorial officer serving in the Singapore Fortress Signals, and he remembered a lecture given by a staff officer in the summer of 1941:

he said, 'Gentlemen, I have dealt with these people and they're very difficult to understand. A lot of them have got an absolutely firm conviction that they are decended from the sun goddess. If ever you should get to know them as long as I have, I'm sure you'll come to the same conclusion that I have, that if what they believe is true, she must have been a pretty remarkable old bitch'.

Even today, boys' comics tend to portray the Japanese as little monkey-faced men with mouths full of teeth, rimless spectacles, all waving bamboo-hilted swords and screaming 'banzai'. All this sort of thing is further emphasised by the preoccupation of television and the cinema with films about martial arts: Karate and Kung-fu tend to form one of the stereotyped images of Japan today.

There is, however, another side of the same coin. This is the 'willow pattern' Japan, the country of miniature trees, lacquer work of exquisite beauty and delicately detailed silk paintings. Through this landscape of paper houses and flawless gardens, the geishas flit, with their elaborate costumes and mask-like faces. This love of ordered formal beauty is difficult to co-ordinate in Western minds with the warlike images of cruelty and passion.

Modern Japan is an industrial giant and her leading firms are respected – and to a certain extent feared. Yet in the 1930s 'Made in Japan' was synonymous with shoddy goods. Much of the discipline and obedience to those in authority that are essentials of the Japanese character have now been harnessed to the production of consumer goods with conspicuous success. It was those very same characteristics, however, that were once the basis of a formidable army.

Any consideration of the role of Japan in the Second World War must inevitably examine the conduct of her troops. Among the surviving Far East prisoners of war (FEPOWs) there is a natural legacy of bitter hatred, and the understandable conviction that all Japanese should have been strangled at birth. But if you probe into the experience of almost every one of them, he will tell you about the 'decent Jap' who showed him some small kindness.

It is a fact that the Japanese committed a number of disgraceful atrocities during the war which can never be condoned – least of all by the Japanese themselves – but an attempt can at least be made to understand them. In books about the war, words such as the *samurai* code and *bushido* are bandied about, but these can only be understood in the context of Japan's long and complex history.

The core of the attitude to the treatment of prisoners of war was based on ancient values, which taught that anyone who was taken captive was not entitled to any consideration – he should have fought to the death. Therefore, his captors were under no obligation to clothe and feed him. If the British officers who surrendered at Singapore had all, solemnly and with one accord, slit their stomachs open, the Japanese would have accorded them every honour.

Japan had never ratified the Geneva Convention, which was based on purely Western Christian values, and they did not feel bound by its provisions. As the Allies found out later in the war, the Japanese practised what they preached, fighting to the end and generally refusing to surrender. Thousands were simply massacred in their foxholes and tunnels on the Pacific Islands. Indeed, in recent years, we have witnessed soldiers wandering out of the jungle, still waiting for the

Emperor to order them to surrender.

The armies that fought the European war had all developed along basically the same lines and subscribed more or less to the same book of rules. The Japanese army was something completely different and it is almost impossible to compare it with, say, the British army of the early 1940s. To provide a somewhat specious analogy, try to imagine the impact of a 12th century Crusading army equipped with firearms, tanks and aircraft, inspired with religious fervour and determined to eradicate as many infidels as possible. We never understood them, and they totally failed to understand us. It was always the complete mystery to the Japanese that the British and Australians could actually laugh about their captivity and could spend time in camp upon such childish pursuits as amateur theatricals.

The foregoing remarks have attempted to look at some of the contrasts as seen with Western eyes. What follows is a brief discussion of Japanese history and of the rise of militarism during the 1930s.

The one constant and thus unifying element in Japanese history is the monarchy, which has survived many centuries of political turmoil. The origins of the country lie buried in myth. Tradition has it that the first Emperor, Jimmu Tenno, who was a descendant of the Sun Goddess, established himself in central Japan in 660BC. Since then, the Imperial line has been unbroken, and thus the present Emperor – within the framework of a constitutional monarchy – still has semi-divine status. Although for many centuries the power of the Emperors was eclipsed, the succession continued. Without the Emperor, one essential part of Japanese culture and belief would have disappeared. The word *Tenno* for Emperor literally means something like 'Heavenly Ruler'.

This divinity stemmed from the supposed blood relationship to the Sun Goddess and gave the ruler a form of priestly status as the father of the family of the Japanese Race. The nation was likened to a tree, whose trunk was the Imperial House, from which grew four main branches representing the four ancient clans or families. From these sprouted the lesser branches and foliage which represented the people. Thus, as the same sap flowed throughout the tree, all could claim a relationship with the line of Emperors. 'Emperor and People are one' was a popular nationalist slogan.

It was a part of this nationalist creed that every Japanese was born with a host of virtues implanted into him by the gods, and the essence of the nation is expressed in the word *kokutai*. This is made up of three elements – loyalty to the Emperor, a sense of mission and the possession of superior inborn qualities. Total defeat in 1945 did not destroy this as the monarchy was preserved intact. But such beliefs have led, from time to time in Japan's history, to rabid chauvinism.

Another strong factor in the Japanese character is religion. In the early years of her existence, Japan absorbed many ideas from China, mainly via Korea. These included the Chinese script and Buddhism – which in time became infused with the native Shintoism. The appeal of Shinto is aesthetic or emotional rather than moral. There is no great breathtaking philosophy behind it, and its attraction to the Japanese lies mainly in its rites and ceremonies. It was Buddhism that supplied the core of theological speculation.

Among the various branches of Buddhism that were imported was Zen – which is naturally difficult to explain in a few words. Essentially it offers salvation through grace – which can only be obtained through self-discipline and meditation. Thus its appeal was essentially to the warrior and aristocratic castes. It fortified the two main ideals of the *samurai* or warriors, which were loyalty and indifference to pain and physical discomfort.

The *samurai* grew out of the turmoil of Japan in what we would term the Middle Ages, and as a warrior aristocracy, they can be equated with European feudal knights. At the end of the 16th Century when times were quieter, they became country gentlemen, forbidden to settle in the cities but still the only class entitled to wear their distinctive hallmark, two swords.

Their sense of what we might term 'chivalry' the ideal of a warrior caste, they termed *bushido*. Although this word first became popular in the 19th Century, its origins are far earlier. Essentially it means the spartan devotion of a warrior caste to war, a readiness to self-sacrifice and devotion to a martial superior – none of which would have been strange to a Norman knight. The problem was that this feudal sentiment survived into the age of the aircraft and the tank, when all such idealism was long dead in the West. *Bushido*, of course, still lingers on among the more extreme devotees of the exotic martial arts disciplines.

Japan's first contact with the West, and incidentally with Christianity, came in around 1542, when some Portuguese were driven ashore in a storm, on an island off the coast of Kyushu. They were followed by others, including Francis Xavier in 1549.

The newcomers were generaly welcome as traders, and their religious fervour was at least tolerated in return for the cannon and muskets which they sold. Then, around 1600, the Dutch and the British appeared on the scene, bringing a different brand of Christianity which must have greatly mystified the Japanese magnates. The mutual animosities of the foreigners, however, soon soured relations and the honeymoon period was a brief one. There were a number of persecutions; the English left in 1623 and the Portuguese were expelled in 1637. The Dutch remained as the only Western nation permitted to trade in a limited fashion, but they were restricted to a small island in

Nagasaki harbour.

Thus Japan voluntarily cut herself off from the rest of the world and those who had the misfortune to be stranded on her shores were often butchered. By the 1850s, however, foreign ships began to appear in Japanese waters in ever-increasing numbers, although if they attempted to land they were politely turned away. The tide could no longer be stemmed, though, as the increase in the number of steam ships led to the need for coaling stations around the world. In addition, the great circle route from California to China brought vessels near to the Japanese home islands.

It was the Americans who were the first to get their feet in the door. Commodore Perry appeared in 1853 at Nagasaki, and in true gunboat diplomacy fashion delivered an ultimatum demanding trading rights – leaving with a warning that he would be back for an answer the following year. There were long debates in Japan, but these were overshadowed by the realisation that Japan had no navy or other modern forces to hinder the entry of outsiders. When Perry returned in 1854, an agreement was signed opening two ports to American ships. This was the beginning of a process of contact that was to transform feudal Japan into a modern industrial power within some fifty years.

For centuries the Imperial house had lived in isolation at Kyoto, and political power had been vested in the hands of the shogunate. The *shogun* was a hereditary commander-in-chief and leader of a governmental system based on a few aristrocratic families. His reception of the Americans and his inability to expel them, led to a movement for the restoration of the prestige of the Emperor.

The ten years after the opening of the country were ones of internal turmoil. Opposition to the *shogun* grew up among other clans, and an anti 'foreign barbarian' movement became linked with the desire to restore the Emperor. In 1868, the forces of the shogunate were finally defeated by an alliance of the four clans based in the west of Japan.

This left power vested in an oligarchy of the heads of these family groupings, and it was they who realised that if Japan was to compete in the modern world, there was no question of expelling the barbarians. They managed at one stroke to abolish feudalism by returning their own fiefs to the Emperor and persuading other families to do likewise. It was only this step that made it possible to establish a central administration in the country and thus for it to become a great power.

There was nothing wrong in such an ambition. The European nations were all caught up in the great late 19th Century technological boom, and it was only natural for Japan to seek to imitate them. Japan could also see what was going on in China, where a great nation, too weak and divided to resist intervention, was being carved up by the powers competing with each other for trading concessions and influence. France had established herself in Indo-China during the 1860s, while, at the same time, the Russians founded Vladivostok.

Inside Japan there was great resentment over the terms of the treaties that had been made with the foreign governments. These were felt to have been disadvantageous as the interlopers were not subject to Japanese law. Revision of these treaties was to become the cornerstone of Japanese politics for some years.

Parallel to this, a modernisation programme got under way. A bureaucracy and a tax system were created from scratch, and railways, telegraphs and industrial plant were built. Although Japan was still politically immature in 1941, by 1880 a Constitution had been granted, there was an elected Diet and a system of cabinet government. Commodore Perry cannot have imagined the genie that he had let out of the bottle.

For centuries, Japan had regarded Korea as being in her sphere of influence, and in 1894, a revolt broke out in that country, which led to intervention by China. The Japanese went to war, armed with modern weapons, and in a nine month campaign, they expelled the Chinese from the Korean peninsula and grabbed large areas of territory around Port Arthur in Southern Manchuria. By a treaty signed in April 1885, China was forced to cede Formosa, the Pescadores, Port Arthur and the Liaotang Peninsula.

But then, the powers intervened in the so-called Triple Intervention – an action that the Japanese never really forgave. She was to be punished for doing what the others had been up to for years. Lacking allies and without sufficient firepower, Japan was forced to back down, and Russia, France and Germany forced her to relinquish her claims to Port Arthur.

She then had to watch while those same powers, joined by Britain and America, proceeded in their turn to annex large areas of 'concessions' in China. The insult was plain to any intelligent Japanese, and the greatest hypocrites were seen as being the Russians, who had seized control of Port Arthur. This has to be borne in mind before one is tempted to castigate the Japanese for their expansionist aims in 1941: what is sauce for the goose is, after all, also sauce for the gander.

One lesson that the Japanese learnt was that might is right, and as a result, the armed forces enjoyed a new prestige. A minor reform carried out under an Imperial edict in 1900, was to have unforeseen results. This laid down that only generals or admirals could fill the posts of Minister of War and Navy Minister respectively. In practice, this meant that the military authorities could hamstring any civilian government by ordering the service ministers to resign over any measure with which the services did not agree, and then refusing to name a successor. The High

Command could thus, in effect, veto cabinet decisions.

It was Russian expansion in Manchuria and a possible threat to Korea that persuaded Japan to sign a treaty with Britain in 1902. This provided that if attacked by Russia, Britain would remain neutral, but if another power joined against Japan, Britain would lend active support. This gave Japan a free hand to deal with Russia, but far more, it gave her back some of the international 'face' which she had lost at the time of the Triple Intervention. For many years, the bulk of the Japanese remained extremely grateful and friendly towards Britain.

In the Russo-Japanese War in 1904, Japan was the victor on land and at sea, and humiliated a European power already being shaken by the tremors of coming revolution. As a result, she gained a free hand again in Korea and virtually ruled Southern Manchuria. This success was not unpopular in Britain, for example, where many people thought that poor little Japan had taught the Russian bully a lesson.

In 1910, Japan annexed Korea, and it was there that the form of Japanese colonialism first became apparent. A rigid and unimaginative administration was set up, mainly run by soldiers who were on their guard for signs of political unrest. Japanese governments in the early part of the 20th Century thought in international terms, but at the same time, a number of ultra-nationalist secret societies began to appear. In Europe, meanwhile, there were mutterings about the 'Yellow Peril'.

The interests of the secret societies lay in a sort of Asian renaissance, led naturally by Japan, and they enjoyed a certain amount of support from within the army. They fondly imagined that theirs was the supreme interpretation and expression of the *kokutai*. Even if the Emperor himself happened to be unsympathetic to their aims, they could justify themselves by believing that he was deluded by his advisers. Thus they could speciously disobey him, while at the same time professing extreme loyalty.

During the First World War, the European nations were otherwise engaged and Japan fulfilled her treaty obligations to Britain. She sent destroyers to help patrol the Mediterranean, and swiftly occupied the German possessions in China and the Pacific. This preoccupation of the powers seemed a heaven-sent opportunity to step into the breach and overawe China.

In 1915, Japan presented the Chinese Republic with the so-called Twenty-One Demands, most of which China was unable to refuse. The effect was, however, that Japan lost much of the international good-will that she had built up, especially in America, which was a strong supporter of the infant Chinese Republic. What Japan could well have achieved by diplomatic stealth she tried to gain by overbearing demands, and henceforth was to be regarded by the Americans as a bully.

During the 1920s, Japanese government was essentially liberal, and it was as one of the victors that she was given a permanent seat at the League of Nations. At the Versailles conference she was confirmed in her possession of the former German area in Shantung, and was given the League mandate over the former German islands in the Pacific North of the Equator.

As we have seen in the previous chapter, Japan took part in the Washington Naval Conference in 1921, which gave her security from an arms race with America which she could not hope to win. At the same time, though, the treaty with Britain was allowed to lapse, and this left a deep wound. Ultimately it would weaken the position of Britain's Far Eastern colonies and the dominions of Australia and New Zealand. Finally, a settlement was agreed with regard to China. The Japanese pulled out of Shantung and the Nine Powers agreed to recognise Chinese territory and sovereignty.

All this international good-will would have seemed to have ushered in a new era of peace and prosperity in the East, but behind the polite smiles, other forces were already at work. In the late 1920s, extreme political and economic views began to take hold of large factions among junior army officers, and in Japan itself, the world slump led to a lack of faith in parliamentary government. As a catalyst, the Kuomintang government in China began a process of national unification and started to look askance at the Japanese position in Manchuria.

It would be a gross over-simplification to regard the rise of extreme nationalism in Japan as just an extension of European fascism. Dictatorship by one man was totally alien to the Japanese mentality, and anyway, the position of the Emperor could not be challenged without destroying the essence of the *kokutai* – in which the nationalists implicitly believed. The Japanese at the time were seeking their own way, but the successes of Hitler and Mussolini could not but confirm to them the essential weakness of the democracies.

In the background, plots were brewing in Manchuria and in Japan itself. The depression brought with it ruin for many farmers, and it was the peasantry that traditionally provided the bulk of the recruits for the army. During 1930 and early 1931 there was growing friction along the line of the South Manchurian Railway which was leased by Japan, and there were clashes with Chinese troops. These incidents persuaded certain Japanese officers on the spot that it was high time to gain control of the area before it was too late. With the foreknowledge of the high command, the Japanese army in September 1931 occupied the city of Mukden – the so-called 'Manchurian Incident'.

The civilian government was taken by surprise and there was a total breakdown of communication between it and the armed forces. While Japanese representatives at the League of Nations protested that the action was only a temporary punitive measure, the army proceeded to occupy the whole of Southern Manchuria – thus earning Japan a reputation for double-dealing and deceit. Japanese public opinion was firmly behind the nationalists, and was cemented by the negative world reaction. The period from then until 1941 is called the 'dark valley' by the Japanese, as it heralded a period of rule by assassination and intimidation, hurrying the country along the road to war.

The following year, fighting broke out in Shanghai between the Japanese and the Chinese, and the former used aircraft to bomb densely-populated areas right under the noses of the international community. At the same time a puppet regime was set up in Southern Manchuria which became known as Manchukuo. As in the case of Hitler's and Mussolini's conquests, the League of Nations proved incapable of doing anything to curb Japanese aggression – which in turn only served to sharpen nationalist attitudes and appetites.

Gradually the Japanese found themselves involved in an all-out war with China. The army, which had behaved with restraint in 1904, was soon shown to the world for what it was. In 1937 Japanese troops captured Nanking and went on an orgy of rape and looting that lasted for several days and received widespread publicity.

It was widely believed at the time that Japan had bitten off more than she could chew in China, and Chiang Kai-Chek was supplied with arms by America. Britain as we have seen, kept aloof: Japan was recognised as a potential but a remote threat, far too involved in China to be able to cast her eyes elsewhere.

But there were plenty of indications of the way Japan's thinking was leading her. In 1936, a book written by a naval officer, Tota Ishimaru, entitled *Japan must fight Britain*, was translated into English and widely read. Its theme was the establishment of an all-Asia movement centred on Tokyo, and the inevitability of a Japanese victory. The author considered that the Singapore base was an insult to his country. However, if Britain made concessions ensuring Japan's domination of the Pacific, all would be well.

In a somewhat later book in the same vein, which was published in 1940 in the West, entitled *How Japan plans to Win*, the author set out the whole catalogue of grievances against America and outlined the steps that would be taken to redress them. He claimed that Japan would first sink the entire US fleet and then occupy Hawaii and close the Panama Canal.

The Western diplomats in Tokyo warned of what was afoot, as a rising tide of anti-foreign agitation swept the country. The colonial powers were being hoist with their own petard and could only register vain protests – which simply served to fuel Japanese disdain and contempt. As far as the dictatorships were concerned, Japan had signed the Anti-Comintern Pact, but was at first unwilling to bind herself too closely, especially to the extent of becoming involved in a European war. After all, she had done nicely out of semi-neutrality during the First World War.

Japan's aims were directed towards a New Order in the East, the so-called 'Co-Prosperity Sphere' which was formulated during the latter 1930s and was laid down in its final form in December 1941. This envisaged the seizure of the British, French and Dutch colonies during the course of a war in Europe. The establishment of this 'smaller Co-Prosperity Sphere' would be followed by a further war within twenty years. In the final phase, certain countries such as Burma and Malaya would become independent monarchies, while Australia, New Zealand and Ceylon would be absorbed into the Japanese Empire. Also to be swallowed were Alaska, the Western States of Canada, the State of Washington, the Central American countries other than Mexico, and the British, French and Dutch West Indies. This was quite a mouthful, and naturally the plan assumed that America would remain neutral during the first phase.

The Russo-German pact put a stop to Japan joining the Axis in September 1939, and it led to a distinct cooling off in relations with Berlin. Instead, Japan busied herself in worming her way into Indo-China, thus setting the stage for the eventual conquest of Malaya. She had seized her chance in 1914–18 while the great powers were busy in Europe and was about to do so again – but this time in a particularly vigorous manner.

4

UNCERTAIN TRUMPET: 1939–41
The strategic debate
September 1939 – October 1940

THE night of 3 September 1939 was a busy one for Corporal 'Pinkie' Evans of the Manchester Regiment. He was on duty in his battalion's canteen in Tanglin Barracks, and was left in no doubt as to his comrades' reaction to the news that Britain and Germany were at war. 'What a night that was,' he recalled.

The canteen was full and all the singing was 'Shout, boys, shout', 'Britannia rules the waves', and 'Up the German army.' No one at that time gave a thought to the Japanese.

Corporal Evans' superiors saw matters rather differently. The Defence Committee, charged with the co-ordination of Malaya's defence, became the War Committee with the outbreak of war in Europe, but the worsened situation and change in title made its deliberations no easier. In September 1939 the Committee consisted of the Governor, Sir Shenton Thomas, the GOC Malaya, Major-General L. V. Bond, and the Air Officer Commanding, Far East, Air Vice-Marshal J. T. Babington. Admiral Sir Percy Noble, Commander-in-Chief, China Squadron, joined the Committee when his headquarters moved from Hong Kong to Singapore. Mr C. A. Vlieland, a member of the Malayan Civil Service, held the influential post of Secretary for Defence, enjoying the right of direct access to the Governor. Indeed, the Defence Committee itself was Vlieland's brain-child, set up as a result of a paper he had written in the summer of 1938.

Vlieland hoped that the institution of the Defence Committee would lead to an improvement in defence planning. Defence would cease to be the sole concern of the GOC, and all three services, together with the civil administration, would be fully involved in the formulation of integrated plans, but Vlieland's hopes were not realised. It soon became clear that there were sharp differences of opinion between committee members, disagreements which were, moreover, worsened by personal antagonism. Bond, a somewhat aloof and distant man, was well aware that his predecessor had concluded that the Japanese were most likely to attempt the conquest of Singapore by landing troops in northern Malaya and Siam. He believed, however, that the forces at his disposal were too small for the defence of the whole of Malaya, and he proposed to defend only southern Johore and Singapore Island itself.

Such views were anathema to Babington. He was a firm devotee of air power, and argued strongly that the prime responsibility for the defence of Malaya and Singapore rested with the RAF: the army's main task was to protect the airfields. Many of these lay in the North – the very area which Bond considered that he had too few troops to defend. Babington did not appreciate that Bond's manpower argument was well-founded, nor did he recognise that his own air forces were inadequate for the role for which he intended them.

Matters were not improved by the fact that Bond was a member of the Legislative Assembly and enjoyed the title 'His Excellency', while Babington, whose responsibilities, were wider, lacked these status-symbols. It was, perhaps, inevitable that Bond and Babington should have clashed, for their views mirrored those of their parent services, which had been engaged in a long-standing dispute over the relative roles of the army and the RAF in the defence of overseas ports.

Vlieland's own attitiude compounded the confusion still further. He agreed with the pre-war army appreciation that the main danger of invasion was from the North, and believed that it was in the North that the invaders must be stopped. These views made him a natural opponent of Bond and, equally naturally, an ally of Babington. Vlieland enjoyed considerable influence with the Governor, and Bond soon found himself in a minority of one. In defence of Vlieland it must be recognised that his strategic appreciation was perceptive and his views were sound, but, like Babington, he over-estimated the capabilities of Bond's troops. Moreover, by giving Babington his vigorous support, Vlieland was straying well outside the parameter of his functions as Secretary for Defence, and was impeding the smooth working of the very body he had helped create.

But what of the navy, which had traditionally been assigned a major role in the defence of Britain's possessions in the Far East, and in support of whose strategy the great naval base at Singapore had been built? Even before the outbreak of war the Admiralty had recognised that the 'main fleet to Singapore' strategy was no longer viable. The Admiralty's war plans, formally approved in January 1939, admitted that the navy was not powerful enough to maintain strong forces in home waters, the Mediterranean and the Far East, and that the Far East came third in order of priority. The only way in which the fleet could be sent to the East in the event of a war with Germany and Japan was by leaving the Mediterranean to the French navy. This was, as we shall see, an option which was no longer open when war with Japan broke out. It was, in any case, recognised that sending the fleet to Singapore would, even assuming a fleet was available, take a considerable time: in July 1939 the Committee of Imperial Defence warned that it would take ninety days for the fleet to arrive. It soon doubled this estimate.

Large though considerations of military strategy bulked in the Governor's mind in September 1939, they were outweighed by other factors. The outbreak of war had increased the dependence of Britain's defence industries on the United States, and the Malayan economy assumed a new importance overnight. Malaya, producing 38 per cent of the world's rubber and 60 per cent of her tin, had immense potential as a dollar-earner, and Thomas was instructed to ensure that this 'dollar arsenal' stepped up its production.

Sir Shenton was later to write that:

The primary role allotted to Malaya . . . (was) the maximum possible production of tin and rubber and the conservation of foreign exchange. She sold more to the USA than any unit of the British Empire save Canada and, whereas Canada bought much from the USA, Malaya bought little. . . . The maximum unrestricted production of tin with the existing plant was estimated by the industry to be rather less than 90,000 tons a year. In 1940, the production was 84,751 tons, and in 1941 to the end of September it was 61,645 tons, equivalent to 82,198 tons in a full year. In that year European supervision had been reduced owing to the demands on manpower. . . . During the quarter ended the 30th of November 1940, no fewer than 137,331 tons of rubber were shipped to the USA alone.

This emphasis on the production and export of raw materials at once sharpened the friction between the military command and the civil administration. The former was concerned with putting Malaya into an efficient state of defence, and the latter with increasing the country's output. In retrospect it is all too easy to accuse the civil administration of striving, ostrich-like, to maintain normal civil and commercial life at the expense of other essential tasks. But as Raymond Callahan ably pointed out in *The Worst Disaster*:

Given the criticism that has been levelled at the civil administration and the business community in Malaya, it is only fair to note that in carrying on business as, or better than, usual, they were simply doing what London had told them to do (even though it doubtless suited the inclinations and bank accounts of many).

The fact that the military and civil authorities were pursuing goals which were, to a great extent, mutually incompatible, led to a series of clashes and to not inconsiderable ill-feeling on both sides. There was, for example, the problem of European manpower. The civil authorities were eager to use the available Europeans to help increase the production of tin and rubber. The military, on the other hand, pressed for the mobilisation of the Volunteer Forces, which formed a substantial part of the army's paper strength. The Governor initially consented to Bond's request for mobilisation, and the Volunteers were called up for training. For most units this mobilisation was not dissimilar to a Territorial Army annual camp. Lieutenant Guy Hutchinson of the Johore Volunteer Engineers, in civilian life manager of a rubber estate, recalled that:

Discipline was very strict, also bounds: no one went outside the camp site, except to the Kota Tinggi Club, without a pass, and there was no week-end leave.
Competitions for drill, turn-out, guard and hut cleanliness were held and the standard of drill, smartness etc was amazing. (Scabbards were polished to look like patent leather).
The Quarter-Guard would have done credit to any regular unit. . . .
As engineers a large programme had to be carried out and by the end of two training periods all ranks had a very good knowledge of all kinds of demolition work, bridging, water-supply and wiring. . . .

But while Lieutenant Hutchinson and his colleagues were engaged in the congenial tasks of bulling bayonet-scabbards and building bridges, their civilian posts were untenanted, which boded ill for the economy. Vlieland persuaded Sir Shenton to change his mind over mobilisation and the Governor later told the Colonial Office that: 'I conceive it to be our duty to give absolute priority to the claims of industry.' He was also opposed to the conscription of labourers for work on defences, and the low rates paid to military labourers were scarcely an incentive to volunteering for such work.

The fact that it was very much 'business as usual' for the civil community in Malaya helped highlight the differences between European civilians in Malaya and the soldiers of units who arrived there after the outbreak of war in Europe. Signalman William Ball, attached to the headquarters of 12th Indian Infantry Brigade, recalled that:

we had a beautiful social life, a jolly good one too. There was no trace of any war there at all, the chaps were out most evenings, dancing, visiting and doing one thing and another.

Corporal William Lee of the RAF, however, found that social distinctions and low pay cast a shadow over his enjoyment of Singapore.

'Eating out,' he noted,

was a rare experience. Finance not permitting. A fortnightly pay meant one good night out followed by visits to local bars, cinemas and at the very bottom, the Corporal's Club on the camp. Socially descending was Lavender Street, brash and notorious. At the Basrah Road end there were about six honky-tonk joints each selling beer, with a small band, a small dance floor where the prostitutes danced, their only reward was to be taken for a 'short time' or 'an all-nighter.'

One conscript complained to the *Singapore Free Press* that:

We would certainly appreciate a club wherein we could sit in comfort and an atmosphere of sociability. Perhaps you cannot realise that we are after all civilians at heart even though we are in uniform and do still look for the comfort of the homes we have left behind in England, mark you, to travel here in defence of Malaya and all who may be therein.

This is not a whine for pity; far from it, and I may add that we don't expect people to rush round us with free beer and fags, but rather want to obtain recognition for ourselves by our fellow countrymen out here.

But wartime British Other Ranks fitted uneasily into the world evoked so brilliantly by Noel Barber, where:

For the white man, life consisted of regular activities taken at a gentle pace. Nobody could hurry in a country where the temperature stayed around the nineties for most of the year. Work started early, finished around five o'clock. There were sports at the clubs before the sun set around 6.30 every day of the year. After that, men would go home, past Government House in its grounds of a hundred acres, often to a big, old-fashioned bungalow in the outskirts; not pretentious, but big so as to give room for the hot air to circulate, and surrounded by a compound with its glimpses of attap huts, palms, broad green banana leaves, all giving the impression of up-country jungle far removed from any city.

While the pre-war regular had been content to divide his free time between sports-field, canteen and dance halls like the New World and the Cadena, the wartime conscript often resented being made to feel a stranger in the European community, a community which, furthermore, played tennis, danced, and drank *stengahs* as if the war in Europe did not exist. To him life was anything but normal, and he may perhaps be forgiven for failing to understand the logic which kept the machinery of the dollar arsenal turning.

In January 1940, with the 'Phoney War' in freezing inactivity in Europe, Sir Shenton asked London to increase the size of the RAF garrison of Malaya, even at the expense of army reinforcements. He stressed that, in the absence of a fleet based at Singapore, the brunt of any defence of the area would fall upon the RAF. RAF reinforcements would also assist to deter the Japanese from taking military action. On 13 March Babington made similar recommendations to the Air Ministry, asking for more aircraft, and emphasising that the successful defence of Singapore implied the defence of the whole of Malaya and, of course, its vital airfields.

These memoranda met with a frosty reception in London. The Foreign Office suggested that Japanese forces were fully occupied in the fighting in China, and that internal strains within Japan made fresh aggression unlikely: Malaya should continue to keep the tin and rubber flowing, and not hamper her economy by making preparations to meet an improbable threat. The Air Ministry, while accepting that there was indeed a need for reinforcement, had its hands full in building up strength to match the Luftwaffe, but hoped to increase its forces in the Middle East and India, permitting the rapid reinforcement of Malaya should the need arise. The War Office was more pessimistic. It suggested that the fact that Britain was at war with Germany opened a window of opportunity for Japan, and that a British reverse in Europe might have dangerous consequences in the Far East, but the War Office, too, had to play the numbers game: although some reinforcements could be spared, Malaya, where war was no more than a possibility, came a poor third after Europe and the Middle East, where military operations were already in progress.

The Overseas Defence Committee's reply to the Governor's dispatch was, therefore, unhelpful. The defenders of Malaya would have to make do with the resources at their disposal. Sir Shenton was ordered to try to improve the effectiveness of the Volunteers, though he was to do so without interfering with the production of rubber and tin. The Committee added that not only were extra aircraft unlikely to be forthcoming in the foreseeable future, but some machines might even have to be withdrawn for use elsewhere.

As this dusty answer winged its way to Singapore, Major-General Bond was putting the finishing touches to a memorandum of his own. Supported, for once, by Babington, Bond pointed out that Singapore was expected to hold out for six months against a substantial Japanese force, which could attack with air support from bases which might be seized in Indo-China or Siam. Bond suggested that the whole of Malaya could only be held by a force of three divisions, two tank regiments, two-machine-gun battalions, and a reinforcement pool amounting to 20 per cent of the total force. Moreover, if the army was to move up into Siam to thwart Japanese landings or seizures of airfields, an extra two divisions would be needed. Although it had been appreciated, as early as 1925, that it was upon the North that a Japanese blow was most likely to fall, this was the first time that a military commander had estimated the force levels required to meet such an attack.

Bond's memorandum would have been unlikely to have aroused much enthusiasm whatever the date of its arrival in London, for the GOC Malaya was suggesting the massive reinforcement of his own command at a time when the British Expeditionary Force in France contained only ten divisions and an armoured brigade. But on 16 May, the very day that the document was considered, Churchill flew to France to hear from the French leaders that the German offensive, launched six days previously, had shattered the Allied Front: defeat in the West was staring him in the face. Bond was told, not surprisingly, that although the Chiefs of Staff were urgently considering the defence of the Far East, the critical situation in Europe precluded the dispatch of reinforcements. The reply also contained the by now familar assertion of the importance of Malaya's tin and rubber.

Having received this gloomy message, Bond at once informed the War Committee that, much as he agreed that the threat lay to the North, he could only afford to hold Singapore Island and Southern Johore, with a battalion on the island of Penang and another covering the airfield at Alor Star in the north-west. He believed that Singapore could be held for only two months, whereas it would take six for a fleet to arrive. Babington disagreed violently, and demanded that the army should be used to garrison the airfields of the North, arguing that, if the RAF lost air superiority over Malaya, successful defence would be impossible.

Sir Shenton Thomas was, at this time, on leave in Britain, having a much-needed rest and profiting from the opportunity to discuss the problems of the Far East with senior officials in London. His deputy, Mr S. W. Jones, upon whom the chairmanship of the War Committee had devolved, felt unable to choose between the plans proposed by Bond and Babington. He expressed serious reservations about the consequences of the abandonment of the North, but trenchantly pointed out that the crux of the problem lay in the strength of forces available. Bond had no doctrinaire objection to garrisoning the North: he simply felt unable to do so with the forces at his disposal. The solution, therefore, lay in the immediate dispatch of reinforcements.

The deepening dispute over the defence of Malaya went on against a background of catastrophe in Europe. Service chiefs and politicians alike were preoccupied with the immediate danger in Europe, and the problems of the Far East, serious though they undoubtedly were, were pushed to the edge of the stage. There was, nevertheless, general agreement that Malaya was in a precarious position. On 4 July the Chiefs of Staff confessed that they were 'extremely apprehensive of the trend of events in the Far East,' and recommended that, on military

44

grounds, war with Japan must be avoided. A diplomatic attempt to persuade America to announce that Japanese aggression would be regarded as a *casus belli* foundered, and Australia and New Zealand, both of whom had agreed to send troops to the Middle East, became 'restive and reluctant to do so' until the strategic situation in the Far East had been made clearer.

Finally, Sir Shenton Thomas, still on leave in England, wrote to the Colonial Office, pointing out that:

it is necessary to decide now what action should be taken in the event of war with Japan. Apparently naval reinforcements are not possible, and in the absence of the Navy the RAF is the only source of help. I know it will be said that sufficient forces of the RAF cannot be spared today. If, then, Malaya should be attacked by Japan within (say) the next two months, is the territory and Singapore to be left to its fate? If so, let us be told and we will do the best we can; but if not let a decision be taken at once as to the size and nature of the relieving air force and let all preparations for receiving it and enabling it to function with the maximum of efficiency be put in hand now.

The War Cabinet met to consider Far East strategy on 8 August. The Chiefs of Staff acknowledged the requirement to defend the whole of Malaya, and admitted that the current RAF strength in the area, 88 aircraft, fell well below the minimum strength thought necessary – 336 aircraft with 168 in immediate reserve. The Chiefs of Staff hoped to replace the aircraft already in Malaya with more modern types in 1940, and also to increase the overall aircraft strength, completing the process in 1941. Once Malaya was fully equipped with modern aircraft and the RAF was able to shoulder the full burden of defence, the army garrison could be reduced to six brigades. But, until this time, the Chiefs of Staff agreed with Bond that three divisions were needed.

Saying that three divisions were required for the defence of Malaya was one thing: providing them was quite another. There could be no question of sending troops from the United Kingdom, whose invasion was believed to be imminent. The Middle East was an active theatre, and units of the rapidly increasing Indian army were already earmarked for service there, rather than in the Far East. Australia, the Chiefs of Staff suggested, should be asked to provide a division, and another one might be cobbled together elsewhere.

A similar paper on the defence of the Dutch East Indies was even more gloomy. Taken together, the documents clearly demonstrated that there was little chance of sending substantial reinforcements – naval, land or air – to the Far East in the immediate future. Indeed, the hope that the RAF's strength would have reached an adequate level by the end of 1941 was almost self-consciously optimistic, bearing in mind the frenzied demands for air defence of the United Kingdom and the only minimally less urgent requests for air cover in the Middle East.

Churchill did his best to reassure the Prime Ministers of Australia and New Zealand that the situation in the Far East was not as desperate as it seemed. Every effort was being made to preserve peace with Japan. Although America had given no firm assurance, she would be unlikely to welcome a renewed burst of Japanese expansionism. Churchill pointed out that although the Mediterranean fleet could be sent to Singapore at any time, he was reluctant to take this step until it was absolutely vital. Nevertheless, he emphasised that if the Japanese embarked upon an invasion of Australia or New Zealand, Britain would at once sacrifice every other interest, save home defence, to move to the support of the Dominions.

The War Cabinet formally accepted the Chiefs' of Staffs recommendations on 28 August, but work had already begun on their implimentation. As the initial appreciations had themselves implied, there was little hope of getting many more men or extra aircraft to Singapore in the near future. The Air Ministry was striving to re-equip the RAF in the Middle East, and the best that it could offer for Malaya was the Brewster Buffalo, an obsolete fighter which was to be hacked mercilessly from the sky by the Japanese Zero. Flight-Lieutenant Tim Vigors, an experienced fighter pilot sent out to Singapore to assist with the formation of new squadrons in late 1940, thought that the Buffaloes:

weren't a bad little aircraft. . . . They'd got nothing like the performance of the Spitfire, but they were very manoeuvrable and had quite a reasonable rate of climb. . . . They weren't bad, and once we got them flying we had quite a lot of fun with them. . . . They were a nice little sporting aircraft.

The War Office hoped that India might be able to provide at least some of the troops it so urgently required. The Indian army had already sent a divisional headquarters and two brigades to the Middle East and another brigade to Malaya, and in October 1940 another brigade went to the Middle East to bring 4th Indian Division up to strength. The 5th Indian Division, two brigades strong, went to the Sudan. This rapid increase in the size of the Indian army – an increase which Churchill never fully appreciated – was carried out only at considerable cost in efficiency and, indeed, in fighting ability. Units were 'milked' of seasoned officers and NCOs to provide drafts for newly-raised units. The 'family' atmosphere which had characterised Indian regiments was imperilled; many young British officers had only the scantiest grasp of the language spoken by their men, and there were growing problems in the selection and training of NCOs.

Major-General B. W. Key, an Indian army officer who was later to play a leading part in the fighting in Malaya, had first-hand experience of the consequences of "milking". 'Every Indian battalion,' he wrote,

lost some 40 per cent of officers, NCOs, specialist and trained soldiers . . . to form the basis of new battalions. These battalions were brought to strength with inexperienced (tho' excellent material) officers who could not speak the language. The men were recruits about 18 years of age who had fired some 50 rounds on the range. They become the riflemen in the platoons. . . .

When, on 4 September, the Chiefs of Staff informed Churchill that they intended to send the 7th Australian Division and two Indian infantry brigades to the Far East as the first wave of reinforcements, the Prime Minister replied in tones which threatened to make nonsense of the August decisions. He told General Ismay that the main defence of Singapore was the fleet, and that the idea of trying to defend the whole of Malaya 'cannot be entertained.' He suggested that the 7th Australian Division should go to the Middle East instead, leaving Malaya to be reinforced only by six battalions. Churchill continued to assert the primacy of the Middle East in the face of opposition from the Chiefs of Staff, and by mid-autumn 1940 there were, as Raymond Callahan pointed out:

really two strategies for the Far East. The official one was contained in the Chiefs' of Staff paper; Churchill's personal policy consisted of relying on America and hoping for the best.

Part of the divergence between the official strategy and Churchill's own view may be explained by the fact that Churchill believed that Singapore was a fortress in the classical sense, like, for example, Verdun or Plevna. This being the case, he failed to see the need for defending Singapore by holding the whole of Malaya. The defences of Singapore were as we have seen, designed to resist only against attack from the sea, and although some work had been carried out on a defence line running across Johore, the project had been abandoned. Had Churchill realised that this was indeed the case, then the logic of the army's desire to hold the whole of the Malayan peninsula would no doubt have impressed itself on him. But, as he himself later made clear, the Prime Minister had no idea of the real state of affairs. 'I cannot understand how it was that I did not know this,' he admitted in *The Second World War*.

none of my professional advisers . . . pointed it out to me . . . I ought to have known . . . the possibility of Singapore having no landward defences no more entered my mind than that of a battleship being launched without a bottom:

By October 1940 the Chiefs of Staff had become convinced that part of the problem in the Far East was the clash of personality between Bond and Babington. Admiral Sir Percy Noble painted a gloomy picture of command arrangements in the Far East on his return to England after his relief by Vice-Admiral Sir Geoffrey Layton, and news of the quarrel trickled in from other sources. On 12 October the Chiefs of Staff decided upon the appointment of a commander-in-Chief for the Far East, and Air Chief Marshal Sir Robert Brooke-Popham was duly appointed five days later.

'Brookham', as he was nicknamed, was a lanky, red-moustached airman with a long and distinguished career behind him. He had qualified as a pilot with the Royal Flying Corps before the First World War, and had joined the RAF on its formation. After a series of increasingly important command and staff appointments he had retired from the RAF in 1937, and spent the next two years as governor of Kenya. Recalled to the active list on the outbreak of war, Brooke-Popham had been employed on liaison visits to South Africa and Canada. In some respects he was a strange choice for the onerous new post of Commander-in-Chief, Far East. He was sixty-two, lacked recent operational experience, and had no special qualifications or attributes which might have been expected to assist him in his new role. True, he was undoubtedly an officer of lengthy seniority and proven ability. Perhaps the RAF was reluctant to spare a more thrusting commander at a time of acute crisis, or possibly Brooke-Popham's colonial service in Kenya was regarded as a valuable asset.

Yet even a younger man, with recent relevant experience might have been daunted by the directive which Brooke-Popham received on 22 October. He was responsible for operational control, in the most general sense, of British land and air forces in Burma, Malaya and Hong Kong, and for the 'general direction of training' of these units. He had no authority over naval forces in his area, although he was responsible for ocean reconnaissance: while the War Office and Air Ministry retained administrative control over their units in the Far East, the Admiralty took care to preserve its authority in operational as well as administrative matters. Finally, he was to enjoy no authority over the civil administration.

These severe limitations on Brooke-Popham's power, together with the minuscule size of his staff, effectively deprived him of the status of commander and reduced him to that of a co-ordinator. His responsibilities were vast, and his powers limited; whatever Brooke-Popham's personal abilities might or might not have been, he was clearly saddled with an impossible task. Matters were not helped by the fact that he received no formal briefing from the Chiefs of Staff before leaving London. When he left England at the end of the month there were still a large number of unanswered questions in Brooke-Popham's mind. It was an inauspicious beginning.

While the strategic debates flickered on along the corridors of power in Whitehall, the situation in the Far East had deteriorated sharply. July witnessed the fall of the Japanese government, and its replacement by a cabinet headed by Prince Fuminaro Konoye. Although Konoye himself was a moderate, his cabinet included two 'hawks': General Hideki Tojo, the Minister of War, and Yosuke Matsuoka, the Foreign Minister. Tojo was leader of the army faction committed to the establishment of the 'Greater East Asia Co-Prosperity Sphere', and Matsuoka was an aggressive nationalist who had brought about Japanese withdrawal from the League of Nations. The Konoye government decided to embark upon a policy of limited expansionism, seeking to gain control of Indo-China, Malaya, Singapore, Siam and the Dutch East Indies, by peaceful means if possible, and to end the war in China.

Japanese foreign policy was perilously close to being locked in the vicious cycle which was eventually to bring war to the East. Gaining control of areas rich in raw materials was a prime motive for Japanese expansionism. But this very expansionism had already led to war with China – a war which itself consumed raw materials – and was to lead the United States to impose economic sanctions which worsened the raw material situation still further. The process might have been arrested in the summer of 1940, but even then the combination of Japanese chauvinism and ambition, and Western failure to understand the nature of the problem, made the situation potentially explosive.

The Fall of France brought Japanese policy closer to fruition, for it left the authorities in French Indo-China isolated and unable to call for assistance. Moreover, despite the efforts of Sir Percy Noble, Admiral Decoux, French naval Commander-in-Chief and subsequently Governor-General of Indo-China, declined to throw his lot in with Free France, and remained faithful to the Vichy regime, now effectively under German domination. Japan demanded military access to Indo-China, and control of some of its airfields, in early August, and on 23 September her troops moved into northern Indo-China, seizing an invaluable jumping-off position for subsequent operations against Siam or Malaya.

Only four days later Japan signed the Tripartite Pact with Germany and Italy. The latter two signatories recognised Japanese ambitions in the Far East, and all three parties bound themselves to assist one another if attacked by a power not already engaged in the fighting in China or in the European war. This clause was a clear warning to the United States, but its consequences were not those that its authors had anticipated. On 16 October the United States government announced the introduction of control of export of iron and steel scrap. About one-third of the iron and steel scrap used by Japanese industry came from abroad, most of it from the United States. This new embargo, coming less than three months after a similar ban on the export of aviation fuel, had the combined effects of tightening the screw on the Japanese economy and irritating the Japanese government, without actually being powerful enough to compel that government to alter its course.

Even before Japanese troops had moved into Indo-China, the Chiefs of Staff had ordered Layton, Bond and Babington to draw up detailed tactical appreciations based on the Chiefs' of Staff August memorandum on the Far East situation, and to assume, in doing so, that the Japanese had complete control of the whole of Indo-China. The eastern commanders replied, on 16 October, that since a Japanese invasion of Malaya was almost certain to come through Siam, it could best be met by a British advance to hold the narrow Kra Isthmus, just across the border in Siam. Bond's April memorandum had already suggested that this operation would require two divisions over and above those employed elsewhere in Malaya. The eastern commanders were less sanguine than their superiors in London about force levels in general. They recommended that 566 aircraft should be deployed in Malaya – 220 more than the number that the Chiefs of Staff had believed satisfactory. When this strength had been attained, the army's garrison could be run down from three divisions. They also asked for three flotillas of MTBs to prevent landings on the long Malayan coastline.

These estimates, frightening enough in themselves, were jacked up still further by a defence conference which met, under Layton's chairmanship, at Singapore in late October. It included Bond, Babington and Vlieland, together with staff officers from India, Burma, Australia and New Zealand. It was assumed that, if war broke out with Japan, the Dutch would be involved from the start, but that the United States would fight only if attacked. Lack of naval strength ruled out an offensive strategy; defence was therefore the order of the day, and the one area believed to be vital to British interests was Singapore and hence Malaya.

The conference then turned its attention to the question of the defence of Malaya, and noted that its current garrison was well below the minimum level required. It was suggested that part at least of the shortfall might be made up by troops from India and Australia. While the conference generally concurred with the estimates of forces required contained in the local commanders' memorandum of 16 October, it emphasised that there were very serious deficiencies at the time, and drew particular attention to shortages in field, anti-tank and anti-aircraft artillery. It then recommended that Burma should be defended by seven battalions and a squadron of aircraft, a suggestion which increased the figure of aircraft demanded to no less than 582, rising, with the inclusion of immediate reserves, to 878. With Britain's defence establishment already creaking and groaning under the strain – a strain which was soon increased by German and Italian advances in the Balkans – the eastern commanders were asking for resources which were simply not available.

Brooke-Popham reached Singapore on 18 November, and set up his small headquarters in the naval base. On 7 December he warned the Chiefs of Staff against taking a soft line with Japan, and suggested close relations with the Dutch, who were resisting, as best they could, Japanese demands for increased supplies of raw materials from the Dutch East Indies. He believed that the Japanese should be left in no doubt as to the risks that any aggression would run, and approved of the recent stiffening of America's attitiude. At a tactical level, he reported that he was considering the plan for an advance to the Kra Isthmus, a scheme which, he felt, had much to recommend it, despite the fact that it would require extra troops.

The unfortunate 'Brookham' soon found himself under pressure from both friends and enemies. When the Chiefs of Staff discussed the Far East on 13 January they were faced with a memorandum from Churchill which baldly stated that:

The political situation in the Far East does not seem to require, and the strength of our Air Force by no means permits, the maintenance of such large forces in the Far East at this time.

Churchill had still not modified his policy of trusting in luck and the Americans, for on 23 December he had wired Australia to emphasise that he thought war with Japan unlikely, but that he was certain that the United States would enter the war at once if Japan attacked British possessions.

Nor were the Chiefs of Staff, who had recommended the reinforcement of Singapore only six months before, prepared to press the Prime Minister on the point. They replied to his 13 January note with an admission that they did not intend to make 'any appreciable diversion' of British war effort to the Far East, where they planned to make only 'a small start in our long-term programme' by forming two fighter squadrons – equipped, in the event, with the lamentable Buffalo – in Malaya.

The Prime Minister and the Chiefs of Staff were not, however, writing off the Far East in a cavalier fashion. Churchill's conception of the problem was admittedly warped by his belief that Singapore was a self-contained fortress, but there were, in any case, problems nearer home. Churchill was convinced of the need to shore up the Greeks against the German threat, even at the expense of diverting forces from the Western Desert, where Wavell's offensive had just bundled the Italians back across Cyrenaica. Moreover, in late January 1941 great emphasis was being placed on persuading Turkey to join the British, and substantial forces would have to be sent to Turkey's assistance in the event of her entry into the war.

The problems facing Britain in the Mediterranean were in themselves an obstacle to the reinforcement of the Far East. They also impeded negotiations with the Dutch, for it was recognised that a clear statement that an attack on the Dutch East Indies would bring Britain into the war would be unwise in view of Britain's very limited resources in the Far East. In late February Brooke-Popham chaired an Anglo-Dutch-Australian conference at Singapore, and a plan for joint action – the ADA Agreement – was drawn up. The Chiefs of Staff, however, declined to accept the conference's definition of a Japanese act of agression, arguing that the British government could not commit itself to co-operate with the Dutch: the decision to assist the Dutch could only be made after the Japanese had actually attacked them.

Another conference, held in April between British, American, Dutch, Australian and New Zealand representatives, considered possible action in the event of a war between Britain and the United States on one hand and the signatories of the Tripartite Pact on the other. Although the conference succeeded in establishing a combined plan – the ABD Agreement – which envisaged Allied co-operation under the general strategic direction of the British Commander-in-Chief, Far East, the American Chiefs of Staff rejected the scheme. Their reasons for doing so were in part political and in part strategic. On the political level they believed, just as the British Chiefs of Staff did with the ADA Agreement, that the United States should not give binding undertakings to enter a war unless she was herself attacked. In strategic terms, they feared that the plan would result in part of the American fleet coming under British control to fight in an area which was not deemed vital to American interests. Subsequent Anglo-Dutch discussions produced a general plan for use in the event of war with Japan, but, although the Americans knew of it, they remained unwilling to pledge their involvement.

While Brooke-Popham strove to formalise joint plans in the face of opposition from both London and Washington, the Japanese continued to strengthen their position. A border dispute between Siam and French Indo-China led to a series of armed clashes in late 1940, and in January 1941 these flared into open war. The French got the worst of the fighting on land, but riposted by demolishing the Siamese navy at Koh Chang on 17 January. The Japanese offered to mediate between the belligerents, and a series of meetings between French and Siamese representatives were held in Tokyo. The mediation plan was not a success, but Japan capitalised upon her newly-won prestige by opening two new consulates in Siam. One of these at the northern railhead of Chiengmai: the other was at the little East coast town of Singora, at the narrowest point of the Kra Isthmus.

For the next eleven months relations between the British, Siamese and Japanese governments, and the French authorities in Indo-China, assumed the air of a complex four-step tango. The Japanese were eager to obtain the right of free passage through Siam and to avoid clashes with Siamese troops. Britain was equally anxious that the Siamese should refuse these concessions, but they were unable, as Brooke-Popham was himself compelled to admit, to offer effective military assistance to the Siamese in the event of a Japanese attack. The French authorities were also involved because they suspected, not without reason, that Britain might support Siamese territorial claims on the Indo-China border in return for Siamese resistance to Japanese demands. It is hard not to sympathise with the Siamese themselves, who were subjected to a mixture of threats and promises from powers for whom Siamese interests were of secondary importance. The situation remained unclear as late as December 1941, but despite the continuation of apparently friendly relations between the Siamese and the Malayan authorities right up until the outbreak of war, events were to show that the Siamese were prepared to bend to the Japanese will. Given Japanese military preponderance, and Britain's inability to guarantee Siam's integrity, it would have been curious had they done otherwise.

The spring of 1941 saw the strengthening of the garrison of Malaya, and the arrival of commanders who were to be the leading actors in the tragedy of Singapore. The Australian government had promised to send a brigade group, and had reached the conclusion that a substantial detached Australian force could not be adequately commanded by a brigade headquarters. Major-General H. Gordon Bennett, commander of the 8th Australian Division, was accordingly dispatched to take control, with instructions which emphasised that the force was to retain its Australian identity and was not to be sub-divided without his consent. If the GOC Malaya insisted on operational dispersion, Bennett was to comply under protest, reporting the full circumstances to Australian army headquarters in Melbourne.

Gordon Bennett himself was already a controversial figure. He was not a regular soldier, but had been commissioned into the militia in 1908, fought with distinction at Gallipoli and on the Western Front, and ended the First World War as a brigadier-general. Between the wars he resumed civilian life but continued to serve as a citizen soldier, taking command of the 2nd Division in 1926. There was a squabble over his promotion to major-general, and a clash between Bennett and the military authorities over the question of Australia's preparedness for war. Although he was the youngest, and most senior, of Australia's major-generals, he did not receive command of a division on the outbreak of war in 1939, and it was not until the summer of 1940 that he at last obtained a division, a command which, Bennett and his supporters suspected, only the opposition of regular officers had previously denied him.

Gordon Bennett arrived by air in Singapore on 4 February 1941, and the 22nd Australian Brigade Group arrived by sea later that month. After a brief period of indecision concerning the role of Bennett and his divsion – whose three brigades were split between Malaya, Port Darwin and New South Wales – the Australian government began to increase its forces in Malaya. By 7 December Bennett had a substantial divisional headquarters and two infantry brigades, some 15,200 men in all, under his command. Bennett enjoyed right of direct communication with Melbourne over administrative matters, and was later requested to report direct to the Australian Minister of the Army. The British Official History, while noting that these arrangements were normal practice when Australian troops were fighting alongside the British, added that it was:

highly desirable that an Australian commander should be sufficiently flexible in his attitude to make adequate allowance for the difference in background and viewpoint between his force and those drawn from other parts of the Commonwealth, and of course that this attitude should be reciprocated.

Shortly before Gordon Bennett's arrival, pressure within the War Committee had come to a head. Brooke-Popham rapidly became convinced that Vlieland was obstructive, and, even before the Governor returned from leave in December 1940, threatened to resign unless Vlieland was replaced as Secretary for Defence. At a meeting of the Committee he accused Vlieland of refusing to co-operate with Bond and with dragging his feet over civil defence. Brooke-Popham was supported by Bond and Layton, and Thomas, usually one of Vlieland's warmest supporters, failed to come to his defence. Vlieland resigned as Secretary for Defence the following day and, hurt and embittered, left the Malayan Civil Service and returned to England. His place was taken by Mr C. W. Dawson.

Vlieland was not the only member of the War Committee to depart in early 1941. Brooke-Popham decided that both Babington and Bond should be replaced. Babington's tour of duty was, in any case, nearing its end, but Bond still had some time to serve in Malaya. Nevertheless, the War Office complied with Brooke-Popham's wishes, and on 14 May Bond was replaced by Lieutenant-General A. E. Percival. Babington had already been succeeded by Air Vice-Marshal C. W. H. Pulford on 24 April.

Percival's name was to be inseperably associated with the tragedy of Singapore, and it is as well to turn our attention to this figure who has attracted both devoted supporters and bitter enemies. Percival had not initially chosen a career in the regular army. The First World War had swept him out of a City office into an infantry battalion. Enlisting as a private soldier, Percival was rapidly commissioned, and served with great distinction on the Western Front, ending the war as a battalion commander. Whatever hard words were subsequently used about Percival, even his most obdurate opponents could not deny the physical courage which won him the DSO and the MC. Nor, in looking at the somewhat effete buck-toothed Percival of 1941–2, should we forget that Percival was a man who had led soldiers with flair and distinction through the maelstrom of the Western Front.

Percival stayed on in the army after the war, holding a series of staff appointments including, as we have seen, the post of GSO 1 to Dobbie in 1936–7. A major-general in 1940, he became one of the three Assistant Chiefs of the Imperial General Staff before, shortly after the evacuation from Dunkirk, he requested command of a division. 'I asked to be transferred,' he wrote,

to a field formation, and was appointed to command the 44th (Home Counties) Division. . . . Perhaps I was influenced in this request by the fact that, having served for the whole of the First World War as a regimental officer in France and Belgium, my leanings were rather towards active service in the field than the more sedentary, though none the less important, work at the War Office.

At the end of March 1941 Percival was ordered to report to the War Office and to procure tropical kit without delay. On arrival at Whitehall he was informed that he was to be GOC Malaya, with the acting rank of lieutenant-general. Percival was ordered to leave for Malaya by flying-boat three days later, but the flying-boat developed a fault and he did not get under way till 1 May, after a delay of some five weeks. The incident is a telling one, revealing as it does the parlous state of the RAF's transport aircraft, and the lack of urgency accorded to Percival's departure.

Percival put the delay to good use, finding out as much as he could from the War Office about the strategic situation in the Far East and the resources that were likely to be available. He gathered that the projected advance into southern Siam was well regarded at the War Office, although he himself had some doubts about it in view of the number of troops required for the operation and the political problems which the move would entail. Delighted though he was at being given an independent command, Percival realised that his future had become, as he put it,

a little uncertain. . . . In going to Malaya I realised that there was the double danger, either of being left in an inactive command for some years if war did not break out in the East or, if it did, of finding myself involved in a pretty sticky business with the inadequate forces which are usually to be found in the distant parts of our Empire in the early stages of war.

Events were to prove Percival's fears to be amply justified: indeed, it would be something of an understatement to describe the situation in Malaya and Singapore as 'pretty sticky.' Percival might have been forgiven for using sharper adjectives.

The new GOC Malaya's arrival coincided with that of the first wave of Indian reinforcements. Headquarters III Indian Corps arrived in May. At its head was Lieutenant-General Sir Lewis Heath, who had recently been brilliantly successful as commander of the 5th Indian Division in the Eritrean campaign. Heath set up his headquarters at Kuala Lumpur, and took over operational control of northern Malaya. Under his command were two Indian infantry divisions, both comprising two instead of the normal three brigades. 9th Indian Division was in the north-western state of Kedah, while 11th Indian Division was deployed on the East coast at Kota Bharu and Kuantan. Heath also commanded detached battalions at Penang and Kroh, the garrison of Penang, and the as yet unmobilised Federated Malay States Volunteers, some four battalions.

To the South, Major-General F. Keith Simmons was responsible for the defence of Johore and Singapore itself. He commanded five battalions on Singapore Island, and the 12th Indian Infantry Brigade in Johore. Percival's general reserve was Gordon Bennett's force, which still comprised only one brigade group, deployed around Port Dickson, about one-third of the way up the western coast.

56

Although the force at Percival's disposal looked impressive on paper and, indeed, was to be further reinforced before December 1941, it suffered from a number of serious flaws. It was, in the first place, a heterogeneous collection of formations – British, Indian and Australian – rather than a homogeneous fighting force. The Indian contingent bore testimony to the stresses created by the 'milking' which had accompanied the Indian army's wartime expansion. It was short of seasoned officers and NCOs, and had a high proportion of young soldiers in the ranks. It also included units of the Indian States Forces, whose morale and training were inferior to those of Indian army units proper.

Something of a psychological gulf stretched between the British and Indian armies. There was a tendency for Indian army officers to look down on the British army as a rather amateur organisation, while some British army officers reciprocated by regarding the Indian army as somewhat socially inferior. Percival, for example, felt that Heath suffered from what he called the 'Indian Army complex' through not having served with British troops or having attended the Staff College at Camberley. He was, thought Percival, more loyal to the Indian army than he was to the combined 'Imperial Army' of Malaya. Indian army officers might, on the other hand, be forgiven for looking askance at the appointment of Percival to a command for which an Indian army officer might have been more suitable. For while Percival had commanded nothing larger than a battalion in action, Heath had recent experience of the command of a division: he was also senior to Percival, still only an acting lieutenant-general.

Practical problems compounded the difficulties created by mutual misunderstanding. The rates of pay of officers in the British and Indian armies were different. As Major-General Woodburn Kirby pointed out:

It might happen therefore that the transfer of to an equivalent or even a higher appointment in another formation would involve a severe reduction in emoluments. This could even result in a British service officer appointed as a first-grade staff officer with an Indian formation drawing less net pay than a third-grade staff officer serving under him. It was therefore almost impossible in practice to ask an individual to accept such a transfer.

In consequence, Kirby observed, Command Headquarters at Fort Canning could not be staffed with the best officers available. It also suffered from being required to act as both command and army headquarters, and there was, in any case, a serious shortage of trained staff officers.

The relationship between Percival and Gordon Bennett's Australians was to prove no easier than that he enjoyed with Heath and his

Indian troops. Percival believed that Gordon Bennett's command was always 'a little top-heavy with a very high proportion of administrative personnel compared to the fighting troops.' He later implied that the system under which Bennett had been appointed to command a division was inherently defective, and complained that he was never really certain of the special instructions under which the Australian force was operating. Friction between Percival and Bennett was clearly visible to Ian Wingfield, a driver at 8th Division's headquarters, who described Bennett as:

an astounding man . . . most capable . . . with very high moral standards. . . . The troops called him 'Ginger' or 'Cocky' – he had red hair. . . . Bennett didn't get on with Percival or Heath. He thought they were too complacent.

There were a number of clashes between Percival and Bennett. In one instance Bennett insisted on the promotion of the relatively junior Lieutenant-Colonel Maxwell to command the 27th Brigade when its commander relinquished his appointment on account of illness. Maxwell, inexperienced in the handling of a brigade, was later to be criticised for locating his headquarters as near as possible to Gordon Bennett's, in order to obtain advice more easily.

The conflict between Bennett and Percival was, to an extent, mirrored by friction between the Australian and British troops. 'Many of the RAF types,' commented H. J. Burn of the RAAF,

were definitely stand-offish. Australians were tolerated. That's about all.

But Charles 'Morrie' March of 2/10th Field Company, Royal Australian Engineers, thought that 'We got on well with the Poms . . . especially the Scots.' Some Australians felt that they had been posted to a backwater. Sergeant Ken Harrison, of the 4th Anti-Tank Regiment, recalled that:

it was very frustrating for us in 8th Division. We never thought the Japs would try it. We prayed for a transfer to the Middle East where there really *was* a war. We used to get letters from the Middle East. They called us Menzies Glamour Boys. Chocolate Soldiers. They told us not to worry, she'll be all right, leave it to them.

But this was not the end of Percival's problems. His predecessor had already drawn attention to the need for organised military labour, and in April 1941 Malaya Command was authorised to raise six labour companies on mobilisation. This was opposed by the civil authorities, and Percival's attempts to raise one Chinese company foundered in the face of the War Office's refusal to pay its members a realistic wage. By December 1941, despite some concessions by the War Office over the pay question, Percival had at his disposal only two Indian labour companies, which had been in Malaya since 1940. Tight financial control by the War Office also impeded the construction of defence works, although, as Brigadier Ivan Simson discovered when he went out to Malaya as Chief Engineer in August 1941, little urgency was attached to the construction of obstacles or defences.

Air Vice-Marshal Pulford wrestled with difficulties which were no less intractable. When he took command he found that his force was well below even the modest initial target of 336 aircraft. By December 1941 he had four day fighter squadrons and a night fighter squadron; two light bomber squadrons, two torpedo-bomber squadrons and one flying-boat squadron, together with support and maintenance facilities. When war broke out Pulford had only 158 first-line aircraft available, and a total strength of no more than 180. As the Official History admits, the total deficiency in Pulford's command, including essential reserves, was no less than 415 aircraft.

Nor was this all. Most British aircraft in the Far East were of obsolete types. The four day-fighter squadrons were equipped with the outdated Buffalo, and many of their pilots were only partially trained. The torpedo-bomber crews, in contrast, were well-trained and experienced, but they flew the elderly Vildebeeste, with a maximum speed of only 137 mph. The two light bomber squadrons were equipped with Blenheims and the reconnaissance squadrons with Hudsons: in order to make the fullest use of the small numbers of both types of aircraft, all these squadrons were trained to carry out maritime reconnaissance missions and bombing by both day and night.

Effective air defence requires an established network of warning and control systems. Wing Commander H. S. Darley (later Group Captain), posted to Malaya in 1941 as wing commander fighter operations, soon realised that these facilities were primitive in the extreme. 'It was not until I got there,' he recalled,

that I realised that there was, practically speaking, no form of air defence organisation as we then knew it in the United Kingdom – even from the basic point of view of radars, the back-up of an observer corps, and no form of operations rooms at all.

There was a warning system covering Singapore from the North, but it proved impossible to do much to cover the airfields in the North, where communications were difficult and there was a shortage of both personnel and equipment.

The lack of adequate warning systems paralleled a shortage of anti-aircraft artillery. In all, four heavy and one light anti-aircraft regiments were available, one of the former a hastily-raised and partly-trained Indian unit. A battery of heavy anti-aircraft guns and a mobile battery of light guns were sent up-country to III Corps, but the majority of guns, together with the one searchlight regiment available, were retained for the defence of Singapore.

The airfields of the North, upon which so much of the RAF's hopes for the defence of Malaya rested, were at best a double-edged weapon. While some had been deliberately sited to maximise the operational range of aircraft, others had started life as civil aerodromes. The main airfield in Kedah was at Alor Star, only thirty miles from the Siamese border, while the base at Kota Bharu in Kelantan was a mere six miles South of the frontier. These airfields, and others at Sungei Patani and Butterworth in Kedah, Gong Kedah and Machang in Kedah, and Ipoh and Taiping in Perak, were all within range of airfields in Siam. Many of them were also vulnerable to swift attacks across the frontier, seaborne assault, or, as in the case of Kota Bharu, both of these. The airfields in central Malaya, at Kuala Lumpur in the West and Kuantan in the East, were more secure, although the latter, only six miles from the coast, was a potential target for attack from the sea. There was one airfield and a landing ground in Johore, and three airfields and a civil airport on Singapore Island.

JAPANESE WAR PLANS 1940–41

While reinforcements trickled into Malaya and the newly-arrived commanders set about grappling with the daunting problems which confronted them, the war-clouds thickened on the far horizon. Fear of Russian intervention in Manchuria had long been a brake on Japanese ambitions, but the signing of a Russo-Japanese neutrality pact in April 1941 removed this menace, for the time at least. The German invasion of Russia on 22 June came as a shock to the Japanese, who had not been informed that the offensive was to take place. A high-level conference three days later decided that Japan would not enter the war against Russia, although she would remain a member of the Tripartite Pact. With the Manchurian flank now doubly secured, attention would be concentrated on the seizure of southern Indo-China by all means up to and including war.

Other pressures conspired to make war more likely. The diplomatic mission sent to the Dutch East Indies returned without having managed to extract the oil supplies which Japan so urgently required, and shortly afterwards the United States placed an embargo on the export of oil to all but a few selected nations, of which Japan was not one. On 21 July the French authorities in Indo-China announced that they would submit to Japanese occupation of the whole of French Indo-China, and by the end of the month this occupation was complete. America reacted, on 26 July, by freezing all Japanese assets in the United States, and the Dutch followed suit two days later. The Japanese had therefore gained military bases from which they could launch sudden attacks on Malaya and the Philippines, but had, in doing so, hamstrung the supply of raw materials upon which Japanese industry depended. Indeed, it was becoming clear to Japanese leaders that a continuation of the American embargo would place Japan in a cleft stick, from which she could only escape by fight or surrender.

In the late summer and early autumn of 1941 the Japanese government negotiated with the United States in an effort to find acceptable concessions which would persuade the Americans to lift the embargo. Discussions were flawed by Japanese reluctance to make major concessions in Indo-China or Manchuria, and by American unwillingness to call off the embargo without a substantial earnest of Japanese goodwill. The military lobby in Japan was, meanwhile, forcing the pace, urging that a decision on war or peace should be made before Japanese oil reserves had reached a critical level. Prince Konoye reluctantly realised that the gulf between Japanese and American terms was too wide to be bridged and, rather than launch his country into a war about which he had the gravest reservations, he resigned on 16 October. His place was taken by the militarist General Hideki Tojo, and Japan hurtled headlong down the road to war.

Japanese preparations for war had, in fact, been going on for some time. With the defeat of Britain and France in the summer of 1940, Japanese strategists focussed their attention on the United States, undoubtedly Japan's most serious potential enemy in the Far East. The American two-Ocean Naval Expansion Act committed the Americans to building a vast number of new warships, including seven battleships and eighteen aircraft carriers. It was clear to senior Japanese naval officers that this would turn a balance of forces which they regarded as favourable to Japan in 1940 into one tipped massively in favour of the United States by 1944. If Japan was ever to have a chance of waging a successful war against America, they argued, it was sooner rather than later.

Many Japanese naval officers, while agreeing with this general assessment of relative strengths, nevertheless felt that war with the United States was, even in 1940–41, an unattractively risky option which should be avoided if at all possible. Amongst them was Admiral Isoroku Yamamoto, a Harvard-educated apostle of carrier-borne air-power, who took command of the Japanese Combined Fleet in August 1939.

Yamamoto remained steadfastly opposed to war with America, warning that:

If it is necessary to fight, in the first six months to a year of a war against the United States and England I will run wild. I will show you an uninterrupted succession of victories. But I must also tell you that if the war be prolonged for two or three years I have no confidence in our ultimate victory.

But if a war with America was inevitable, Yamamoto believed that Japan's only chance lay in administering a massive knock-out blow, delivered by carrier-borne aircraft, against the American Pacific Fleet in its base at Pearl Harbor.

Yamamoto's plan was not finally approved till 3 November 1941, only thirty-five days before the attack was launched. By this time Japanese plans for action in other sectors were well advanced. Ever since the Japanese invasion of Manchuria the main emphasis of Japanese army training had been on fighting in the cold, open terrain of Manchuria. With the likelihood of a thrust into South-East Asia, study began of the problems of jungle warfare. The 'Taiwan Army Research Section' was set up on Formosa on New Year's Day 1941, and, in the words of Colonel Masonobu Tsuji, one of its members:

was allotted the task of collecting, in approximately six months, all conceivable data associated with tropical warfare – the organisation of Army corps, equipment, campaign direction, management and treatment of weapons, sanitation, supply, administration of occupied territory, and military strategy, tactics and geography.

Tsuji and his colleagues received excellent intelligence from Japanese officials and agents who had visited Singapore and Malaya. They soon realised that:

Singapore Fortress was solid and strong on its sea front, but the rear facing Johore was practically defenceless. . . . Styling Singapore the Gibraltar of the Orient and boasting of its impregnability might possibly indicate a show of strength – or bluff. But the absence of rear defences of the fortress constituted a very grave defect.

It also appeared that the RAF was seriously under strength, and that the army numbered approximately 80,000 men, about half of whom were European.

The results of this research were tested in exercises in South China in June: troops were embarked on transports and disembarked across open beaches to move through tropical terrain. A simple training pamphlet, 'Read This Alone – And The War Can Be Won,' summed up the lessons of the first six months of 1941. The booklet described the area of operations, stressing that the 'treasure-house of the Far East' had been seized by tryannical Europeans who were terrorising the native populations. It went on to advise soldiers how to behave on the transports and during the assault, and gave practical hints on such matters as weapons cleaning and personal hygiene in the tropics.

There can be no doubt that the work of Tsuji and his colleagues was a major contribution towards initial Japanese success. Many Japanese soldiers came from urban environments, and few had experience of the jungle, but their realistic training and forceful doctrine made them into formidable adversaries. After the initial Allied setbacks it became convenient to regard the Japanese as supermen before whom conventional troops were helpless, but the truth is that the roots of Japanese success lay in solid training and indestructible morale.

The invasion of Malaya was to be carried out by Lieutenant-General Tomoyuki Yamashita's 25th Army: Lieutenant-General S. Iida's 15th Army was to consolidate in Siam in preparation for an attack into Burma. Yamashita had three divisions, the Imperial Guards, and the 5th and 18th Divisions in his first wave, and the 56th Division in reserve. He was also able to count on support from the 15th Army for operations in Siam.

Yamashita planned a combined assault by land and sea. The Imperial Guards Division was charged with securing Siam, moving overland from southern Indo-China and seizing Bangkok before moving by rail into Malaya. Two regiments of the 5th Division would land at Singora and one at Patani, and were to take Perlis and Kedah before advancing down the western side of Malaya. The East coast was entrusted to the 18th Division, one of whose regiments was to land at Kota Bharu and capture the airfields of Kelantan before moving southwards. Another of the division's regiments would follow in support.

As the first wave of the attack went in, the 15th Army's 55th Division would co-operate by landing on the Kra Isthmus, securing the airfields North of Singora and controlling the Singora–Bangkok railway. If the British moved forward into Siam, as the Japanese expected they might, the 5th Division would postpone its landing and assist the 55th Division in the capture of the airfields in the Kra Isthmus. Only when these were in Japanese hands, and air superiority in the sector was assured, would the 5th Division resume its primary task in Malaya.

Yamashita's second wave, consisting of the uncommitted regiment of the 5th Division and the bulk of the 18th Division, was to land at Singora as soon as possible after the initial assault. This force would provide Yamashita with an immediate reserve, while his remaining division, the 56th, remained in Japan for use if required. In the event, Yamashita was able to carry out his mission without calling upon it.

There was a sharp contrast between Yamashita and his British adversary. Commissioned into the infantry in 1908, Yamashita graduated from Staff College in 1916 and did well in a series of command and staff appointments. In the 1920s he became heavily involved in one of the military cliques, the 'Imperial Way', and his protégés played a leading part in the military insurrection of February 1936. Yamashita was punished by being struck off the list for promotion to lieutenant-general, and was sent off to command a brigade in Korea. Promoted in late 1937, Yamashita was recalled to Tokyo in the summer of 1940 to be inspector-general of aviation, but was almost immediately sent off on a liaison mission to Germany and Japan. On his return Tojo, with whom he had clashed during the 1920s, posted him to command the Kwantung Defence Army in Manchuria. He remained there until given command of the 25th Army in November 1941.

Yamashita was a plump, rather unprepossessing man. Tsuji, who joined his staff when the 25th Army formed in early November, wrote that the general was:

Quite unlike a hero in appearance, perhaps he was at that time the most clear-headed type of politician.

This was an apt description, for Yamashita had more than a little of the politician's astuteness: one contemporary described him as 'halfway between clever and cunning.' Like Yamamoto, he disapproved of the war, but felt that it was the inevitable result of Japan's economically-motivated expansion, which had brought her into conflict with other powers. Both ruthless and ambitious, Yamashita was nevertheless a devotee of the *samurai* tradition: he had advised his protégés to commit suicide in front of their troops after the failure of the February 1936 coup.

Yamashita and Percival shared one problem in common: they did not enjoy unruffled relations with their subordinates. While Percival had to contend with the difficulties created by the diverse nature of his force, Yamashita was forced to cope with a command structure which gave abundant evidence of the factionalism which beset the Japanese army. Lieutenant-General Takuma Nishimura, commander of the Imperial Guards Division, was a headstrong officer who had clashed with Yamashita on previous occasions and who resented being under his command. The Imperial Guards had not been in action since the Russo-Japanese war, and Yamashita warned Nishimura that his division made a poor showing on manoeuvres and urgently required more training. Nishimura was an ally of Yamashita's opponents, Field-Marshal Count Terauchi, overall Japanese commander in the area, and General Sugiyama, Chief of the General Staff. Tsuji's presence on the staff was also unsettling, for he was believed to report direct to the Prime Minister himself, Yamashita's old rival Tojo. The army commander was on far better terms with Lieutenant-General Renya Mutaguchi, who led the 18th Division. Mutaguchi had served briefly as Yamashita's chief of staff, so the two men were well acquainted: both had also been members of the 'Imperial Way', and had fallen into disfavour after the February 1936 plot.

Yamashita's assault force set off on 4–5 December, its convoys screened by powerful naval forces and given close air protection during daylight hours. After a rendezvous in the Gulf of Siam early on the night of the 7th, the force of twenty-eight transport vessels and their escorting cruisers and destroyers set off on the last leg of their journey under cover of darkness. The landings were to take place in the small hours of 8 December.

THE DILEMMAS OF DEFENCE: 1941

The Japanese plan for the invasion of Malaya and the assault of Singapore conformed, with surprising accuracy, to the assumptions made by General Fraser in the 1920s and by General Dobbie and Percival himself in the late 'thirties. British plans were, therefore, geared to meet the very sort of attack which was unleashed against northern Malaya in the second week of December 1941, and it is to these plans that we must turn our attention.

Percival had some 88,600 men under his command on 7 December, 19,600 of them British, with 15,200 Australians, 37,000 Indians and 16,800 locally enlisted Asians. They formed three divisions – 9th and 11th Indian and 8th Australian – each of two brigades; two reserve brigade groups; two fortress brigades for Singapore, and a battalion in garrison in Penang. There were also coastal and anti-aircraft batteries, local volunteer units, and some airfield defence battalions. These forces were, as we have seen, very much a mixed bag, in terms of recruitment, experience and training.

The question of training was particularly important. Angus Rose, then a captain in the Argyll and Sutherland Highlanders, recalled that in late 1939 the tradition of certain country being 'impassable to infantry' died very hard. In fact, as he soon discovered, although:

The casual observer got the impression that the whole jungle was one dense mass of impenetrable foliage . . . this was not the case. Along the borders of roads, where the trees had been cut down and light had come in, the jungle grew up again in great density. This was known as secondary jungle. Once inside this narrow belt, which went only to a depth of a score of yards, there was the real, or primary, jungle. It was not normally necessary to cut through primary jungle, except in river courses or over water-logged ground. . . . Tourists and office-bound staff officers, who never had time to leave the road, got a completely wrong impression of what jungle really was and 'impenetrable jungle" was, of course, a complete myth.

The extent of jungle training varied very much from unit to unit. Gordon Bennett's Australians, particularly those of the 22nd Brigade, had taken jungle training seriously, and had been in Malaya long enough to have acquired considerable skill. But other units were less fortunate. In some cases wide peacetime deployment made training difficult, and in others recent arrival in Malaya impeded both acclimatisation and training. Lieutenant Peter Kemmis-Betty's 2nd Gurkha Rifles, for example:

prior to our departure from India . . . had been practising, doing all our training for open desert warfare with a platoon here and one three hundred yards away. . . . Literally two or three weeks before we embarked we were told: 'No, that is off: you are going to Malaya. . . .' We did jolly little training in jungle warfare and what there was was pretty unimaginative. . . . We did drive into the jungle and make a show of training . . . but, I thought, in a fairly amateurish way.

Anti-tank training was in an even worse state. Brigadier Simson discovered, to his surprise, that unopened bundles of the War Office pamphlet on anti-tank defence were lying in cupboards in Fort Canning, and had not been issued to units. Simson drew Percival's attention to the matter, and was instructed to produce a single illustrated booklet which embodied all information contained in the numerous War Office instructions. The pamphlet, aimed particularly at Indian and Australian troops, most of whom had never seen a tank, was ready by 6 December, but was not issued until after the Japanese attack had begun. By then it was, as Simson ruefully admitted, 'really too late and virtually useless. . . .'

Lack of serious jungle and anti-tank training was, in part, accounted for by the air of complacency which enveloped pre-war Malaya. The insistence on 'business as usual', logical though it was from the economic point of view, made it difficult for the authorities to obtain permission to train or construct defences on privately-owned land. Even after the outbreak of war these attitudes changed slowly: one irate planter tried to expel a field ambulance from his estate, and Australian gunners hacked down rubber trees to clear their fields of fire, muttering 'to hell with the $5 fine.'

This unwillingness to change the habits of peacetime was itself closely linked with a widespread underestimation of the fighting qualities of the Japanese armed forces. When Colonel G. T. Ward,

British Military Attaché in Tokyo, lectured to the officers of Singapore garrison in April 1941 he warned his listeners that the Japanese army was a first-class fighting machine, composed of tough, determined soldiers and led by an experienced and efficient general staff. He concluded by cautioning his audience against underestimating the Japanese, and by suggesting that the Japanese had an accurate picture of British strength and deployment in Malaya. At the conclusion of the lecture General Bond took the floor to assure the assemblage that Ward's views were:

far from the truth. . . . What the lecturer has told you is his own opinion and is in no way a correct appreciation of the situation. . . . I know exactly what the Japanese are up to and just how much or how little they know about us. If this is the best that the Japanese can do, I do not think much of them and you can take it from me that we have nothing to fear from them.

Ward later assured Bond that he had not overestimated the quality of the Japanese army. Bond thereupon warned him that 'we must not discourage the chaps and we must keep their spirits up.'

Not surprisingly, the 'chaps' cherished bizarre ideas of the inferiority of the Japanese, scorning them as squat, simian creatures with protruding teeth and thick spectacles. Angus Rose recalled that:

It was held that their pilots were as blind as bats and couldn't hit a thing.

Fighter pilot Tim Vigors remembered that:

there was this theory that they couldn't fly above a certain height without passing out even on oxygen. . . . This was actually what we were told in an intelligence lecture, you can't believe it! And their aircraft were supposed to be very, very inadequate. . . . Stuck together with rice paper and all this type of thing.

'Somehow,' recalled H. J. Burn of the RAAF, seconded to 34 Squadron RAF at Tengah,

we all expected the Japs to be flying biplanes. The fact that they weren't came as a big surprise.

The rank and file expected to find the Japanese easy meat. Corporal Gabby Gavin of the East Surreys remembered the shouts of 'Tokyo, here we come' and 'Look out, you yellow bastards' which enlivened his platoon's departure from barracks after the outbreak of war. Gunner G. K. Topping of the 80th Anti-Tank Regiment encountered similar enthusiasm when passing through an Australian position:

as we passed in our vehicles the Aussies came out to greet us. 'Where are the little yellow bastards,' one of them shouted. 'We'll show them who's boss and send them back to hell where they came from.'

William Ball summed up British attitudes concisely:

we never considered the Japs were people worth bothering about. . . . What were a few little orientals, the way we treated the Indians, the Malays, the Chinese, almost as a sort of subnormal race. That's the way we looked at the Japanese, we never looked at them as soldiers.

When Percival arrived in Malaya he found Heath's III Indian Corps responsible for the defence of the North, with its headquarters at Kuala Lumpur. Major-General Barstow's 9th Indian Division held the East coast against seaborne assault and attacks on the vital airfields, with Brigadier Key's 8th Brigade in Kalantan and Brigadier Painter's 22nd Brigade around Kuantan in the state of Pahang. For two brigades to defend a coastline over 200 miles long, littered with potential landing-places, was, as the Divisional History admitted, 'dispersion run riot.'

The north-western sector was defended by Major-General Murray Lyon's 11th Indian Division, one of its brigades, Brigadier Garrett's 15th, at Sungei Patani in South Kedah, and the other, the 6th Brigade under Brigadier Lay, at Tanjong Pau in North Kedah. Heath also had two battalions up in the frontier region, one in the extreme north-western state of Perlis and the other at Kroh. Penang was garrisoned by a volunteer infantry battalion and some static units, but much of the equipment which had been ordered with the intention of turning the island into a self-contained fortress had not yet arrived. One of Heath's battalions was quartered in Penang, but was not intended to form part of the garrison and was to move to the mainland in the event of hostilities. III Corps' reserve, a single battalion, lay South of Kuala Lumpur. This reserve was later increased to a brigade, on the arrival of Brigadier Carpendale's three Gurkha battalions of 28th Brigade, and was moved up to Ipoh, where it was better placed to support the forward divisions. The four battalions of the Federated Malay States Volunteer Force, under the commander of Heath's lines of communication area, Brigadier Moir, were, as yet, unmobilised, and were earmarked for the defence of aerodromes and other key points.

Major-General F. Keith Simmons, commander of the Singapore fortress, was responsible for the defence of Singapore and eastern Johore. This was a substantial task, including as it did the defence of the little East coast port of Mersing, some eighty miles from Singapore and connected to it by a good road. The 12th Indian Infantry Brigade, under Brigadier Paris, was entrusted with the defence of eastern Johore. Percival described this as "probably the best trained and most experienced brigade in the country." It included 2nd Battalion the Argyll and Sutherland Highlanders, which had taken jungle training very seriously under the energetic leadership of Lieutenant-Colonel Ian Stewart.

The 12th Brigade had an alternative role on Singapore Island, whose permanent garrison consisted of Brigadier Williams' 1st Malaya Brigade, of only two battalions, and the three-battalion 2nd Malaya Brigade of Brigadier Fraser. Keith Simmons also had the Straits Settlements Volunteer Force at his disposal, less the battalion garrisoning Penang.

Percival's command reserve was provided by Gordon Bennett's 8th Australian Division, stationed South of Kuala Lumpur. 'It was,' Percival noted, 'to be prepared to operate anywhere in Malaya.' Finally, there were a number of battalions of Indian States Forces deployed in Malaya. These were elements of the personal forces of various Indian rulers, and as such distinct from the Indian army, properly speaking. Most of these units – like the 1st Bahawalpur Infantry and the 1st Hyderabad Infantry – were employed in the defence of airfields, and came under the authority of the commanders of the areas in which they were deployed. Percival was to acknowledge that the Indian States troops were somewhat patchy in quality. 'Some units,' he wrote,

showed themselves fully qualified to take their place with other fighting troops in the general scheme of defence; others found their lack of training and of war experience a great handicap in operations which were a severe test for even the most highly skilled troops.

Percival had heard of the proposed scheme for an advance into Siam even before he had left London, and it was one of the first problems to which he turned his attention on reaching Malaya. The scheme's immediate advantages were obvious. The Japanese could be met on the beaches, and denied the use of the facilities at Singora and Patani: the airfields of southern Siam could also be secured against them. But the disadvantages were also striking. Time was of the essence: Britain could not move into Siam before it had become clear that the Japanese had already violated Siamese neutrality, but, if they were to be effective, British troops would have to be established in Siam before the arrival of the Japanese. There was also the question of force levels. Any advance into Siam would require extra troops, and soldiers were, as we have already seen, a commodity in very short supply.

The project was studied in detail immediately after Percival arrived, and a compromise solution was adopted. The study indicated that there were insufficient forces available to occupy both Singora and Patani. Singora could, however, be occupied, provided that the operation took place during the north-east monsoon, between October and March, when Japanese armour would be road-bound, and provided also that the advance began at least twenty-four hours before a Japanese landing at Singora. In order to prevent the Japanese from moving down the Kroh road from Patani, outflanking the units which had advanced to Singora and imperilling the defence of Kedah and Perak, a force would move to occupy a position known as the Ledge, where the road crossed a steep ridge thirty-five miles across the Siamese border.

This plan, christened Operation Matador, was very much of a gamble. Not only could it be employed only during part of the year, but it also relied on getting a head start of at least twenty-four hours. It was, as Percival acknowledged, only natural for the British government to hesitate granting permission to violate Siamese neutrality, an act which was certain to alienate American opinion. Even if the requisite permission was forthcoming, and the advance began twenty-four hours before the first Japanese landings, armed opposition might be expected from Siamese frontier guards, and this, combined with demolitions on the roads and railways, could only slow up the British advance. Given the conspiracy of imponderables which surrounded Matador, it is, perhaps, surprising that Percival and Brooke-Popham continued to entertain the scheme.

But press on they did. In August Brooke-Popham informed the Chiefs of Staff that he was considering Matador, adding that it would require three brigade groups with air support. He also sent selected officers, in a variety of improbable disguises to reconnoitre South Siam. This led to what Percival called 'curious incidents', for they encountered Japanese officers who were obviously doing the same thing. 11th Indian Division's History tells how:

On one occasion the precision with which a comedian changed step in order to march with his companion, a commercial traveller, raised a smile from a party of Japanese officers. On another occasion the interest of a retired tight-rope acrobat in a previously unknown landing-ground near Singora led to his arrest by the Thai police; his contention that he was only taking a walk was eventually accepted, but for a while he was indeed walking on a tight-rope.

Brooke-Popham's superiors warned him of their doubts about Matador, but the Commander-in-Chief assured them it was practicable, and that sufficient forces would be available from 1 October.

Far from being satisfied, the Chiefs of Staff cast new doubts on the plan in mid-September. They stressed their anxiety to avoid conflict with Japan, told Brooke-Popham that they had no intention of violating Siamese neutrality, and asked him how much warning he needed to launch Matador. They added the gloomy footnote that they saw no prospect of bringing the garrison of Malaya up to the required level in the immediate future. Brooke-Popham replied that he needed only thirty-six hours warning before implementing Matador: four days would, in the opinion of the campaign's Official Historian, have been a more realistic estimate. 'It was at this point,' he continued,

that the whole idea should have been dropped, unless Percival's demand for a reserve division for III Corps could have been met at once and the RAF could have been brought up to the agreed strength in 1941.

With Matador on its books, 11th Indian Division had the confusing task of preparing for alternative roles. 'What fun', remarked Murray-Lyon's GSO1, 'we now don't know whether we're Angus or Agnes.' On the one hand, it might have to lunge forward into Siam and carry out Matador, a task which, as Percival acknowledged, was 'naturally the more attractive and as such apt to receive the greater attention.' On the other, it was to prepare for the defence of the airfield at Alor Star and those in South Kedah and Province Wellesley. The former aerodrome had, like that at Kota Bharu in the north-east, started life as a civilian airfield, and lay North of the best potential defensive positions in Kedah.

Because the frontier area was badly infested by malaria, Percival chose an intermediate position between the frontier and Alor Star at Jitra, where the Perlis road left the main road to Siam. It was a wretched position, and Percival agreed that 'nobody ever really liked it.' Most of the defences were constructed across the two roads and the area between them: the ground to the West, between the main position and the sea, was intersected by water courses and defended only by a chain of pill-boxes. Work on the position was impeded by the dismal weather, which caused the bogging of the mechanical diggers brought up to construct the anti-tank ditch, and by the shortage of civilian labour. Eventually the troops had to do most of the work themselves, and their digging was interrupted by training for Matador. When war broke out the Jitra position, bad at the best of times, was only partially complete.

In the centre, around Kroh, the situation was scarcely better. The road forked just West of the frontier, one branch running West towards Butterworth and the other going South, through Grik, to Kuala Kangsar. Defences were constructed to cover the Butterworth road, but it was impossible to hold both roads from one position without going forward into Siam. It was to overcome this problem that the advance to the Ledge was decided upon, for occupation of this feature would block the road well North of the Kroh fork. It should be noted in passing, however, that the failure of the Ledge operation would result in this centre road lying open before an invader. Between Kroh and the coastal belt lay a number of jungle tracks, impassable to vehicles but perfectly practicable to infantry. They were watched by a locally-recruited platoon attached to one of the Volunteer battalions.

The north-east coast of Malaya, the preserve of the 9th Indian Division, contained numerous sandy beaches upon which landings could be made. Studies, carried out as early as 1937, had revealed that it was possible to land on these beaches even at the height of the monsoon, although Percival suspected that the risks entailed in such an operation would deter the Japanese from attempting landings between December and February.

Considerable discussion surrounded the deployment of 9th Indian Division. Brooke-Popham and Percival agreed that the defenders should concentrate their main efforts on the beaches, but other senior officers favoured keeping the bulk of the division inland to strike concerted blows at the Japanese once they had got ashore. In Kelantan, Brigadier Key's men were posted to cover the beaches, although a strong reserve was kept on the main road, between Kota Bharu and Kuala Krai. A similar policy was adopted for the defence of the airfield at Kuantan: one of 22nd Brigade's battalions guarded the beaches while another held the Kuantan River, between the coast and the airfield. The brigade's third battalion was temporarily detached to 8th Brigade in Kelantan.

III Indian Corps' dual mission and wide deployment would, in themselves, have taxed the ability of a battle-hardened and experienced formation. But the corps was, as we have seen, neither experienced nor fully trained. The process of 'milking' its units to send trained men to India as a nucleus for new units went on right up until the outbreak of war. Much-needed equipment was slow in arriving: three field artillery regiments with 25-pounders joined the corps in November, as did the 80th Anti-tank Regiment. Prior to the latter's arrival the only anti-tank artillery in the corps had consisted of seven captured Italian Brada guns, manned by the 22nd Mountain Regiment. If these units were capable of carrying out their tasks, the same cannot be said of the corps reconnaissance regiment, the 3rd Cavalry, which came out in October. It had only recently been mechanised, and lacked experienced drivers and mechanics. There were no armoured vehicles available for it, so it was equipped with 15 cwt trucks instead. Most of these were wrecked by their enthusiastic but untrained drivers on their first operational move.

The defence of Johore, initially the responsibility of Keith Simmons of Singapore garrison, became an Australian task in August 1941. Gordon Bennett moved his headquarters to Johore Bharu, just across the causeway from Singapore Island, sent his 22nd Brigade to dig itself in at Mersing, and posted his newly-arrived 27th Brigade around Jemalaung, on the Mersing–Singapore road. The excellent 12th Indian Brigade, now freed from its duties in Johore, moved up to Port Dickson as command reserve.

Percival's dispositions have been the subject of detailed criticism, notably from Major-General Woodburn Kirby, whose *Singapore: The Chain of Disaster*, was rather more hostile to senior British commanders than the Official History, of which he was also the author. Kirby suggests that the plan was flawed in its conception. Given the low strength of the RAF by the summer of 1941, it was, he argued, unreasonable to expect that British aircraft would be able to prevent a Japanese landing. This being so, the airfields of the North were bound to fall to ground attack within a matter of days. Rather than spreading troops thinly in an attempt to hold them, Kirby believed that Percival would have been better advised to have left only a few troops around the airfields, to destroy them as the Japanese approached.

The army would then, in Kirby's words, 'have been free to work out a plan of defence without being tied to the apron-strings of the RAF.' Such a plan might, he suggested, have involved the abandonment of Perlis and Kedah, and the defence of a number of natural defiles on the main West coast road and railway. He drew attention to the efforts of the energetic and perceptive Brigadier Simson to bring about the construction of defences in Johore, noting that Percival was opposed to such proposals, basing his resistance partly on the belief of Sir Shenton Thomas and Brooke-Popham that war with Japan was unlikely.

It is difficult to resist being seduced by the remorseless logic of Kirby's argument. One should nevertheless remember that the abandonment of the North would have been an improbable option in view of the political and military realities prevailing in the summer of 1941. It would have been impossible for Thomas to have sanctioned a plan which gave up the states of Kelantan, Perlis and Kedah with scarcely a shot fired in their defence: it is not hard to imagine the effect that the news of such a scheme would have had on the native rulers or European residents of these states. Moreover, in military terms alone it had long been accepted that the defence of Singapore meant the defence of Malaya, and that the defence of Malaya hinged on that of the northern airfields. It was not clear until the Chiefs of Staff mid-September letter that the RAF would not be brought up to strength: even after this date the presence of an RAF officer as Commander-in-Chief militated against a radical change in strategy.

It must also be acknowledged that Thomas and Brooke-Popham were not alone in believing that war with Japan could be averted, a confidence which tended to discourage a major strategic reappraisal. In June 1941 Sir Archibald Clark-Kerr, British Ambassador to China, suggested to the government that a civil administration, headed by somebody of considerable standing, should be set up in the Far East to implement a co-ordinated policy even if communications with London were cut off. In July the War Cabinet gave Mr Alfred Duff Cooper, Chancellor of the Duchy of Lancaster, the task of examining the relationship between military and civil authorities in the Far East and reporting on how communications and consultation could be improved. Duff Cooper arrived in Singapore on 9 September, and spent the next seven weeks examining the problem. On 29 September he presided over a high-level conference, attended by Thomas, Brooke-Popham, Layton, Clark-Kerr, the British Ambassador to Siam and an Australian representative.

The conference suggested that the presence of a British fleet based on Singapore would be a prime deterrent to Japanese aggression, although the belief that Japan was concentrating her forces for war against Russia persuaded the conference that war was unlikely to break out in the near future. Recognising that it would be difficult to send a substantial fleet to Singapore, the conference pointed out that even one or two battleships would have an enormous propaganda value, particularly if their arrival was reinforced by a combined announcement by the British, Dutch and United States governments that a concerted plan existed for use in the event of a Japanese attack.

Duff Cooper submitted his formal report on 29 October, a month after the conference. He suggested the appointment of a civil supremo, called the Commissioner-General for the Far East, to provide a link between the War Cabinet and the Far East and carry out some of the political functions which had previously been conducted by the commanders-in-chief. Duff Cooper's suggestions would undoubtedly have resulted in the improvement of the command structure in the Far East. His report, however, took nearly a month to reach London, and no decision had been made on its proposals when war broke out.

Not long after Duff Cooper had been briefed for his Far East mission, the War Cabinet considered the replacement of Brooke-Popham by a younger man with more experience of modern war. Churchill agreed to this in early November, wiring Brooke-Popham that he was to be replaced by 'an army officer with up-to-date experience.' Brooke-Popham was shortly afterwards informed that his replacement would be Lieutenant-General Sir Bernard Paget. Churchill planned to send Paget to liaise with Stalin before going out to the Far East, a fact which would have delayed his departure, but eventually a high-level reorganisation in the War Office made it necessary for Lieutenant-General Sir Henry Pownall, a capable staff officer who had served as chief of staff to the BEF in France, to be found a billet. Pownall was accordingly appointed Commander-in-Chief Far East, with a directive similar to that given to Brooke-Popham. Pownall left London in early December, but he was not to arrive in the Far East until after the outbreak of war.

Duff Cooper and the members of his 29 September conference were not alone in believing that the dispatch of a naval squadron to

Singapore would act as a powerful deterrent. In early August the Chiefs of Staff had instructed the Joint Planning Staff to give special consideration to the question of reinforcing the Far East with capital ships, and the Naval Planning Staff reported that four obsolete R class battleships could be sent to form a nucleus of a force in the Far East, and reinforced by early 1942. The Admiralty stressed that this fleet could not hope to take on the Japanese navy in a direct confrontation, but believed that it would provide a deterrent and, if war came, protecting shipping in the Indian Ocean.

Churchill disliked the proposal. He told the First Sea Lord that the old R class battleships were ill-suited for their task.'The old ships,' he wrote,

are easy prey to modern Japanese vessels, and can neither fight or run. . . . I am however in principle in favour of placing – a formidable, fast, high-class squadron in the aforesaid triangle (Aden–Singapore–Simonstown) by the end of October, and telling both the Americans and the Australians that we will do so.

The Admiralty replied by reminding Churchill that the Atlantic was the vital area, and recommended that Britain's modern battleships should be retained in home waters in case the *Tirpitz* forayed out into the Atlantic.

There the matter rested until the fall of the Konoye cabinet in mid-October lent new urgency to the question of naval reinforcements for the Far East. Churchill again demanded that modern capital ships should be sent to the East, pointing out that the *Repulse*, a battle-cruiser laid down in 1915, was already in the Indian Ocean, where she could be joined by the modern battleship *Prince of Wales*, which had recently carried the Prime Minister to a meeting with Roosevelt. On 20 October the Admiralty at last gave way. The First Sea Lord, Sir Dudley Pound, suggested a compromise: *Prince of Wales* would go to Cape Town, where she would have considerable propaganda value, but whence she could quickly be recalled to home waters if the need arose. She would be joined en route by the new aircraft carrier *Indomitable*, which was still on her 'working up' trials in the Caribbean.

Prince of Wales, flying the flag of Admiral Sir Tom Phillips, Commander-in-Chief designate of the eastern fleet, left England on 25 October. By this time the 20 October compromise had already been eroded, for the Admiralty had agreed that both *Repulse* and *Prince of Wales* would press on to Singapore. Just over a week after *Prince of Wales*' departure, *Indomitable* ran aground off Jamaica. Churchill's 'formidable, fast, high-class squadron' was now reduced to two vessels, one of them decidedly elderly and the other, in the words of a leading naval historian:

still a new ship, still not yet fully worked-up for combat in the important role allotted to her.

The dispatch of Force Z, as it was known, typifies the whole dismal tale of overstretched resources and tangled strategy which had governed British defence policy in the Far East in 1939–41.

Lieutenant General A. E. Percival DSO, OBE, MC, new GOC Malaya (replacing Lieutenant General L. V. Bond) as he stepped out of the aircraft on arrival.

HMS *Repulse* hit by bombs from Japanese aircraft, 10 December 1941.

above: Blenheim bombers flying over a grounded Bufflalo fighter in Malaya.

below: One of the Singapore coast defence guns camouflaged.

above: Japanese troops mopping up in Kuala Lumpur.

below: Japanese forces storm into Johore Bahru.

above: A famous Scottish regiment on manoeuvres in Malaya before the Malay Campaign. The end of the crossing.

below: Soldiers of the Manchester Regiment building beach defences.

Admiral Sir Tom Phillips *(right)* who subsequently went down with his ship (HMS *Prince of Wales*), with Rear Admiral Palliser.

GHQ Conference, 29 September 1941. Air Marshal Sir Robert Brooke-Popham, C-in-C Far East, with the Rt Hon Alfred Duff Cooper.

below: General Wavell with his two Commanders-in-Chief at a conference in Singapore, 3 November 1941.

General Percival surrenders to the Japanese, 15 February 1942.

Children about to be evacuated.

5

THE BLOW FALLS
6 December 1941–31 January 1942

AT 2.00 on the afternoon of 6 December 1941, a Hudson aircraft of No. 1 Squadron RAAF, flying at maximum range from its base at Kota Bharu, sighted Japanese troopships and their naval escorts some eighty miles south-east of Cape Cambodia, steaming West. This sighting was no mean feat, for the weather was wretched, with the low cloud and frequent heavy rainstorms of the north-east monsoon. It was clear from the Hudson's three reports that a substantial Japanese force was at sea, and although its precise destination was unknown, it was likely to be heading for Siam, Malaya, or both.

Brooke-Popham held a conference immediately the report arrived. He consulted Admiral Leighton and Rear-Admiral A. F. E. Palliser, Chief of Staff to Admiral Sir Tom Phillips. Phillips himself had left Singapore for Manila on 4 December to consult American commanders. His force – *Prince of Wales*, *Repulse* and their escorting destroyers –had arrived at Singapore on the 2nd. *Prince of Wales* had remained in port, but *Repulse* had set off for Port Darwin to show the flag in Australia. Phillips began his return to Singapore when he heard that a large Japanese fleet had left Camranh Bay in southern Indo-China, and Palliser ordered *Repulse* to return at the same time.

News that the Japanese were at sea presented Brooke-Popham with a cruel dilemma. Since February 1941 he had been pressing the Chiefs of Staff for permission to launch Matador on his own authority, without further reference to London. Such permission was at last granted on the afternoon of 5 December, but, coming as it did on top of repeated warnings of the danger of precipitating war with Japan or alienating American opinion by a premature move into Siam, it did little more than emphasise the great weight of responsibility now lying on Brooke-Popham's shoulders. Brooke-Popham was aware that he no longer enjoyed the Government's confidence: he was, furthermore, tired by his numerous long journeys in an oppressive climate. He eventually decided not to launch Matador, but to order his forces to assume the highest degree of readiness. Percival, who was up at III Corps headquarters, received this news at about 3.15 pm: he at once ordered Heath to place his troops on alert, bringing 11th Division to half an hour's notice to move. This, as the Division's history noted, 'meant practically one foot on the running board'. It added, with commendable understatement: 'The weather broke. There was little sleep for the troops that night.'

Although Brooke-Popham had ordered Pulford to maintain contact with the Japanese convoys, the atrocious weather in the Gulf of Siam severely hampered air reconnaissance. Various aircraft were sent up during the night of the 6th–7th and on the 7th itself, but not until mid-afternoon were further sightings made. These were inconclusive, and the information which reached Brooke-Popham at his headquarters at about 9.00 that night left him in doubt as to Japanese intentions. The British ambassador in Bangkok had that day warned him, in the strongest terms, not to violate Siamese neutrality, and there remained the possibility that the Japanese vessels sighted on the 7th might be part of an attempt to induce Brooke-Popham to launch Matador prematurely. If, on the other hand, the vessels were part of an invasion force, it was likely that they would be in a position to land troops by midnight on the 7th–8th. Matador required a head start of at least twenty-four hours if it was to have any chance of forestalling Japanese landings in Siam. Brooke-Popham therefore remained reluctant to order Matador, but at 11.20 that night he warned Heath to be prepared to begin the operation at dawn the following day. 11th Division was condemned to spend another sleepless night in the rain.

Angus Rose, now a major and GSO2 at Headquarters Malaya Command, went on duty in the War Room at 0001 on 8 December. Whatever Brooke-Popham's doubts, Rose felt that 'it looked pretty obvious that the Nips were "coming a' shootin' "' that night.' He had been on duty for about an hour and a quarter when a telephone message from Kota Bharu announced that there were ships off the coast. The message was soon amplified.

> 'Someone's opened fire,' said Kota Bharu.
> 'Who, us or the Japs?' queried the Ops. officer.
> 'Us, I think. No it wasn't – it was the Japs.'

Pulford chipped in to order the Hudson squadron to take off and attack. The telephone conversation continued without interruption.

Our aircraft had apparently met with heavy and accurate 'flak' over the Jap fleet. Kota Bharu wanted to know whether they should bomb the cruisers or the transports.

'Go for the transports, you bloody fools,' shouted the Ops. officer down the telephone.

'Dear God,' I thought. 'Didn't they even know that.'

The three transports of the Japanese invasion force and their warship escorts arrived off Kota Bharu at about midnight, and work began on loading the first of the three assaulting waves into landing craft. Although the night was cloudy, visibility was good; lights could be seen on shore, and the harbour light at Tumpat, at the mouth of the Kelantan River, could be seen clearly. There was a heavy swell running, which made it difficult to get the infantry aboard their landing craft: some of these vessels capsized and a number of troops were lost. Nevertheless, the first wave was on its way by 1.30, and half an hour later signal lights and flares could be seen on the beach.

The Kota Bharu area was the responsibility of Brigadier Key's 8th Brigade. Two of his battalions, 3/17th Dogra and 2/10th Baluch, were dug in along the beaches, the Dogras just north-east of Kota Bharu itself and the Baluchis along the coast to the South, as far as Kuala Besut. The beaches were mined, wired, and covered by fire from pillboxes. Key had an Indian mountain battery and the 25-pounders of 73rd Field Battery to support his forward battalions, and his other two battalions, 1/13th Frontier Force Rifles of his own brigade and 2/12th Frontier Force Regiment, attached from 22nd Brigade, were a few miles inland, at Peringat and Chondong respectively.

But Brigadier Key's position was far less favourable than it might seem. The beaches were intersected by streams and creeks, and the area behind them was difficult and swampy. Battalion frontages were wide: the Dogras, holding the vital Padang–Sabak sector, covering the airfield, were responsible for nearly ten miles of front, while the Baluchis covered no less than twenty-five.

The Japanese assault fell squarely on 3/17th Dogra between Sabak and Badang. 'The enemy pillboxes,' wrote Colonel Tsuji,

which were well prepared, reacted violently with such heavy fire that our men lying on the beach, half in and half out of the water, could not raise their heads. . . . The enemy soldiers manning the pillboxes fought desperately.

By about 3.45, however, after savage fighting with heavy losses on both sides, the Japanese had captured two of the strong-points in the centre of the Dogras' position around Kuala Pa'amat, and were pushing infiltration parties into the maze of creeks and lagoons behind the beach.

The landing craft had returned from the beaches to pick up the second wave of attackers when, at about 3.30, British aircraft began bombing and strafing attacks on the convoy. The Japanese escort commander feared that the aircraft would inflict severe damage on his ships, and argued in favour of withdrawal, while the army commander insisted that it was vital to continue with the landings, reinforcing those troops who were already ashore. The commanders eventually agreed to withdraw at 6.30, by which time the third wave would have been landed.

A renewed air attack, at 5.00, led to confusion in the launching of the third assault wave: one British aircraft was shot down, but the transport *Awaji-San Maru* was hit and set on fire. The aircraft returned at 6.00, did further damage to *Awaji-San Maru*, left *Ayato-San Maru* with 130 men dead and wounded and a gash just above her water-line, and hit *Sakura Maru* twice. Yet another air attack forced the naval commander to suspend the landings for a time, and to transfer most of the men remaining on the crippled *Awaji-San Maru*. 'The damage inflicted by a handful of Hudsons and old Vildebeeste aircraft stationed at Kota Bharu,' wrote Louis Allen,

is a clear indication of what might have happened had the RAF in Malaya been reinforced to the 336 aircraft promised for the end of 1941 by the Chiefs of Staff. Heavier, more persistent and wider-ranging attacks might well have destroyed the Japanese invasion fleet, or at any rate a portion of it large enough to tip the scale in favour of the British Army defenders in North Malaya. As it was. . . .

The Japanese had three battalions ashore by dawn, established in a bridgehead at Kuala Pa'amat, and their patrols were active in the area between the beach and Kota Bharu airfield. Brigadier Key decided to counter-attack to pinch out the bridgehead. He had already moved the Frontier Force Regiment to Kota Bharu, and he now ordered it to attack the Japanese position from Sabak, while the Frontier Force Rifles attacked along the beaches from Badang. Sound though the plan was, it failed to take into account the nature of the ground behind the beaches and the limited standard of training in the two battalions. The attacks shuddered to a halt amongst the rivers and lagoons, and confused fighting, which went on all day, left the Japanese in secure possession of the bridgehead.

While Major-General Takumi's men struggled to establish themselves at Kota Bharu, their comrades of the 5th Division, accompanied by 25th Army headquarters, had a far easier time at the little Siamese port of Singora. Here the landing was unopposed, and the leading wave got ashore despite the heavy seas, without serious incident. Things went less smoothly once they were ashore. They were to have been met by Major Osone, who had been working 'undercover' in the Singora consulate. When Osone failed to appear, Tsuji set off for the consulate, to be met by the Consul, Katsuna, with the lapidary comment 'Ah! the Japanese Army!' From the persimmon-like odour of the consul's breath Tsuji deduced that 'he had probably been drinking freely the previous evening.' Osone then appeared, rubbing his eyes: it transpired that the message giving details of the date and time of the landing had not been decoded, and Osone had neither produced plans for the seizure of motor vehicles nor made arrangements with the Siamese police and army.

Tsuji set off in a car with the consul, an interpreter and an orderly, to negotiate with the Siamese police, but as they approached the police station they were briskly engaged, and made off on foot, with the orderly clutching a large bundle of Siamese money which had been brought along in case, as Tsuji put it,

it might be possible, and much better, to solve certain problems by payment of money rather than by hurling projectiles.

A Japanese battalion moved off down the road, in column of fours and with a large white flag at its head, but was soon pinned down by Siamese machine-guns. Yamashita was by now ashore, and he ordered the area to be secured regardless: the airstrips were taken without resistance, and Japanese aircraft began landing on the waterlogged runways shortly after dawn. The Siamese Army kept up a desultory shelling till midday, when it was announced that, at Premier Pibul's command, resistance was being suspended for the time being. Shortly afterwards a Siamese army negotiator, rumoured to be the illegitimate child of a Japanese nobleman, arrived at Yamashita's headquarters to negotiate a more permanent cease-fire. The Japanese had planned to spearhead the advance to the Malayan frontier with a force dressed in Siamese uniforms, but the chaos surrounding the landing now rendered this stratagem impossible. The soldiers involved changed back into Japanese uniforms, and before long 5th Division, led by three medium tanks, was moving rapidly to the south-west. By nightfall on the 8th the Japanese had landed some 12,000 troops, 400 vehicles and five tanks in Siam, mainly at Singora and Patani, while a regiment of the 55th Division had landed further North to secure the Kra Isthmus.

Things had, meanwhile, gone from bad to worse at Kota Bharu. During the day the Japanese had mounted several air attacks on the northern airfields, destroying a number of British aircraft refuelling and rearming on the ground. At about 4.00 pm a rumour went round the airfield at Kota Bharu that the Japanese had broken through the defensive perimeter, and this story was all too readily believed in view of the damage done by previous air attacks and the fact that stray rounds of small-arms fire were cracking over the runways. Air Headquarters at Singapore was informed that the airfield was under infantry attack, and Pulford ordered the surviving aircraft of the Hudson squadron to withdraw to Kuantan. The ground staff set fire to the operations room and some of the stores, and although Brigadier Key accompanied the wing commander on a reconnaissance which proved that the airfield was in no immediate danger, the damage was done. The ground staff departed in local transport for the railhead at Kuala Krai, having failed to destroy stocks of bombs or fuel, or to render the runways unusable. The Official History commented, not unfairly, that although the weight of Japanese air attacks on the airfields of Kelantan justified the withdrawl of the aircraft, 'the hurried evacuation of the airfield at Kota Bharu was premature and not warranted by the ground situation.'

The withdrawal did, however, make Key's task somewhat easier, as did the fact that much of the population of Kota Bharu, together with the Sultan of Kelantan and his entourage, had by now been evacuated by the civil authorities. When Japanese transports reappeared off the beaches at about 7.00, Key obtained his divisional commander's permission for a retirement, and an hour later he decided to fall back to a position between the airfield and the town of Kota Bharu, with his left flank buttressed by the Kelantan River. While his three forward battalions – the Dogra, the Frontier Force Rifles and the Frontier Force Regiment – held this position, 2/10th Baluch would leave its defences on the beaches and concentrate at Peringat. Help was already on its way, for that morning Key had heard that 4/19th Hyderabad, part of 12th Infantry Brigade, in Percival's command reserve, had been ordered to move by rail to Kuala Krai, where it would come under his orders.

Key's withdrawal took place in the rainy darkness of the night of 8–9th December, and by dawn the new position was occupied, although the troops were exhausted after a harrowing retirement across difficult country, often in contact with an aggressive and enterprising enemy. Soon after dawn the Japanese opened a determined attack against the right flank of the new position, and infiltration parties began to seep through weak spots. Key decided that his troops were too widely dispersed to hold the position with any prospect of success: moreover, the evacuation of Kota Bharu meant that there was no longer any real need to cover the town. He accordingly disengaged, pulling back, on the afternoon of the 9th to the line Peringat–Mulong, with the Hyderabads in support at Ketereh. He then withdrew through the Hyderabads to Chondong. Things were reasonably quiet on the 10th, and a number of stragglers, who had been cut off by the Japanese or who had simply got lost during the trying night retirements, rejoined their units. But news of fresh Japanese landings at Kuala Besut, behind his right flank, together with the realisation that the airfields at Machang and Gong Kedah were

82

now of little use to the RAF, persuaded Key to continue his retreat, and on 11 December his brigade withdrew in good order to a position South of Machang.

THE BRITISH RESPONSE: FORCE Z AND MATADOR

The first wave of assaulting Japanese troops were still pinned down on the beach between Badang and Sabak when Sir Shenton Thomas was awakened by a telephone call from Percival, with the unwelcome, but not unexpected, news that the Japanese had landed. 'Well,' replied the Governor, 'I suppose you'll shove the little men off!' He then telephoned the police to order them to seize all Japanese males, spoke to several of his senior officials on the phone, ordered some coffee, and dressed in slacks and an open-necked shirt.

The Governor was walking in the garden of Government House when, about three hours later, he was called to receive the second alarming phone call of the morning. It was Air Vice-Marshal Pulford, informing him that Japanese aircraft were on their way to the city. The incoming aircraft had been detected by Fighter Control Operations Room at 3.30, and service establishments and anti-aircraft defences were at once alerted. It was less easy to notify the civilian Air Raid Precautions organisation or, indeed, the civilian population. Once Thomas had given his authority for the alarm to be sounded – a decision which seems to have taken some 30 minutes – it proved impossible to find the ARP officer who had the keys to the box which contained the alarm.

The Japanese aircraft, seventeen naval bombers based in southern Indo-China, appeared over Singapore at 4.00. As no air-raid warning had been given, the city was a blaze of light, and the Japanese pilots had little difficulty in locating their targets, Tengah and Seletar airfields. Little damage was caused to the airfields, but some bombers overshot their targets and bombed the heavily-populated centre of Singapore, causing about 200 casualties. There were night-fighters available, but these were not sent up after the raiders, for fear of confusing the anti-aircraft gunners and searchlight operators. None of the Japanese aircraft were shot down.

The bombing of Singapore came as a profound shock to the civilian population. Dicky Durrant, an official of the Post and Telegraph Department, and on call in the event of an emergency, was telephoned by the superintendent of the main telegraph office with the news that there was an air raid. 'So I said,' he recalled,

completely sure of myself, 'Oh no, it can't be an air raid – I'm looking out from my house and all the lights are on down through Tanglin and Orchard Road . . .

it must be just an air-raid practice. . . .

And then my superintendent in the telegraph office said: 'Sir, it is an air raid, not an air raid practice. . . .'

So that's how unsuspecting we were. We never dreamed when we went to bed on the previous evening that war was going to hit us on 8 December. . . .

An Englishwoman, thrown from her bed by a 'near miss' which badly damaged Guthrie's import house, telephoned the police, only to be reassured that it was merely a practice. 'Well,' she replied:

tell them they're overdoing it. They've just hit Raffles Place and knocked Guthrie's for six.

At 6.30 that morning Brooke-Popham issued an Order of the Day, prepared long in advance, which made ironic reading in view of the events of the past few hours. 'We are ready,' it trumpeted.

We have had plenty of warning and our preparations are made and tested. We do not forget at this moment the years of patience and forbearance in which we have borne, with dignity and discipline, the petty insults and insolences inflicted on us by the Japanese in the Far East. . . . Now, when Japan herself has decided to put matters to a sterner test, she will find out that she has made a grievous mistake. We are confident. Our defences are strong and our weapons efficient.

Deciding to what use these weapons should be put was no easy task for British commanders. Percival's staff, understandably eager for a decision on Matador, telephoned Brooke-Popham's headquarters just after 8.00 a.m., only to be told that no decision could be made until a report had been received of air reconnaissance over Singora and Patani. By 9.45 Brooke-Popham knew that the Japanese had landed at both places and were using the airfields in southern Siam. He therefore decided to cancel Matador: 11th Division would concentrate on the Jitra position, but the detachment based at Kroh – *Krohcol* – would advance into Siam to secure the Ledge, and a small force would advance into Siam in an effort to delay the Japanese.

A routine meeting of the Straits Settlement Legislative Council had been scheduled for 10.00 that morning, and Percival, believing that it would be as well to brief the Council's members on the current situation, left his headquarters to address it. He returned an hour later, and gave orders for the cancellation of Matador almost immediately. It took some time for these to be relayed to III Corps headquarters, and it was not until 1.30 that afternoon that 11th Division, whose commander had spent the day pressing for a decision on Matador, at last heard that the operation was off.

The delay had serious consequences. A day's work on the Jitra position was lost: indeed, no work had been carried out on this position since 29 November, when the Division had been placed on six hours' notice to implement Matador. The Divisional History observed that this:

caused the troops avoidable fatigue. It resulted in rushed moves. . . . Worst of all, it lowered morale; the sudden change from the offensive to a defensive role before battle was joined made the troops wonder. The Leicesters, who with the 1/14th Punjabis had spent the morning dashing out of and into their trains as the Japanese aeroplanes came and went, murmured: 'Hell! Back to the effing mud hole.' These two battalions passed the Alor Star aerodrome on their way to assume their Jitra dispositions, and saw the results of the raid. That did them no good.

Worst of all, the Japanese were given a head start of ten hours over III Corps: this delay was to prove little short of disastrous.

Krohcol, the force detailed to march into Siam and secure the Ledge, was intended to consist of 3/16th Punjab, based at Kroh, 5/14th Punjab, at Penang, a company of engineers, a field ambulance, and the light battery of the Federated Malay States Volunteer Force, all under the command of the CO of 3/16th Punjab, Lieutenant-Colonel H. D. Moorhead. But 5/14th Punjab was unable to join the column until after the operation had started, and even then it had to leave a company behind in Penang. The FMSVF battery failed to mobilise in time, and was replaced by an Indian Mountain battery.

When, at 1.30 on the 8th, Moorhead received the coded order 'Operate LEDGE', his force was well below the strength required for such an important task, and much valuable time had already been lost, for the Japanese were pressing on down the Patani road, their advance spearheaded by tanks. Moorhead's men smashed the frontier barrier with axes at 2.00, still hoping that there would be no armed opposition from the Siamese. But as the leading scout of 3/16th Punjab crossed the border, a volley crashed out and he fell dead: it was clear that the Siamese would resist the incursion.

Krohcol's advance was methodical. The bren-gun carrier platoon of the 3/16th moved down the road, with two rifle companies cutting their way through the jungle on either flank. There was a road-block of felled trees, covered by rifles and machine-guns, around the first bend, and the defenders were not prised out until the flanking companies had worked their way round the obstacle. The same process was repeated at every turn in the road, and at intervals the Siamese put in vigorous bayonet-charges, supported by fire from the jungle. By dusk the column had advanced only three miles, at a cost of 15 casualties. The Punjabis got little sleep that night, as the Siamese prowled round the company perimeters, sniping constantly.

The advance was resumed at first light, and during the morning the fighting was very much the same as it had been on the previous day, with vicious little actions taking place around Siamese road-blocks. The opposition miraculously ceased as the afternoon drew on, and Moorhead entered the town of Betong at 3.00. It was lavishly decorated with white flags, and a local official explained that the resistance put up by the Siamese gendarmerie had been an unfortunate mistake. 5/14th Punjab joined the column that day, and Moorhead initially held it back at Kroh, as he considered that little would be gained by trying to move two battalions along the narrow road.

On the 10th the advance again began at dawn, although the absence of Siamese resistance now allowed the troops to move in 3-ton trucks manned by the 2/3rd Australian Reserve MT Company. Moorhead had reconnoitred the Ledge in peacetime, and knew that there was only one turning point for lorries within many miles of it, some six miles South of the Ledge itself. His leading elements accordingly debussed at 1.30 that afternoon to trudge the last six miles on foot. The advanced guard had covered only two thousand yards when they encountered light opposition which, a mile or so further on, stiffened into heavy resistance. But this time the Punjabis were not up against lightly equipped Siamese gendarmerie: they were facing the Japanese army, clear winner in the race for the Ledge.

Krohcol's advance had ground to a halt by late afternoon. A Company 3/16th Punjab had pressed on down the road and had disappeared, and Moorhead had also lost touch with B and D Companies, which were trying to feel their way round the Japanese flanks. The battalion's adjutant went forward in an effort to locate A Company, crossing a ramshackle bridge which the sappers were trying to make passable for the carriers. About five hundred yards forward of the bridge he saw two Japanese tanks, and at once ran back, warning the sappers, who 'immediately reversed their tune and started frantically pulling the bridge to bits.' The tanks appeared almost immediately, but were driven off by the fire of anti-tank rifles.

One of the lost flanking companies appeared after dark, and a section of the missing A Company rejoined the battalion shortly afterwards. Moorhead heard how A Company, under Subedar Shar Khan, had encountered a Japanese company led by two tanks. Two similar detachments followed. The Subedar allowed the first tanks to pass, and then charged the leading Japanese company. He was wounded almost immediately, but his men dispersed the enemy company before they were themselves cut up by the tanks ahead of the second Japanese detachment. Shar Khan, kneeling by the road and cheering his men on, was crushed by a tank. The company fought on for thirty minutes, after which it had, for all practical purposes, ceased to exist.

Moorhead warned his divisional commander, Major-General Murray-Lyon, that he was faced by a substantial Japanese force – he estimated three battalions, supported by light tanks – and believed that withdrawal might be called for. Murray-Lyon replied that Moorhead's mission was to stop the Japanese, not merely delay them, and drew his attention to the fact that 5/14th Punjab was as yet uncommitted. Moorhead had, in fact, already ordered the 5/14th to occupy an intermediate position nine miles North of Betong, with the 10th Mountain Battery in support.

The fighting on 11 December bore out Moorhead's fears. Although the other missing flanking company reappeared at 10.00, the battalion was subjected to fierce attacks all day, and by dusk it had suffered another thirty casualties, making a total of 200 since it had crossed the frontier. Moorhead decided that, with mounting casualties and lack of sleep, his men could not go on much longer, and a retirement on the 5/14th was essential if his battalion's disintegration was to be avoided. He told divisional headquarters of his intention to fall back, and shortly afterwards received an emissary from Murray-Lyon, with a message granting him permission to withdraw at discretion, but emphasising the importance of blocking the Kroh road.

Moorhead began to fall back, under heavy pressure, shortly after 9.00 on the morning of the 12th. Another of his companies was destroyed during the withdrawal, but Moorhead managed to break clear with the debris of his battalion. Moorhead himself, armed with a rifle, came out on the rearmost surviving bren-carrier, having carried a wounded lance-naik along the road to the vehicle under a brisk fire. The three hundred survivors of 3/16th Punjab passed through the position held by 5/14th Punjab at 3.00 and that evening took up a prepared position near Kroh. Moorhead ordered Lieutenant-Colonel Stokes of the 5/14th to delay the Japanese for as long as he could, and then to fall back on the main position at Kroh.

While *Krohcol* was receiving its baptism of fire, another small column, consisting of two companies and the carrier platoon of 1/8th Punjab, an anti-tank section and a detachment of sappers, under the command of Major Andrews of the 1/8th, advanced into Siam on the afternoon of the 8th in an effort to delay the Japanese force moving down from Singora. An armoured train, manned by a platoon of 2/16th Punjabis and an engineer detachment, set off from Padang Besar, and came under Andrews' command when it crossed the frontier. Andrews halted for the night at Sadao, nine miles inside Siam, and prepared to hold the village until his sappers had completed their demolitions. Andrews was subsequently to earn a reputation for bravery during his captivity, but he was, perhaps, more gallant than tactful: his cheery announcement that 'If we're caught here at dawn we'll be bombed to hell,' scarcely inspired his unblooded and nervous troops.

At 9.00 that evening a large force of lorried infantry led by tanks approached Andrews' position along the main road from Singora. The road was covered by the anti-tank guns and the carriers, and the defenders waited until the Japanese were only 100 yards away before opening fire. The anti-tank guns knocked out the three leading tanks, and rifles and bren-guns poured fire into the trucks. But the Japanese reacted swiftly. They had mortars in action within minutes: one of the carriers was set on fire, and as its flames lit up the rainy night, Japanese soldiers could be seen working their way through the jungle round Andrews' right flank. By this time the sappers had finished preparing the bridges for demolition, and Andrews ordered his companies to embus while the carriers and anti-tank guns fought on.

The force withdrew at about 11.00, and had recrossed the frontier within two hours. Andrews' casualties were light, and although Japanese losses had been far heavier, the clash did not delay them for long. When Andrews reported to divisional headquarters early on the 9th he gave a verdict on the fighting ability of the Japanese which contrasted starkly with pre-war mythology. 'They struck me,' he said,

as being absolutely first-class. The speed with which they tumbled out of their lorries, and commenced an enveloping operation against us was incredible.

The armoured train had been more fortunate: its engineer detachment destroyed a 200-foot girder bridge at Khlaung Ngae, and it returned to Padang Besar without interference.

The bulk of 11th Indian Division spent the first two days of the war preparing for the defence of the Jitra position. This was easier said than done: the concentration areas for Matador were in some cases a considerable distance from Jitra, and there were numerous frustrating problems with the transport of personnel and defence stores. It took 155th Field Regiment Royal Artillery until mid-morning on the 9th to get all its guns from Sungei Patani to its gun positions at Tanjong Pau: one section spent an hour moving along two hundred yards of track from the main road to its final position. 1/14th Punjab, tasked with setting up a delaying position on the main road at Asun, arrived there at midnight on the 8th, and immediately set to work on their defences: they were to have had little rest by the time the Japanese arrived. Of the battalions around Jitra itself, 2/9th Jats stumbled into the main position, after a march across wet paddy fields, at 2.00 on the morning of the 9th, and immediately set to work:

putting sodden defences in order; erecting wire in paddy fields which were knee-deep in wet, warm cloying mud; carrying ammunition and rations; and carrying and laying mines.

Their story was little different from that of many other battalions in the 6th and 15th Brigades. The corps reserve, the three Gurkha battalions of Brigadier Carpendale's 28th Brigade, spent the night of the 8th–9th moving up to join 11th Division: once there they found, in the Divisional History's bald words, 'plenty of work awaiting them.'

The deployment of 11th Division for the Jitra battle took place against a backcloth of constant Japanese air activity. On 8 December the Japanese hammered the airfields of the North, often catching British aircraft on the ground. The RAF had some 110 machines in northern Malaya on 7 December: by last light on the 8th only 50 operational machines remained. All the airfields in Kelantan, and that at Sungei Patani in Kedah, had been evacuated: Alor Star was still operational, but the Blenheim squadron based there had lost all but two of its aircraft.

On the 9th, Pulford was reinforced by three squadrons of Dutch Glen Martin bombers and a squadron of Buffaloes. These assets were, however, soon cancelled out by a fresh wave of disasters. Kuantan airfield was crowded with machines which had been withdrawn from Kelantan. No sooner had Pulford decided to thin out this concentration than the Japanese struck, destroying seven aircraft on the ground. Pulford withdrew the remainder to Singapore.

The dismal performance of the RAF on these first crucial days was largely a result of the poor quality of many of its machines and the uneven state of its training. There were some discreditable incidents, like the premature evacuation of Kota Bharu airfield, but there seems to have been little wrong with the morale of RAF aircrew, who flew their ageing machines from water-logged runways to take on an enemy who was both technically and numerically superior.

On the morning of 9 December six Blenheims flew from Singapore to attack Singora. They were to have collected fighter cover as they crossed northern Malaya, but the aircraft that should have joined them were at full stretch trying to defend their own airfields. The Blenheims pressed on in the face of heavy anti-aircraft fire and repeated attacks by Japanese fighters. Only three of them recrossed the border and landed at Butterworth, where they refuelled and rearmed in preparation to renewing their attack, assisted by the Blenheims of 62 Squadron which had survived the raids on Alor Star.

Squadron Leader A. K. S. 'Pongo' Scarf had just taken off in the leading Blenheim when a formation of Japanese aircraft bombed the airfield and destroyed the remaining Blenheims. Although Scarf could have justifiably cancelled his mission and landed elsewhere, he flew on alone and bombed Singora at low level, with his rear gunner, Flight Sergeant Cyril Rich, strafing the rows of parked Japanese aircraft. Scarf made his way back at treetop height, with Japanese fighters in hot pursuit. With his left arm shattered and his back smashed, Scarf, held in his seat by Flight Sergeant Rich, managed to bring the aircraft down in a paddy field only 100 yards from the hospital at Alor Star where his wife Sally was a nurse. Scarf was carried into the operating theatre, squeezed his wife's hand and said 'Keep smiling, Sal.' Then he died. Squadron Leader Scarf was posthumously awarded the Victoria Cross in 1946, when the full story of his courage became known.

By the end of 9 December the RAF had only ten aircraft in the North, concentrated at Butterworth. Pulford decided that daylight bombing operations over northern Malaya were no longer feasible, and he sent the three Dutch squadrons, trained only for daylight work, back to the East Indies to retrain. Alor Star and Kuantan joined the list of abandoned airfields, and by 11 December only a solitary photo-reconnaissance Buffalo remained at Butterworth. The air battle over the North had been lost, leaving III Corps to fight its defensive battle beneath skies dominated by Japanese aircraft.

Events at sea were no more encouraging. During the morning of 8 December Admiral Phillips discussed the situation with his senior staff officers in his 'cuddy' aboard *Prince of Wales*. Phillips outlined the situation, and suggested that Force Z might attack the transports which would probably be landing reinforcements in Siam or northern Malaya. The possibility of withdrawing without a fight remained a possibility, but it was a plan so alien to the instincts of Phillips and his officers, and to the traditions of their service, that it was not seriously discussed.

Phillips decided that his force would leave shortly before dusk, to minimise the chance of being intercepted by patrolling submarines, steam East of the Anambas Islands to avoid minefields, swing North until it was some 150 miles South of Cape Cambodia, and then turn west-north-west so as to arrive off Singora at daybreak on the 10th. Having wreaked havoc amongst the Japanese transports and their escorts, Force Z would return at best speed along the coast. Phillips believed that this plan offered good chances of success, and considered that it depended on speed, surprise, adequate air reconnaissance and fighter protection over Singora. With this in view, he submitted to Pulford a written request for reconnaissance 100 miles North of the force during daylight on the 9th, reconnaissance to Singora on the 10th, and fighter cover over Singora while the raid took place.

Pulford already knew that his airfields were being subjected to repeated attacks, and at 4.00 he told Phillips that while he hoped to be able to provide reconnaissance as requested, he was unable to guarantee fighter cover over Singora. No sooner had he given this cautious assent than his position deteriorated still further, for at 4.30 he was informed that the RAF commander at Kota Bharu considered the airfield, vital for the protection of Force Z, untenable.

Prince of Wales and *Repulse*, together with their four escorting destroyers, slipped out of harbour at 5.35 that evening and steamed north-east. Admiral Leighton, who had handed over to Phillips as Commander-in-Chief Far East that morning, watched Force Z depart with a heavy heart: he had many good friends aboard, and he did not expect to see any of them again. Phillips left his Chief of Staff, Palliser, behind at Singapore to act as a link with the other services: he would not, however, be able to reply to any of Palliser's messages, for Force Z was to maintain radio silence to minimise the chances of detection.

The arrival of Force Z at Singapore, intended as it was as a deterrent to Japanese aggression, had naturally been well publicised, and the Japanese were well aware of its presence. Measures had been taken to deal with the Force if it ventured out: naval aircraft of the 21st and 22nd Air Flotillas, their pilots specially trained in anti-shipping missions, were stationed on airfields near Saigon. Not only were Japanese troop convoys strongly escorted, but a force of four heavy cruisers and a number of destroyers under Vice-Admiral Takeo Kurita, provided them with close cover. To make assurance doubly sure, Vice-Admiral Nobutake Kondo, with two battleships, two heavy cruisers and ten destroyers, furnished the invasion force with distant cover.

Surprise, Phillips' strongest ally, evaporated on the afternoon of the 9th when a Japanese submarine, one of twelve picketing the East coast of Malaya, reported the presence of Force Z. Phillips had already heard from Palliser that fighter cover over Singora would definitely not be available, although Pulford still hoped to be able to provide reconnaissance. On receipt of the submarine's sighting report, Kondo ordered Kurita to search for Force Z with his cruisers' spotting aircraft, and ground-based aircraft also joined the hunt. Kurita's aircraft were seen by Phillips' flagship late that afternoon, and at 8.15 p.m. Phillips reluctantly decided to abandon his mission and return to Singapore. More messages from Palliser, which spoke of the damage to the northern airfields, contributed to his decision.

Shortly before midnight Phillips received another signal from Palliser. 'Enemy reported landing in Kuantan,' it read, 'latitude 3° 50' North.' Not only was Kuantan well to the South of Phillips' initial objective, but it was not far from his return route to Singapore. The message placed Phillips in a quandary. He recognised the strategic importance of Kuantan, whose seizure would permit the Japanese to outflank III Corps. He considered that Palliser would have sent him the message in the assumption that he would act on the information it contained, and was also sure that, this being the case, Palliser would have arranged fighter cover. At 1.00 in the morning of the 10th Force Z altered course for Kuantan. In order to preserve surprise, Phillips decided to maintain radio silence, and no news of his change of plan reached Palliser.

Force Z reached Kuantan at dawn and found nothing, which was hardly surprising in view of the fact that the report of the Japanese landing had been false. The next scene of the drama was, meanwhile, unfolding. A Japanese submarine had sighted Force Z early on the morning of the 10th: it had, unbeknown to Phillips, fired a number of torpedoes at his ships and radioed to Kondo that the British were falling back. But the submarine lost contact at 3.00, and Kondo had no information available which suggested that Force Z was doing anything other than making for Singapore as quickly as it could.

Soon after dawn, reconnaissance aircraft, bombers and torpedo-bombers of the 22nd Air Flotilla left their airfields in southern Indo-China to resume the hunt for Force Z. Their search concentrated upon the area some 80 miles West of the Anambas Islands, where Phillips would have been had he been steaming straight for Singapore. By 11.00 the Japanese seemed to have drawn a blank: all of their aircraft had reached the limits of their operating range and had turned back. There had been a brief flurry of excitement at 10.00 when a bomber squadron sighted and attacked *Tenedos*, an elderly destroyer which Phillips had ordered back to Singapore the previous evening. *Tenedos* had been instructed to inform Palliser of the abandonment of the Singora plan at 8.00 on the morning of the 10th, by which time her radio transmissions would not give away the position of the main force. *Tenedos* duly sent the message, but the information it contained was already well out of date, and made no mention of the Kuantan project.

It was at shortly after 11.00 that Phillips' luck at last ran out. Ensign Hoashi, in a 'Babs' reconnaissance aricraft – the single-engined Navy 98 monoplane – was flying the last leg of his search pattern when he glimpsed warships far below through a gap in the cloud. Hoashi banked his plane to starboard and lost height as he took a closer look. A few minutes later he transmitted the general alert that was, in effect, the death sentence of Force Z: 'Sighted two enemy battleships seventy nautical miles south-east Kuantan course south-east.'

The anti-aircraft gun crews on the battleships had been on the alert ever since *Tenedos'* disturbing report that she was under air attack, and sat, sweating in their flash protection hoods, on the rapidly-warming decks. *Prince of Wales* led *Repulse* in line ahead through the calm waters, with the three destroyers ahead and on either flank. *Repulse*'s radar picked up Hoashi's 'Babs' at 11.00, and shortly afterwards the aircraft itself came into sight, well out of range. But already a more sinister smudge was visible on British radars as large numbers of bombers approached from the South.

The first wave of aircraft, twin-engined 'Nell' bombers, ran in at high level through a sky speckled with the bursts of the ships' anti-aircraft guns. Eight bombs narrowly missed *Repulse*, and one crashed through her deck, bursting below in the Marines' mess and starting a fire. The damage control parties soon had the blaze under control, and *Repulse*'s effectiveness was undiminished. Rear-Admiral Sadaichi Matsunaga, commander of 22nd Air Flotilla, had intended that the high-level bombing would damage the superstructure of the British ships and distract their gunners' attention while torpedo-bombers delivered the knock-out blow. But Matsunaga's force had been split up during the hunt for Force Z, and the torpedo-bombers arrived on the scene some fifteen minutes after the first wave of bombers had departed.

The torpedo attack may have been late, but it was nonetheless effective. The Japanese pilots flew in through a fearsome barrage to drop their torpedoes. Captain Tennant of *Repulse* managed to turn his ship through 45 degrees, offering only its stern to the oncoming torpedoes, but the flagship was less fortunate: at 11.44 two torpedoes slammed into *Prince of Wales* near the stern, damaging her rudder and propellor shafts, and seriously affecting her engines. The great battleship at once listed heavily to port, and began to steam in a circle, signalling that she was not under control.

Seeing the crippled state of the flagship, Tennant decided that he should inform Singapore of the progress of the action as it seemed likely that *Prince of Wales* could no longer transmit messages. He was surprised to hear from his Chief Yeoman of Signals that the flagship seemed hitherto to have sent no messages, and he at once sent the emergency signal 'Enemy aircraft bombing', together with the ships' position. Another wave of aircraft approached just before 12.00. This time the attack was perfectly co-ordinated, with the bombers and torpedo-planes arriving almost simultaneously. Although the bombing was as accurate and the torpedo attacks as determined as before, Tennant, manoeuvring *Repulse* with great skill, eluded the torpedoes and his vessel escaped without damage. He then closed the flagship to ask if he could offer any assistance and to enquire if her radio was still working. *Prince of Wales*, circling like some mortally-wounded beast, made no reply.

The two ships were still close together when, at 12.20, the third wave of attackers approached. Three of the oncoming torpedo bombers peeled off to attack *Repulse*, while the remaining six carried straight on for *Prince of Wales*. Tennant managed to swing *Repulse* round to face the torpedoes launched by the first group, but he then saw that three of the other planes had altered course to attack *Repulse* from the beam. There was, he knew, little hope of avoiding torpedoes coming in from two directions, and Tennant warned his crew over the Tannoy to 'Stand by for torpedo'. A torpedo hit *Repulse* square amidships at 12.23, but although the old battle-cruiser began to list to port, she could still fire all her guns and make good speed. But *Prince of Wales*, making less than 15 knots, had offered a far easier target to the aircraft which had pressed on to attack her. She was hit by all three, and her list diminished as water poured in through the gaps torn in her hull.

The Japanese still had uncommitted aircraft on the scene, and the success of the previous attack on *Repulse* left them in little doubt as to how to continue the battle. The next squadron split up and attacked from several directions, making co-ordinated air defence almost impossible. Four torpedoes slammed into *Repulse*, and Tennant realised that his ship was doomed. He ordered everyone to come up on deck and to clear away the Carley floats. 'Men were now pouring up on the deck,' he recalled.

When the ship had a thirty degree list to port I looked over the starboard side of the bridge and saw the Commander and two or three hundred men collecting on the starboard side. I never saw the slightest sign of panic or ill-discipline. I told them from the bridge how well they had fought the ship and wished them good luck. The ship hung for at least a minute and a half to two minutes with a list of about 60 or 70 degrees to port and then rolled over at 12.33 pm.

The destroyers *Vampire* and *Electra* picked up Tennant and forty-one out of his sixty-nine officers, together with 734 of the 1,240 ratings.

Just after *Repulse* slipped beneath the waves nine high-level bombers attacked *Prince of Wales*. Although they hit her only once, it was by now obvious that she was sinking, and at 1.10 her captain gave the order to abandon ship. Ten minutes later the battleship shuddered and began to roll to port, almost capsizing *Electra*, which had come in close to take off survivors. Her huge red underside showed briefly amongst the oil and debris, and then she too disappeared. Most of her crew were saved, ninety of the 110 officers and 1,195 of the 1,502 ratings. Both Phillips and his flag-captain, John Leach, went down with the ship.

Tennant's emergency report that the force was under air attack was received at Singapore at 12.04, and it arrived at the Operations Room at

Air Headquarters a few minutes later. Eleven Buffaloes of 453 Squadron, which had been detailed to provide air protection for the fleet, took off from Sembawang at 12.26, and arrived at the scene of the battle at about 1.20. Flight-Lieutenant Tim Vigors described the scene:

It was obvious that the three destroyers were going to take hours to pick up those hundreds of men clinging to bits of wreckage and swimming round in the filthy, oily water. Above all this the threat of another bombing and machine-gun attack was imminent. Every one of those men must have realised that. Yet as I flew round every man waved and put up his thumb as I flew over him. After an hour lack of petrol forced me to leave, but during that hour I had seen many men in dire danger waving, cheering and joking, as if they were holiday-makers at Brighton waving at low-flying aircraft. It shook me, for here was something above human nature.

Vigors' report was to be accepted with less than enthusiasm by some survivors, and there were subsequently suggestions that the men in the water were shaking their fists in anger at the RAF's inactivity. Whether or not this is true, it can be seen that little blame attaches to the RAF, which reacted promptly when told of Force Z's plight. Indeed, the arrival of eleven Buffaloes would scarcely have had a decisive effect upon the battle, although it would undoubtedly have made life more difficult for the Japanese pilots.

The key to the disaster lies with Phillips himself. Like so many naval officers of his generation he failed to understand the potential of aircraft, and over-estimated the ability of the anti-aircraft guns on *Prince of Wales* and *Repulse* to deal with them. His relationship with Palliser is also of pivotal importance. Phillips assumed that his Chief of Staff would do what he himself would have done, sending aircraft to Kuantan in the belief that Force Z would certainly steam there after the receipt of the warning of Japanese landings. Palliser, for his part, was not unreasonable in expecting Phillips to risk breaking radio silence in order to notify him of something as important as the decision to investigate Kuantan. Tom Phillips' decision to take Force Z on an admittedly difficult mission to attack the Japanese landings was taken in the highest traditions of his service, traditions which were, alas, to be sorely bruised as Japanese naval aviation announced the end of an era of maritime history.

Churchill was spending the weekend at Chequers, the Prime Minister's country residence, when he heard of the Japanese attack on the American fleet at Pearl Harbor. He telephoned Roosevelt to ask him if the news was true. 'It's quite true,' he replied.

They have attacked Pearl Harbor. We are all in the same boat now.

The news lifted a great burden from Churchill's shoulders. England no longer stood alone: with the might of America to assist her, Churchill had no doubt as to the final result. 'So we had won after all,' he thought, and 'went to bed and slept the sleep of the saved and thankful'.

The Prime Minister's euphoria was short-lived. Churchill was sitting up in bed opening his dispatch-boxes on the morning of the 10th – it was mid-afternoon in Singapore – when the bedside phone rang.

It was the First Sea Lord. His voice sounded odd.

He gave a sort of cough and a gulp, and at first I could not hear quite clearly.

'Prime Minister, I have to report to you that the *Prince of Wales* and *Repulse* have been sunk – and we think by aircraft.Tom Phillips is drowned'.

'Are you sure it's true?'

'There is no doubt at all.'

So I put the telephone down. I was thankful to be alone. In all the war I never received a more direct shock.

DISASTER IN THE NORTH

On 10 December, against a backcloth of growing Japanese superiority, the Far East War Council was formed at Singapore. It was chaired by Duff Cooper, newly elevated to the post of Resident Minister for Far Eastern Affairs, with Cabinet rank. He was charged with relieving the commanders-in-chief of their extraneous responsibilities, giving them broad political guidance, settling emergency matters on the spot when time did not permit reference to Whitehall, and authorising certain essential expenditure. His terms of reference stated, however, that he was not to interfere with the normal command functions of the commanders-in-chief, who were to continue to correspond directly with their respective departments in London.

The Council's members included the Governor, Brooke-Popham and the three commanders-in-chief: Admiral Layton was hurriedly reappointed Commander-in-Chief, Far East Fleet, on 11 December. Mr. V. G. Bowden represented Australia on the Council, and Gordon Bennett was told that he was at liberty to attend meetings if he wished to do so. Sir George Sansom, responsible for propaganda and Press control, joined the Council later. When Duff Cooper and Sansom left in January, Sir Shenton Thomas took over the chairmanship of the Council and Mr. Robert Scott assumed responsibility for propaganda and Press control.

The Council met daily at 9.00 a.m., and its meetings usually lasted for two hours. Although it was originally intended to examine British strategy throughout the Far East, the Council soon tended to concentrate on events in Malaya and Borneo. As Percival himself observed:

Hong Kong was fighting an isolated battle and really nothing much could be done to help the garrison there. The responsibility for the defence of Burma was, on 15 December, transferred from the Commander-in-Chief Far East to the Commander-in-Chief India.

Although some critics suggested that the composition of the Council meant that discussion was centred too much on what was happening in Malaya at the expense of wider issues, Percival felt that the Council's balance was about right, although it would have been more convenient if meetings had taken place later in the morning, to give commanders more time to discuss matters with their staff and with each other.

Duff Cooper and his colleagues found little comfort in the news from the North. Even as the Council held its first meeting. 11th Division was straining every nerve to complete the preparation of the sodden position at Jitra. Murray-Lyon planned to hold Jitra with two brigades, 15th and 6th, forward, and the 28th in reserve. The position lay about thirty miles South of the frontier and ten miles North of the airfield at Alor Star, indeed, it was the defence of this airfield which was the prime *raison d'etre* for the occupation of what was generally regarded as an abysmal position at Jitra.

On the right, 2/9th Jats and 1st Leicesters of 15th Brigade held a 6,000 yard front astride the main road on the northern edge of Jitra, their position running from the wooded hills on the Jats' right, through flooded paddy-fields to rubber estates in the Leicesters' sector. Brigadier Garrett's remaining battalion, 1/14th Punjab, was mainly concerned with the provision of a screen on the main road, well North of the position, and holding an outpost position at Asun. His fourth battalion, 3/16th Punjab, was, as we have seen, already committed to *Krohcol.*

The 18,000 yards separating the Leicesters' left flank at Rimba from the coast was the responsibility of Brigadier Lay's 6th Brigade. Much of this ground was swampy, with the exception of a cultivated belt on either side of the railway and a relatively firm area between Jitra and the railway. This latter sector was held by 2nd East Surreys, while 2/16th Punjab was entrusted with the broad marshy front between the railway and the sea. Lay's third battalion, 1/8th Punjab, had been reduced to two companies by the detachement of two companies and the carrier platoon to Major Andrews' force which had been sent into Siam to delay the Japanese advance. Lay posted the two remaining companies of 1/8th Punjab at Kampong Imam on the Perlis road, in order to screen his position in the same way that 1/14th Punjab was covering 15th

Brigade's.

Three battalions of 28th Brigade were to come under Murray-Lyon's command on their arrival in the Alor Star area, the brigade's remaining battalion was to remain behind to cover the lines of communication between Alor Star and Sungei Patani. Murray-Lyon's divisional artillery consisted of two 4.5 inch howitzer batteries of 155th Field Regiment, parts of a mountain regiment and an anti-tank regiment, and a 16-gun light air defence battery. 137th Field Regiment, equipped with 25-pounders, was on its way up. There remained, of course, the divisional reconnaissance regiment, the 3rd Cavalry, mechanised only in the sense that it had been deprived of its horses and equipped with an inadequate number of soft-skinned vehicles which its troopers were, in the main, unable to drive. So unfitted for its role was this unit that Murray-Lyon wisely left it out of the battle. Its absence meant, however, that the task of screening the position and reporting on the progress of the Japanese advance had to be entrusted to the infantry of 1/8th and 1/14th Punjab, who were ill-equipped to participate in a tough and fast-moving battle.

The advanced guard of the Japanese 5th Division, a tank company, two infantry battalions, a light battery and some engineers, moved South down the main road with headlights blazing, and at about 9.30 on the night of the 9th it collided with the first of 1/14th Punjab's blocking positions, some ten miles inside Siam. The anti-tank guns with the Punjabis hit the two leading tanks, and the advance ground to a halt. The Punjabis then withdrew as planned, destroying culverts as they went, to an intermediate position at Changlun, six miles south of the frontier. It was intended that they should give the Japanese another bloody nose at Changlun before falling back to the outpost position at Asun, which would be then have been prepared for defence by the remainder of 1/14th.

Murray-Lyon realised, however, that the delays resulting from the cancellation of Matador meant that his main position would not be ready in time to meet the Japanese attack unless Brigadier Garrett's men could buy more time on the main road. He therefore ordered Garrett to hold the Japanese North of Jitra till dawn on the 12th, and when Garrett pointed out that this could only be achieved by stripping Asun to concentrate the whole of 1/14th at Changlun, Murray-Lyon at once agreed, giving Garrett three companies of 2/1st Gurkhas to hold Asun.

The Gurkhas reached Asun, after a trying day's digging and moving, after dark on the 10th, enabling Lieutenant-Colonel Fitzpatrick of the 1/14th to concentrate astride the road at Changlun, covering a bridge over a stream. At 9.00 on the morning of the 11th the Japanese launched the first of a series of attacks against 1/14th, supported by mortar fire whose accuracy gave rise to growing rumours of Fifth Column activities. Just after midday a determined Japanese assault broke into the centre of the position, capturing the partly-demolished bridge and two Breda anti-tank guns. Fitzpatrick, who was becoming increasingly worried by signs that the Japanese were working round his right flank, decided to pull back, and managed to extract the bulk of his battalion in good order.

Brigadier Garrett had been wounded in the neck by mortar fire while visiting 1/14th that morning. Having had the wound dressed he returned to the front, arriving at Fitzpatrick's headquarters shortly before Murray-Lyon himself. After a brief discussion the divisional commander ordered 1/14th to fall back to a position covering 2/1st Gurkhas at Asun, giving the Gurkhas time to finish work on their own position. Fitzpatrick briefed his company commanders and went off to look for gun positions, and company orders groups began to assemble. As the battalion began its move back, with most of its senior management engaged in receiving orders and carrying out reconnaissance, the worst happened.

Lieutenant Greer, commanding the anti-tank section attached to 1/14th Punjab, gave perhaps the most coherent account of the next few minutes, minutes which saw the extinction of 1/14th as a fighting battalion. 'It was raining,' said Greer

Well, as you'll remember, it hadn't stopped for days. Then suddenly there was the devil's own deluge. I had never been in such a storm. You couldn't see more than twenty yards.

I was with my carriers in a hide . . . One of my sections was forward. It was about quarter to five. Suddenly I saw some of my trucks and a carrier screaming down the flooded road, and heard the hell of a battle a short way to the North. It sounded as though guns and machine guns had got right into our position. The din was terrific.

I wasn't given any time to wonder about this because almost immediately a medium tank roared past me. I dived for cover. I reckon that within the next two minutes a dozen medium tanks and a couple of one-man tanks passed me. They had crashed right through our forward companies, but most of these must have been on the move . . . In the middle of the tanks I saw one of my carriers; its tail was on fire and the No. 2 was facing back firing his LMG at a tank twenty yards behind him. Poor beggar.

The Japanese column, consisting of lorried infantry led by tanks, had broken through the rearguard and ploughed down the length of the Punjabi battalion, most of whose soldiers had never seen a tank before. Some 200 men, including Brigadier Garrett, managed to rejoin the division the following day.

The Japanese sped on, overrunning a detachment of 2/1st Gurkhas which had gone forward to support the Punjabis, and nearing the bridge at Asun, the last major obstacle before Jitra. The bridge had been prepared for demolition, but as the leading tank roared towards it, blazing away with its cannon and machine-gun, the Indian Viceroy's Commissioned Officer in command of the firing party was hit. Major Bate, commander of 23rd Field Company, ran forward to fire the charge, but nothing happened when he pressed the plunger, and a burst of fire cut him down almost instantly. Although the Gurkhas had no anti-tank guns, for they were to have received those with the 1/14th when the Punjabis withdrew through Asun, they had anti-tank rifles, and one of these, manned by Havildar Manbahadur, covered the bridge. Manbahadur stopped the leading tank just short of the bridge, and hit the second as it tried to worm its way past. When two more appeared the Havildar damaged the first, persuading the other to withdraw. Manbahadur then profited by a brief lull in the fighting to sprint out to rescue Major Bate, but the officer died as he was being carried back.

The check at the bridge did not hold up the Japanese for long. Their lorried infantry quickly debussed to attack the Gurkhas' flanks, and by 7.30 there was heavy fighting all over the position. Lieutenant-Colonel Fulton, who had initially dismissed reports that the Japanese were on the bridge as 'wind-up', warned brigade headquarters that:

The Japs have got through the 1/14th and are on my front. They've got tanks and seem to be . . .

At this point the line went dead. As the *Divisional History* commented sombrely, 'few survivors of this battalion ever rejoined the Division.'

The laceration of the Gurkhas and Punjabis was not the only damage suffered by 11th Division on 11 December. On the division's left, the covering and outpost troops of 6th Brigade were withdrawn after dark. As the column approached the bridge over the stream at Manggoi, on the left of the Leicesters' position, the officer in command of the demolition, fearing that the approaching vehicles were Japanese, blew the bridge on his own initiative. There were no materials available locally for its repair, and the column had to abandon all its transport and most of its carriers, together with seven anti-tank and four mountain guns.

Murray-Lyon did what he could to repair the damage by ordering Brigadier Carpendale of 28th Brigade to assume command of the 15th in place of the missing Garrett, and by placing 2/2nd Gurkhas, from 28th Brigade, at his disposal. This left only one battalion in 28th Brigade and, since Murray-Lyon had already deployed this for the protection of the

Alor Star–Sungei Patani area, it left him with no divisional reserve. Morale had been bruised by the events of the 11th, and the troops had already become uncomfortably aware that the RAF seemed to have lost the war in the air. On the morning of the 10th a huge pall of smoke could be seen hanging over the airfield at Alor Star, and Carpendale telephoned Murray-Lyon:

The RAF have hopped it. They seemed to be in a great hurry. What's happened? You might have let me know.

Murray-Lyon was understandably pained. He had taken up the poor position at Jitra in order to defend Alor Star, and now, with the battle for Jitra about to break, Alor Star had been evacuated.

The Japanese advance guard, Lieutenant-Colonel Saeki's detachment of 5th Division, gave the defenders of Jitra no time to recover from the events of the 11th. The ubiquitous Colonel Tsuji was with the column – Saeki was an old friend – and he had driven with Saeki in a commandeered civilian car through the battles on the main road, firing his revolver through the car's windows. Saeki's men were in contact with 2/9th Jats by the early evening of the 11th, and at about 8.30 his tanks tried to force their way down the main road through the Leicesters. They overran a forward patrol, but were soon brought to a halt, with two tanks knocked out by the 215th Anti-Tank Battery.

The Jats were heavily sniped all night, their positions pinpointed by 'the Japanese barber of field rank' – yet another instance of the efficiency of Colonel Tsuji's agents. Fearing that the Japanese would envelop his right flank. Carpendale obtained assistance from 6th Brigade in the shape of two companies of 1/8th Punjab and two of 2/16th Punjab. Carpendale also ordered up his reserve battalion, 2/2nd Gurkhas. At 3.00 on the morning of the 12th the Japanese rushed the roadblock on the main road and wrested a lodgement in the Leicesters' position, only to be driven out by a counter-attack. About three hours later a Japanese company, supported by tank fire, managed to drive a wedge between the Leicesters and the Jats, and an immediate counter-attack failed. Carpendale believed that it was vital to restore the integrity of his front, and he again turned to Brigadier Lay for assistance.

Lay sent up the remaining two companiess and battalion headquarters of 1/8th Punjab. Murray-Lyon had visited Carpendale's headquarters and was on his way to brief his senior commanders at the nearby peace-time HQ Mess of 6th Brigade as one of the 1/8th companies plodded past. He was not impressed:

The men looked hang-dog and tired, and gave no sign of response to the Divisional Commander's words of encouragement. When they had passed he spoke to the GSO 1:

'I haven't seen that look on men's faces since March 1918,' he said.

The attack was doomed from the outset. The Punjabis were shot at by the Jats as they moved forward: this shock proved too much for the tired troops, some of whom bolted. Lieutenant-Colonel Bates of the Punjabis did his best to rally his men, and led them forward, recapturing a pill-box between the Leicesters and the Jats. They pressed on into a hail of fire: Bates, his adjutant, and the commander of the leading company were shot dead, and the attack petered out.

As the Punjabis launched the hopeless counter-attack, Murray-Lyon briefed his brigade commanders. He had decided that 11th Division would break clear to a position at Gurun, the other side of Alor Star, that night, and the preliminary moves would start immediately. The news from *Krohcol*, where the badly mauled 3/16th Punjab was falling back through 5/14th Punjab convinced him that the position would soon be outflanked, and in any case the news from the Jats seemed depressing. But even as Murray-Lyon was answering his brigadiers' questions, his GSO 1 was called to the phone to receive a personal order for Murray-Lyon from Percival himself. 'The Jitra position,' ordered the Commander-in-Chief, 'will be held to the last man and the last round. There must be no thought of withdrawal.' Murray-Lyon was called from the conference to receive the order, and returned looking relieved and confident. The grave faces of his subordinates relaxed as he told them that the withdrawal was cancelled, and the divisional commander agreed with his Commander, Royal Engineers, that disarming some of the demolitions would encourage the troops as it would show that they were to stand and fight. Only Brigadier Carpendale, the man whose troops were bearing the brunt of the battle, seemed unhappy. He muttered to the GSO 1 before he started back to his headquarters through the rain:

The troops are too tired. That's how it is. The troops are too tired.

Murray-Lyon's adversary, Major-General Sanro Kawamuru, whose 9th Infantry Brigade was moving behind the Saeki Detachment, was also taking stock of the situation. He decided to launch a major attack that night, sending an infantry regiment up each side of the road. But while this assault was being prepared, the Saeki detachment made further progress, penetrating as far as the Sungei Bata and coming into contact with 15th Brigade's rearmost battalion, 2/2nd Gurkhas. Nevertheless, both the Leicesters and the Jats held firm despite the widening gap between them, and when Murray-Lyon visited Carpendale at about 3.00 that afternoon he found him full of confidence and convinced that the Japanese had shot their bolt for the day. Carpendale proposed to withdraw the Jats about a mile to the South, while the Leicesters regrouped for a counter-attack, in which they would be assisted by the East Surreys of 6th Brigade. Murray-Lyon approved these plans, although he refused to sanction the involvement of the East Surreys, as he intended to use them to hold two bridges between Jitra and Alor Star, where they would also be available as a divisional reserve.

Carpendale subsequently decided that, without the help of the East Surreys, the Leicesters' counter-attack would be likely to make little headway, and he decided to use them for a defensive task instead, ordering them to pull back to a new position curling round from Rimba along the Sungei Jitra, and thence to Tanjong Pau. The Leicesters protested most strongly that the new line was some 2½ miles long, and ran mainly through flooded rice-fields. The position had not been reconnoitred, and had no depth. On the other hand, the battalion had so far suffered only thirty casualties, and was confident of holding fast in its prepared positions. Carpendale stressed, however, that his orders were final, and Lieutenant-Colonel Morrison of the Leicesters duly issued instructions for withdrawal.

Murray-Lyon, meanwhile, had visited Brigadier Lay's headquarters and briefed him on the future role of the East Surreys. He then returned to the main road, considerably delayed by his car becoming bogged and then, after a lengthy extrication, breaking down. Few divisional commanders can have seen more depressing sights than that which confronted Murray-Lyon when at last he reached the road.

It was a scene of panic. Lorries were screaming down the road . . . Broken down lorries already overcrowded were being besieged by excited men fighting for a lift . . . a carrier rattled by . . . someone fired . . . the carrier crashed off the road into a tree and overturned . . . a lorry skidded into the ditch . . . the next lorry hit it . . . a man clinging to the side of a lorry yelled 'Back to Alor Star!' . . . another shouted madly from the back of a lorry: 'Tanks across the bridge!' . . . a staccato of rapid fire close to the road urged crazy lorry-drivers to accelerate their insane career . . .

Murray-Lyon spoke to Lieutenant Coombe, whose section of 350th Field Battery was in action on the road, firing in support of 2/2nd Gurkhas a thousand yards forward, and then decided, on the urging of his GSO 1, to return to divisional headquarters to gain a broad view of the situation.

Things at divisional headquartrs were scarely less depressing. Murray-Lyon heard that the Leicesters had been caught as they were withdrawing, and that the Jats on their right had been overrun. Moreover, 3/16th Punjab of *Krohcol* had staggered back to Kroh with only 350 men. Murray-Lyon decided that he must retreat as soon as possible. The Japanese would soon be debouching down the Kroh road to his rear, and a determined frontal attack might easily smash its way down the main road. At 7.30 he asked III Corps for permission to withdraw to a new position covering Gurun, and his request was forwarded to Singapore, where Heath was visiting Percival. Heath replied, reminding Murray-Lyon that his task was to fight for the security of North Kedah and suggesting that he was opposed by only one Japanese division. He was, though, given permission to withdraw from Jitra, and was told that *Krohcol* would cease to be under his command from midnight that night.

Although Murray-Lyon made a reasonable decision on the basis of the evidence currently available to him, the situation was by no means as bad as he had been led to believe. The panic on the road had largely involved only lorry-drivers, rear echelon personnel and stragglers from Asun, and, although the withdrawal of the Jats to their new position had been impeded by communications problems which had resulted in the loss of one company, both the Jats and the Leicesters were still effective fighting units. Nor was *Krohcol* in quite as desperate a plight as it appeared to be.

For much of 11th Division, the withdrawal represented a leap from a moderately uncomfortable frying-pan into a raging fire. The troops were desperately tired after days of digging and fighting in heavy rain, and some battalions were widely dispersed and in close contact with an aggressive and enthusiastic enemy. For 15th Brigade the withdrawal was particularly nightmarish. Companies were ambushed as they fell back, and strong parties of Japanese worked their way deep into the Brigade's position. Major Emsden-Lambert of 2/16th Punjabis – lent to Carpendale by 6th Brigade – gave a vivid account of his experiences as he tried to form his detachment, at the right rear of 15th Brigade's position, into a defensive perimeter for the night:

a devastating fusillade arose. At least I thought it was devastating – it was my first experience of being under fire, and I estimated that at least one battalion was letting drive. Then it ceased and I walked round my post to find out what the damage was. The third platoon of my Sikh company had vanished but there was not a single casualty. I decided that my foreboding of devastation had been a bad 'un. In future I'd know better.

The withdrawal order failed to reach some units. Captian Holden's D Company 2/16th Punjab, holding an outpost position on 6th Brigade's front, was out of radio contact. Divisional headquarters tried to procure a boat to send the order by sea, but the navy was unable to help. The RAF was asked to drop a message, but replied that there were no aircraft available. Still ignorant of the changed situation, D Company stood fast, and when attacked, fought, quite literally, to the last man and the last round.

Other units were more fortunate, and received the order in time to break contact and make their way southwards. Some, fearing that the Japanese would push tanks down the main road, moved across country. Gabby Gavin of the East Surreys' mortar platoon had been looking for the remains of a Japanese patrol engaged by his mortars, but found nothing.

We found plenty when we got back to our guns though. Everybody was running hither and thither and most of them were yelling orders or information. A frantic 'withdraw' order had come through and the panic was on. We had no trucks and anyway the enemy were said to be on the road in force, so we had to carry what we could and destroy what we couldn't and make our way over ten miles of sodden padi field, and rubber plantations. It was a slithery, sloppy, exhausting ten miles burdened each with full marching order plus one part or another of the mortar and bombs.

It was dusk on the 13th by the time that Gavin and his section reached the bridge at Alor Star. Some detachments marched South along the railway line to Alor Star: others made for the coast, hoping to be taken off by ship. One party, commandeering a small craft, managed to reach northern Sumatra. It is, perhaps, surprising that the division managed to break clear as well as it did. 2/2nd Gurkhas covered the bridge over the Sungei Bata long enough for it to be blown, at about 2.00 on the morning of the 13th, in the faces of the advancing Japanese. 2/2nd withdrew through a rearguard furnished by 2/9th Gurkhas and, after a brisk action at about 4.00, contact was temporarily broken. One of the saddest footnotes to the whole dismal episode was the case of a battery of 155th Field Regiment, which had had such a laborious time in getting its guns the short distance from the road into their gun positions four days previously. The battery was heavily sniped while trying to haul its guns back on to the road over the same stretch of boggy track. Two of the 4.5s became irrevocably stuck: the gunners rendered them useless, and left them.

We have examined the Battle of Jitra in some detail, devoting more attention to it than we shall to subsequent similar actions. This is because Jitra set the tone of so much of what was to follow, and amply illustrates the problems which beset British commanders and their troops. The army's prime strategic function in Malaya was to defend the airfields, a requirement which forced its commanders to adopt a series of blocking postions in the North, of which Jitra was the first. Since these positions were of no abstract value in themselves, but were only useful in relation to the airfields they protected, British commanders were understandably sensitive to threats to their flanks, threats which might – and, indeed, sometimes did – indicate that the Japanese were working their way around the main position, cutting off its defenders and pushing on towards objectives in the British rear, and, ultimately, towards Singapore itself. Thus there was never a 'last ditch' mentality amongst the defenders of the North: it made far more sense to delay the Japanese from a series of blocking positions, falling back from one to the next and obstructing the enemy line of advance with demolitions, than to make a 'last man and last round' stand in a position which could in any case be outflanked.

But whatever the military logic of Britain's plans, their consequences were, in both moral and material terms, disastrous. British and Indian troops, many of whom were young and inexperienced, were speedily disillusioned by the all too evident signs of preparation for withdrawal and the frequency with which plans appeared to be changed. The Japanese were, conversely, elated by the fact that the British seemed intent on falling back, and actions like Asun boosted their morale just as they depressed that of the defenders. Ironically, the Japanese attack on Jitra was the result of a tactical misappreciation. A patrol led by Second-Lieutenant Oto had reported that the Jitra position was lightly held, inducing Saeki to continue his attack without waiting for the main body of the 5th Division to arrive. As Tsuji later admitted:

The breakthrough in the Jitra line was due to extraordinary tactics and to an error in the report of our first patrol. If we had judged this well-fortified position correctly, launched a full-scale attack with the whole strength of the division, and become locked in the struggle, it would have taken more than ten days to break through, and we would have had to be prepared for over a thousand casualties.

As it was, Saeki lost only 110 killed and wounded, and reaped a rich harvest of prisoners, equipment and rations. His men pressed on southwards, pockets crammed with food and tobacco, chatting about the delights of receiving 'Churchill's allowance.' Young Oto was less fortunate. Wounded in the shoulder on the night of the 12th-13th, he died in hospital at Saigon after gangrene set in.

11th Division never fully recovered from Jitra. Tsuji's claim that the British abandoned fifty field guns, fifty heavy machine-guns and 300 trucks and armoured cars is somewhat extravagant, but the facts of the situation were serious enough. Two battalions, 1/14th Punjab and 2/1st Gurkhas, had effectively been destroyed, and others had been badly mauled. Murray-Lyon had lost a mountain battery, two 4.5s and a number of anti-tank guns: the loss of the latter was particularly serious in view of the bold use which the Japanese were making of their tanks against Indian troops who had no idea of how to deal with them.

But perhaps the most serious casualty of all was British prestige. Both Indian soldiers and Malayan inhabitants could be forgiven for believing that there was more than a little truth in the Japanese propaganda leaflets, one of which showed what Murray-Lyon's GSO 1 called 'a crowd of muscular Japanese brandishing Samurai swords and wearing Fee-Fi-Fo-Fum expressions.' This made a sharp contrast with another leaflet depicting a strange figure which:

sported a gaudy vest which rivalled a tattooed lady's torso – half of it was composed of the Union Jack and the other half of the Stars and Stripes. The creature was brandishing a fistful of £ notes in one hand and a wad of $ bills in the other. It was wearing a pipe on the British side of its face and a cigar on the lease-and-lend side: it was simultaneously drinking a bottle of champagne, cuddling a Taxi girl and treading firmly on a prostrate half-starved Oriental. It wore no School tie. It was quite revolting.

Such crude propaganda amused many British, but there was no doubting its impact upon a population which was witnessing what looked uncomfortably like the beginning of a long retreat.

The battered *Krohcol* came under the direct command of III Corps at midnight on the 12th–13th, falling back across the frontier to a prepared position West of Kroh on the 13th. This had been sited to cover the road, but it left unguarded a narrow, muddy track which ran southwards through Grik to join the trunk road near Kuala Kangsar. British commanders had decided, after studying reconnaissance reports, that this track was impassable to infantry. But while it may have been an effective obstacle to British or Indian battalions with their wheeled transport, it was certainly usable by lightly-equipped Japanese infantry. The excellent Japanese espionage system had furnished Japanese commanders with details of the track, and the regiment which landed at Patani had been ordered to use it to seize the crossings of the Perak river near Kuala Kangsar, thereby neatly outflanking the defenders of Kedah.

At the same time that Heath took direct responsibility for *Krohcol*, Percival placed the command reserve, Brigadier Paris' 12th Brigade, at his disposal. Two of Paris' battalions – the Argylls and 5/2nd Punjab – arrived on the 13th and 14th, but his third unit, 4/19th Hyderabad, was still with Brigadier Key in Kelantan. The arrival of 12th Brigade enabled Heath to strengthen Krohcol and to take steps to cover the vital track. He sent a company of the Argylls, with some armoured cars, to Grik, while the rest of the battalion was ordered up to Baling to extricate *Krohcol*.

While the deployment of 12th Brigade took some of the pressure off his threatened right flank, things continued to go badly for Heath's main force on the trunk road. 11th Division had, as we have seen, made a difficult and costly withdrawal from Jitra, and dawn on December 13th found it South of the Kedah River, reorganising and picking up stragglers, covered by the two surviving Gurkha battalions of 28th Brigade. The bridges over the river had not been prepared for demolition, but work was put in hand immediately, and Murray-Lyon ordered them to be blown when, on the morning of the 13th, two Japanese motor-cyclists appeared. The road bridge was successfully demolished, but although the railway bridge was badly damaged, it refused to collapse. An engineer officer decided that the structure would not support the weight of the armoured train used for the advance into Siam, and Lieutenant Burns of 2/16th Punjab volunteered to drive it on to the bridge. 'I was shown how the thing worked,' he wrote, and

stepped into the cab and pulled the requisite lever. When the train was well under way, puffing noisly in protest at its impending demise . . . I jumped for it. The train gained speed as it approached the spot where it was destined to perform its gallant deed of self-immolation; it reached the dent; it passed over it unscathed, its cry changing to a piercing whistle of triumph as it continued its way southwards.

Burns dashed after the train, scrambled aboard and managed to stop it. But its reprieve was short-lived: the sappers blew it up at Ipoh a short time later. The episode had sinister implications, for Murray-Lyon's engineers had now run out of explosives, and, although his division was safely behind the Kedah River, it was obvious that the Japanese could make good use of the damaged bridge.

Murray-Lyon planned to make a stand behind the river, but Japanese infantry crossed it on the afternoon of the 13th, and although the Gurkhas drove them back across the river Murray-Lyon felt he could not sustain a major attack in that position. He accordingly issued orders for a withdrawal to Gurun, some twenty miles southwards, where a position had been reconnoitred but not prepared. The retirement took place in pouring rain, impeded by orders going astray and by the increasingly brittle morale of some units.

Gunner G. K. Topping, driving a truck with B Echelon of 80th Anti-Tank Regiment, wrote:

That night will live in my memory as long as I live. Such a night of confusion I have never witnessed before nor ever hope to again. Six hours it took us to make the journey by lorry from Alor Star to Sungei Patani over a stretch of road of about 25 miles. The highway was so congested with traffic, troops and refugees that it was impossible to move at more than walking pace. . . . At the outset of this nightmare journey all the vehicles moved off in convoy, but soon the column was so spread out that it was impossible to keep the lorry ahead in sight: other vehicles came between, severing connection with the lorry in front so that eventually each vehicle became a separate unit striving to reach its destination. I could well imagine . . . the quiet unruffled voice of the BBC announcer broadcasting the news to the British public: 'Our forces have made another strategical withdrawal in Malaya, carried out according to plan'.

Japanese aircraft were active during daylight hours. Gabby Gavin, moving back with the remnants of the East Surreys' mortar platoon, watched a Japanese aircraft working its way down the trunk road with bombs and machine-guns forcing the retreating troops to take cover.

All, that is, except a little Gurkha who planted himself in the middle of the road to wait for the third run of the plane. He had a Bren gun with him . . . The first plane came down the road, machine-guns rattling, and the Gurkha took aim. We watched him as the plane zoomed closer. I never noticed him fire but suddenly the plane disintegrated and burning petrol and plane showered over us. The Gurkha looked as if he was on fire for a moment and then he rolled over towards the ditch . . . He died quietly and without complaint.

It was not until midday on the 14th that the last of Murray-Lyon's exhausted units stumbled into Gurun.

While 11th Division made its painful way southwards, senior British commanders were forced to take hard decisions. Although Brigadier Key's force in Kelantan was falling back steadily towards the railhead at Kuala Krai, checking the Japanese advance from a series of defensive positions, its position was precarious in the extreme. Should the single line railway between Kuala Krai and Kuala Lipis be cut either by air attack or by an outflanking move through the jungle, the whole force would be lost. On the other hand, a withdrawal would have a bad effect on morale, and would free the Japanese forces in that area for operations elsewhere. Nevertheless, when Percival and Heath consi dered the matter on 12 December they resolved to withdraw the Kelantan force as soon as rolling stock could be made available. Brooke-Popham approved the decision the same afternoon.

The withdrawal from Kelantan was carried out with a skill which merited a better cause. All spare stores and equipment had been sent back by the 16th. 4/19th Hyderabad was sent back to rejoin 12th Brigade, now with 11th Division, and 2/12th Frontier Force Regiment rejoined its own brigade at Kuantan. By 22 December 8th Brigade was safely concentrated around Kuala Lipis and Jerantut, its withdrawal admirably covered by a composite detachment of Pahang Volunteers and the Malay Regiment, know as Macforce from its commander, Lieutenant-Colonel McKellar.

No sooner had he decided upon a withdrawal from Kelantan, than Percival was forced to consider the problem of Penang. Although the island had been delcared a fortress in 1936, it had only the most sketchy fixed defences, and no anti-aircraft guns: its garrison consisted of a battalion of the Straits Settlements Volunteer Force, a company of 5/14th Punjab, an independent company and an assortment of administrative detachments. On 11–12 December the Japanese bombed George Town, setting part of the town on fire, damaging the docks and causing heavy civilian casualties. The Fortress Commander and the Resident Counsellor decided to evacuate all European women and children on the night of the 19th, together with such of the sick and wounded who could be moved. The evacuation was carried out with the help of 50 survivors from the *Repulse* and *Prince of Wales,* who manned the ferries, most of whose crews had disappeared.

The Far East War Council discussed Penang on the morning of the 14th. The prime object of garrisoning the island had been to secure the anchorage against attack, and Layton now pointed out that the anchorage was no longer of any use to the navy. Percival had initially planned to throw more troops into Penang if his forces on the mainland had to fall back. But he had now come to the conclusion that it was on the mainland, where 11th Division was already running short of men, that the campaign would be decided: he simply could not spare the troops to reinforce Penang. The Council recognised that an evacuation would have a bad effect on morale, but there seemed no practicable alternative. A message was sent to Heath, authorising him to evacuate the garrison, remove what stores he could and destroy the remainder. The Governor sent similar instructions to the Resident Counsellor.

The situation on Penang had deteriorated still further by the time that the message reached Heath. On the 14th the municipal commissioners of George Town warned the Fortress Commander that the breakdown of civil administration made epidemics likely.

Montague Selfe, a Penang businessman, attended a meeting at the Resident Counsellor's house on the 16th.

I remember someone saying, 'The services have packed up, you know. The streets are stinking to high heaven. It's up to the merchants, the bankers and everyone to get the place cleaned up. And I said 'What's more to the point, it's time we started to get out of the place,' . . . and with that the few at the meeting woke up to the fact that things were a bit hot.

Heath had already come to the same conclusion. On 15 December he issued orders for the evacuation of the island on the night of the 16–17th. This left little enough time for the destruction of raw material and equipment that might be of use to the Japanese: no centralised plan had been made, and the authorities were desperately short of labour. Some damage was done: the civil airport and the power station were destroyed, and much of the equipment in the defences was rendered useless. But a great deal was destined to fall intact into Japanese hands.

110

The Japanese were able to seize no less than 3,000 tons of tin, a substance of which they were very short. The radio station was left undamaged, and was soon back on the air, pumping out virulent anti-British propaganda. Worse still, many small craft were left at their moorings, providing the Japanese with the capacity to launch amphibious operations along the coast.

There was, nevertheless, a shortage of vessels for the evacuation, and only the troops and European civilians would be taken off. Montague Selfe was told, like other Europeans,

that we should meet at the wharf somewhere about 5 in the evening, not telling anybody except Europeans. Otherwise we would have been bogged down with Chinese and Malays. We all walked along to the Wharf, no cars of course. I walked past my office in Beach Road, which had been bombed, hoping to get in as I had the keys. It was my intention to collect some business records, and my wife's jewellery and so forth from a private safe. However this was not to be as there were Indian troops guarding the buildings as looting had been rife. Although I showed my keys to the Sergeant in command, he would not let me in, and he had orders to shoot.

The evacuation of Penang was, as the authorities had feared, a severe blow to the morale of civilians, both European and Asian. Noel Barber believed that the news had:

a more stinging effect even than the loss of the *Prince of Wales* and the *Repulse* . . . Suddenly, instead of being treacherous and cunning, the Japanese had become monstrous and inhuman. Penang in a dramatic sort of way crystallised to ordinary people in Singapore a new and terrifying picture of the Japanese. It was as though the enemy had been invested in the eyes of both civilians and soldiers with superhuman qualities.

On 22 December Duff Cooper broadcast from Singapore, speaking of the loss of the *Prince of Wales* and *Repulse* and the fall of Penang. Although the broadcast was well-received in some quarters – Ann Scott thought that he was 'frank, sincere and honest,' – many people shared Sir Shenton Thomas' horror that the Resident Minister had spoken of the successful evacuation of the population of Penang when, of course, he meant the European population only. Thomas feared that there would be a very bad Asiatic reaction, and held a meeting at which he tried to reassure leading Chinese, Indian and Malay representatives. But, as Barber was to write:

The damage was done, and a wave of defeatism swept down to Singapore, to white and coloured alike.

11th Division's position at Gurun had considerable potential, which is more than could be said for that at Jitra. It squarely blocked the main

111

Japanese axis of advance, where the road and railway ran through a narrow neck of open country, with the high ground of Kedah Peak to the West and thick jungle to the East. But although Murray-Lyon had given orders, as early as 8 December, that the position should be prepared for defence, a crucial shortage of labour meant that nothing could be done until the exhausted troops of the division arrived there after the gruelling withdrawal from Jitra. Thus, instead of occupying trenches sited with care and dug by civilian labour, they were forced to set to work themselves immediately they arrived. 1/8th Punjab, the last troops to reach the position, arrived at 10.00 on the morning of the 14th: they swallowed, as their history puts it, 'half a chappati and immediately moved off to work.'

Murray–Lyon gave Brigadier Lay's 6th Brigade, of three under-strength battalions, the task of holding the road and railway North of Gurun, with 28th Brigade, once more under the command of Brigadier Carpendale, on its right. 15th Brigade, under Brigadier Garrett once again, was in reserve around Gurun itself. No sooner had the troops finished digging, on the afternoon of the 14th, than Japanese tanks and lorried infantry, having crossed the Kedah River by the damaged railway bridge, appeared in front of the position. One tank was knocked out by an anti-tank gun and the other two withdrew, but the infantry promptly debussed and were soon in close contact with the exhausted men of 1/8th Punjab astride the main road.

Lieutenant-Colonel Napier of 88th Field Regiment, whose command included the anti-tank guns forward with 6th Brigade, called in on Brigadier Lay after visiting the forward positions. 'I've just come back from the line,' he said.

and things look bad there. There's a good deal of retrograde movement, and I don't think the troops are going to stand.

Lay at once ordered an immediate counter-attack by a squadron of the lorry-mounted 3rd Cavalry. This went wrong from the start. The Japanese had already made good progress, and the squadron was heavily sniped and mortared before its troops could debus. The Brigadier then organised and led a counter-attack with a mixed bag of East Surreys, Punjabis and gunners, and this checked the Japanese advance, for the time at least.

While Brigadier Lay was contending with the growing Japanese threat to his Brigade, Murray-Lyon met Heath at divisional headquarters, in the club house of the Harvard Estate, four miles South of Gurun. Murray-Lyon warned the Corps Commander that many of his men were weary and demoralised, and that he feared that a continuation of short retreats and hasty defences would lead to disaster.

Moreover, the situation around Kroh seemed dangerous: it was likely that the Japanese would soon debouch from the Grik road in the Division's rear. He suggested that 11th Division should be withdrawn in 'long hops' by road or rail, to permit the troops to rest between battles and to construct proper defensive positions. Heath broadly agreed, but told Murray-Lyon that, since the Corps' role was to delay the Japanese advance as much as possible, 11th Division's immediate task was to hold Gurun. He reassured Murray-Lyon about the threat from Kroh: a detachment of the Argylls had already been sent to cover the Grik road, and the remainder of 12th Brigade would soon follow.

Murray-Lyon briefed his brigade commanders at Lay's headquarters, and then retired to divisional headquarters for what turned out to be the first quiet night since 7 December. Things were rather less quiet at the front, for at 8.00 on the morning of the 15th an officer from 28th Brigade arrived with unpleasant news:

The East Surreys and 1/8th Punjabis have been completely overrun: so has the HQ of 6th Indian Brigade: there is no news of 2/16th Punjabis.

The Japanese had attacked at about 1.30, overwhelming the battalion headquarters of the East Surreys, and killing the commanding officer. 6th Brigade's headquarters had shared the same fate, but Lay, fortuitously absent when the Japanese attacked, had managed to escape. 1/8th Punjab had broken out westwards leaving the road undefended, and only the energetic action of Brigadier Carpendale had prevented the complete collapse of the position.

Murray-Lyon went forward as soon as he received the news, and decided that the Gurun position was no longer tenable. He initially planned to fall back to a position seven miles to the South, but, upon realising that 28th Brigade was now the only reliable formation at his disposal, he decided to withdraw behind the Muda River on the night of the 15–16th. The Japanese, mauled by the accurate defensive fire put down by Murray-Lyon's artillery, did not follow up closely, and by the morning of the 16th the remnants of 11th Division were behind the river-line.

The withdrawal of 11th Division threatened to expose 12th Brigade's rear, and Brigadier Paris accordingly decided to fall back from Baling along the Kroh road to conform to the general rearward movement. This brought the Brigade into 11th Division's position behind the Muda, and on 16 December Heath placed Paris under Murray-Lyon's command. At the same time he recognised that the Muda position could easily be outflanked by Japanese moving down the Kroh road or the Grik track, and accordingly ordered Murray-Lyon to retire some twenty-five miles to a new position behind the Krian River.

He also ordered 6th and 15th Brigades to be sent back for reorganisation and re-equipment, and at the same time disbanded *Krohcol,* placing its units under Murray-Lyon's command.

This new structure did not survive for long. On the 17th Heath, realising that the troops he had sent to Grik would be unable to hold the Grik track if the Japanese advanced down it in force, took 12th Brigade from Murray-Lyon and sent it back to Kuala Kangsar, to secure the vital junction between the trunk road and the track. This phase of disengagement went reasonably well. 11th Division pulled back behind the Krian, and the Japanese seemed in no hurry to follow up. 12th Brigade withdrew to cover the Grik track, though not before the Argylls have given a good account of themselves in a baptism of fire at Titi Karangan on the 17th, in which they killed some 200 Japanese for the loss of only ten men.

This brief lull in mid-December gave Percival a chance to reapprise his strategy. He slightly over-estimated Japanese strength, believing that the Japanese had landed a division at Singora, one at Patani and one in Kelantan, and had a fourth moving through Siam to join the fighting. The Japanese also had numerous tanks – a regiment of about 150, thought Percival, with another to follow soon – giving rise to obvious tactical problems. He acknowledged that the Japanese air force, with a considerable technical edge and a numerical superiority of about 4:1, had won undisputed command of the air over the North, and that the Japanese navy was in a similarly strong position in the waters East of Malaya. It seemed certain that the Japanese intended to attack Singapore from the North, and their strength at sea and in the air permitted them to mount amphibious operations against British communications or even to attack Singapore itself.

British forces were, on the other hand, already badly over-stretched. 11th Division was, in Percival's own words, 'very exhausted by almost continuous fighting and movement.' Nevertheless, much as he sympathised with those who argued that a concentration in Johore was the only viable policy, he believed that such a course of action failed to take account of long-term strategy, which remained the defence of the Singapore naval base. Retirement on Johore would give the Japanese still more airfields from which to attack Singapore and convoys of reinforcements and, as Percival acknowledged, 'our only hope of turning the tables on the enemy was to get these reinforements in safely.'

Percival conluded that 11th Division would have to delay the Japanese in northern Malaya for as long as it could, and on 17 December, when Heath telephoned him to warn of sinister developments on the Grik track, Percival gave permission for a withdrawal on the Perak River only when Heath considered it to be absolutely essential. Percival's decision, however unpopular it may have been with the shattered troops of 11th Division, was approved of in other quarters. On 18 December Duff Cooper chaired an inter-Allied conference, with Dutch and Commonwealth representatives, at Singapore. The conference concluded that the Japanese should be kept as far North in Malaya as was possible, and should be prevented from acquiring territory, and particularly aerodromes, from which they could threaten the arrival of reinforcements.

At the same time as the conference gave added weight to his decisions, Percival met Heath at Ipoh and made plans for the next phase of operations. He confirmed that Heath could withdraw behind the Perak River when he deemed it necessary, and ordered him to prepare a series of blocking positions South of it. The battered 11th Division was to be reorganised. 12th Brigade once again came under its command, and 6th and 15th Brigades were combined to form a single brigade, 6/15th. A number of under-strength Punjabi battalions were amalgamated: the East Surreys and the Leicesters were combined to form the British Battalion. All three of the division's original brigadiers were replaced, a command reshuffle which was to culminate on 24 December with the replacement of Murray-Lyon by Brigadier Paris of 12th Brigade. Percival acknowledged that Murray-Lyon was 'a brave and tireless leader', but felt that Paris, 'who had been in Malaya for two and a half years and commanded what was probably at that time the best trained brigade in the country,' was the man of the moment.

Although Percival was prepared to reorganise 11th Division, and to do what he could to safeguard its left flank by asking the navy's Perak flotilla to prevent Japanese amphibious hooks, he was unwilling to send reinforcements to the north-west. He assigned to Major-General Barstow's 9th Division the dual tasks of continuing to deny the Kuantan aerodrome to the Japanese and of securing 11th Division and its communications against attack form the east coast. This decision was highly questionable. Percival was already well aware that the main Japanese thrust was developing along the West coast. The poor communications on the eastern side of the central mountain ridge made it improbable that the Japanese would operate in strength on that side of the country. Important though the airfield at Kuantan was, its significance was not so great as to justify the stationing of 9th Division East of the ridge. It would have been wiser to have destroyed the airfield and its facilities, and swung the main weight of 9th Division on to the western axis, where the decisive battle of the campaign was likely to take place.

6

THE LOSS OF MALAYA
23 December 1941–31 January 1942

THE complexion of the campaign changed in late December. As Heath had foreseen, the Japanese continued to advance down the Grik track, using the regiment which had landed at Patani, without its tanks. Although 12th Brigade gave a good account of itself, the Japanese worked their way round successive blocking positions and soon posed a threat to the communications of 11th Division. On 21 December, therefore, Heath authorised Murray-Lyon to fall back across the Perak River, a manoeuvre which the latter successfully carried out on the night of 22–23 December.

Once the Division was safely across the river, its tactical situation was dramatically altered. The existence of the Kroh road and the Grik track, which had enabled the Japanese to mount flanking operations in support of their main thrust. had made the defence of north-western Malaya particularly hazardous. South of Kuala Kangsar, however, the road and railway lay close to the central ridge, and broad outflanking operations against Murray-Lyon's right were no longer possible.

But there remained the seaward flank. In asking for the assistance of the Perak flotilla Percival had shown that he was well aware of the threat to 11th Division's left flank. Japanese planners were, though, one jump ahead. The forty or so craft used in the Singora landing had been taken overland to the Alor Star River, where they were launched again. They were then collected at the mouth of the Perak River, together with the motor-boats captured at Penang. Colonel Watanabe's 1st Manoeuvres Unit – one and a half battalions of the 11th Infantry Regiment, a section of mountain guns and a section of engineers – was formed specially to carry out amphibious hooks along the coast using this flotilla of small craft.

The uninspiring performance of British and Indian troops in the early stages of the campaign, together with the evidence that British commanders appeared to have, as Tsuji put it, 'no consistent policy,' persuaded Yamashita to adhere to his initial strategy and press on as rapidly as possible to achieve 'the prompt reduction of Singapore.' In order to throw more weight behind his push along the trunk road, he ordered the Imperial Guards Division to be brought down by rail from Bangkok, and intended to leapfrog the 5th and Imperial Guards Divisions down his main axis of advance.

Freddie Spencer Chapman, until recently an instructor at a Special Training School for irregular warfare, was with a small party behind the Japanese lines, and gave a vivid description of the Japanese reinforcement of the Perak River bridgehead.

The majority were on bicycles in parties of forty or fifty, riding three or four abreast and talking and laughing just as if they were going to a football match. Indeed, some of them were actually wearing football jerseys. They seemed to have no standard uniform or equipment and were travelling as light as they possibly could. . . .
The general impression was one of extraordinary determination. They had been ordered to go to the bridgehead, and in their thousands they were going, though their equipment was second-rate and motley and much of it had obviously been commandeered in Malaya.

Spencer Chapman noted wryly that this was in very marked contrast to British soldiers, who were, as he put it, 'equipped like Christmas trees . . . so that they could hardly walk, much less fight.'

Not only was the campaign on land fulfilling Yamashita's most sanguine expectations, but the war in the air was also going consistently in his favour. Large numbers of local Malays and Chinese were impressed to act as labourers at the captured airfields at Alor Star, Butterworth and Sungei Patani, quickly repairing the damaged runways. The fighter and bomber squadrons based at Singora and Patani were moved forward to these airfields by 20 December, enabling new pressure to be put upon the surviving RAF squadrons. On 21–22 December the Japanese attacked the airfield at Kuala Lumpur, destroying twelve of the eighteen Australian-manned Buffaloes based there. Pulford withdrew the surviving aircraft to Singapore, and thereafter concentrated on the defence of Singapore Island and the protection of convoys bringing reinforcements. Logical though this policy undoubtedly was, it enabled the Japanese to concentrate on providing air support for their advancing ground formations, adding further to the difficulties facing 11th Division.

Reinforcements had indeed been requested. Brooke-Popham warned the Chiefs of Staff on 8 December that he could only hope to win the war in the North with substantial air reinforcements, and urged that these should be sent as soon as possible. Admiral Layton, for his part, asked the Admiralty for such destroyers, submarines and aircraft that could be spared. On 16 December, with 11th Division, already battered at Jitra, reeling back from another defeat at Gurun, Brooke-Popham asked for substantial land reinforcements: a brigade group complete, and 400 men for each of 11th Division's battalion's. The conference of 18th December echoed these demands.

The news from Singapore struck Whitehall like an icy shower. The acute conflict of priorities which had prevented the reinforcement of the Far East before the outbreak of war still remained, and decision-making was hampered by the fact that there was no general agreement as to how serious the threat to Singapore actually was. That there was clearly sharp conflict amongst the defenders of Singapore did not help. Duff Cooper clashed sharply with Brooke-Popham and Thomas at the first meeting of the War Council on 10 December. He told the Prime Minister of his doubts about his colleagues:

Sir Robert Brooke-Popham is a much older man than his years warrant and sometimes seems on the verge of nervous collapse. I fear also that knowledge of his own failing powers renders him jealous of any encroachment on his sphere of influence. . . . The Governor, Sir Shenton Thomas, is one of those people who finds it impossible to adjust their minds to war conditions. He is also much influenced by the last person he speaks to. . . . General Percival is a nice, good man who began life as a schoolmaster. I am sometimes tempted to wish he had remained one.

Brooke-Popham was, in any case, in the unenviable position of fighting a campaign in the full knowledge that he had lost the government's confidence, trying to do what he could without unduly committing his successor, Sir Henry Pownall, who at last reached Singapore at midday on 23 December.

London's initial response to demands from the East was hesitant. On 11 December the Chiefs of Staff agreed to send some land and air reinforcements, though nothing could be done to help Layton. Burma was removed from Brooke-Popham's sphere of responsibility, and placed instead under that of General Sir Archibald Wavell, Commander-in-Chief India. Wavell was told that he could retain 17th Indian Division, previously earmarked for service in the Middle East, and that 18th Division, together with a number of anti-tank and anti-aircraft regiments and four fighter squadrons, was being sent to him. Wavell was ordered to use these and his existing forces to form an 'Eastern fighting front.'

Attempts were made to meet Brooke-Popham's demands for extra aircraft. Twenty-six Hudsons and Blenheims were to be flown in from

Australia and Egypt, while another fifty-two Hudsons took the air reinforcement route from England. The capture, on 15 December, of the airfield at Victoria Point, a vital link in the chain of air reinforcement airfields, meant that aircraft could subsequently only be flown in by way of Sabang in Sumatra, or sent by sea. On 17 December the chiefs of Staff ordered that fifty-one crated Hurricanes, currently in a convoy at the Cape, should be diverted to Singapore.

But all this activity produced only a meagre result. Over half the Blenheims sent from Egypt crashed or became unserviceable on the way, though the eight Hudsons from Durban did arrive safely. As late as 6 January only twenty-three Hudsons had actually left Britain for Singapore, and few of these actually arrived. The crated Hurricanes were initially more fortunate. They arrived in a convoy on 13 January, and were quickly assembled and tested. When unescorted Japanese bombers attacked Singapore a week later, the Hurricanes accounted for no less than eight of them.

But this success did not last for long. Many of the Hurricane pilots were only partly trained, and their aircraft, intended for use in the Middle East, were equipped with air filters which reduced their speed. When the Japanese bombers reappeared the following day, escorted by Zeros flown by battle-hardened pilots, five Hurricanes were shot down without loss to the Japanese. But even if the Hurricanes had proved more effective, it was already too late, for the battle on the ground, fought under the Japanese air umbrella, had been lost.

A final attempt at air reinforcement proved equally abortive. At the end of December the aircraft carrier *Indomitable* was ordered to sail from Durban to Port Sudan and take on board forty-eight Hurricanes. She was then to proceed to Java or Sumatra, whence the aircraft could be flown to Singapore. The first phase of the operation went as planned, but by the time that the aircraft left *Indomitable* for Java on 26 January the campaign in Malaya was already over.

Steps were also taken to meet Brooke-Popham's demands for troops. The early disasters led the Chiefs of Staff to order two brigades of 17th Indian Division from India to Singapore, and to send all available reinforcements for 9th and 11th Indian Divisions. In addition, 18th Division was to be diverted to Singapore, and the Australians were to provide extra troops for 8th Australian Division. Impressive though this scheme looked on paper, it was riddled with flaws. The reinforcements sent to the two Indian divisions already in Malaya were, if anything, worse trained than the young soldiers who made up the bulk of the divisions on the outbreak of war: they were, moreover, injected into a battle which would have sorely tried the morale of even the most seasoned troops. 18th Division was an altogether different matter.

Composed mainly of East Anglian Territorial Units, it was an enthusiastic, well-equipped formation. But it had been trained for desert warfare, and its soldiers would, in any case, require some time to recover from a long voyage and to acclimatise themselves.

Sir Henry Pownall at least had the comforting knowledge that reinforcements were on their way to the Far East when he assumed command on 23 December, although he would, no doubt, have been anything but comforted if he had known how long it would take many of them to reach Singapore, or the sort of condition that they would be in on arrival. Pownall was not destined to retain his responsibilities for long, but he certainly did his best to restore the situation during his brief period of command. He departed up-country to see things for himself, and on his return wired the CIGS that middle-rank officers had generally performed well, although junior leaders were raw. He told General Brooke that he was much struck by the distances involved in Malaya, and advised him, when considering problems on a small scale map, to have a map of England to the same scale alongside. Pownall also made another percipient observation, this time in his diary: 'none of this country need stop good lightly equipped infantry.' He might almost have been describing that commodity which Yamashita possessed in such abundance.

Brigadier Ivan Simson, Malaya Command's Chief Engineer, was also up-country in late December, visiting senior commanders to discuss anti-tank obstacles and field defences. The business of the anti-tank pamphlets had already shown Simson to be something of a Cassandra, offering sound advice to which few were prepared to listen, and he was to retain this reputation for the remainder of the campaign. He called on Heath at his command post at Ipoh, and was given a message for Percival:

The message was to the effect that he, General Heath, believed that he could no longer hold the enemy for long at any point, and he therefore hoped that General Percival would have constructed successive lines of defences by the time he had retreated by stages to the Johore area. These defences were essential, General Heath maintained, for it was impossible for his troops to fight, then retreat, dig in and wire, and to go on repeating this process without ceasing.

Simson took the message down at Heath's dictation, and then read it back for Heath to verify its accuracy. Heath made some minor amendments to the message but, for some reason refused to sign it.

Simson arrived at Flagstaff House, Singapore, Percival's residence, at 11.30 p.m. on 26 December. Although Percival accepted the accuracy of Heath's message, he firmly rejected the idea of constructing defence works in Johore into which III Corps could retire. Simson, now convinced that the Japanese would soon be nearing the approaches to Singapore Island, strongly urged Percival to authorise the construction of defences on the North shore of the island. Percival remained obdurate, telling Simson that: 'Defences are bad for morale – for both troops and civilians.'

The discussion went on for some two and a half hours, and at the end of it Percival yielded to the extent of agreeing that Simson could put the case for defences on the North shore to Keith Simmons, commander of Singapore Fortress. Simson breakfasted with the Fortress Commander that morning, but his arguments made little impact on Keith Simmons, who argued, as Percival had, that defences were bad for military and civilian morale. Simson left the house convinced, in his own words, 'that Singapore was as good as lost.'

But not all Simson's urgings were wasted. Percival changed his mind a few days later, arranging that surplus officers from the Public Works Department, working under the State Engineers, would organise the building of defences and anti-tank obstacles to the rear of III Corps. On 29 December he informed Heath and Gordon Bennett that the State Engineers would report to them for instructions. The effort proved fruitless. III Corps' staff was preoccupied with fighting the battle, and had no time to spare for consideration of positions well behind the front: the PWD was hamstrung by lack of labour. What is saddest about this episode, however, is that Simson, who as Percival's Chief Engineer was responsible for the construction of defences, was never informed of what was afoot, and heard of it only with the publication, sixteen years later, of the *Official History*. There were nearly 6,500 military engineers available and, working under the direction of the trained specialists on Simson's staff, they could have built formidable obstacles in Johore and on Singapore Island itself.

THE LOSS OF CENTRAL MALAYA: KAMPAR AND THE SLIM RIVER

Heath planned to hold two main defensive positions South of Ipoh, one at Kampar, some twenty miles to the South, and the other just North of Tanjong Malim. Intermediate positions would be taken up at Tapah, Bidor and on the Slim River. The reorganised 6th/15th Brigade would occupy the Kampar position while 12th and 28th Brigades held the Japanese further North. 6th/15th Brigade duly moved to Kampar on 23 December, and began work on its defences. The Kampar position had great natural strength. The trunk road and the smaller Sahum road forked past the steep, jungle-covered Bujang Meleka, which dominated both routes. To the North and West the ground was open, giving good fields of fire to infantry weapons, and the slopes of the Bujang Melaka provided useful artillery observation posts. Better still, it was difficult to outflank the position: the only practical way was by an amphibious operation via Telok Anson.

While the men of 6th/15th Brigade were digging and wiring their position around Kampar village on the trunk road, 12th and 28th Brigades strove to buy time for the completion of the position. Yamashita, correctly appreciating that the British would endeavour to hold a series of blocking positions, was determined to press on as rapidly as possible, maintaining constant pressure so as to prevent the defenders from gaining a breathing-space. Japanese troops crosssed the Perak River unopposed and, spearheaded by 4th Guards Regiment, advanced down the trunk road. On 26–27 December 12th Brigade gave the Japanese advanced guard a bloody nose at Chemor, North of Ipoh, but Major-General Paris realised that a sustained defence of this area would result in the laceration of troops which he required for the Kampar battle. On 27–28 he fell back through Ipoh, 28th Brigade moving directly to the Kampar area, where it began to dig in on the Sahum road, with 12th Brigade acting as rearguard.

The Japanese never let up. They continued to smash their way down the road, their infantry and tanks maintaining constant pressure on the exhausted 12th Brigade. The Official History quotes an eyewitness:

The troops were very tired. Constant enemy air attacks prevented them from obtaining any sleep by day. By night they either had to move, obtaining as much sleep as was possible in crowded lorries, or had to work on preparing yet another defensive position. The resultant physical strain of day and night fighting, of nightly moves or work, and the consequent lack of sleep was cumulative and finallly reached the limit of endurance. Officers and men moved like automata and often could not grasp the simplest order.

But there was nothing listless about the Brigade's performance. On 28 December, for example, Captain Bal Hendry of the Argylls, accompanied by Sergeant-Major Bing and an orderly, rushed the Japanese-held railway station at Kota Bharu. Lieutenant-Colonel Stewart, until recently CO of the Argylls and now commander of 12 Brigade, described the scene.

When within twenty yards of the station they charged. CSM Bing kicked in a door of the ticket office and ran into five Japs. He let them have a whole magazine from his tommy-gun at point-blank range and killed the lot. Another Jap jumped up in front of him from an overturned wardrobe and fired at him from less than twenty feet. The bullet missed, and the CSM clubbed his tommy-gun and bashed in the Jap's head. In the excitement he didn't realise that his barrel was almost red-hot, and it wasn't until the last Jap was *hors de combat* that he painfully surveyed two blistered palms.

The three Argylls accounted for thirteen Japanese in all.

The last phase of 12th Brigade's withdrawal, to a bridgehead at Dinang, North of Kampar, which was held by a company of 2/9th Gurkhas of 28th Brigade, was fraught with peril. Japanese tanks, headlights on and firing tracer down the road, got in amongst the rearguard and, crippling the Kedah armoured car company in what turned out to be its first and last battle, almost repeated their performance at Asun. But 12th Brigade managed to stagger across the Dipang bridge, where Stewart met Lieutenant-Colonel Selby of 28th Brigade. 'I've come to hand over the business to you,' he said. 'It's a running concern.' The survivors of the Brigade then withdrew to Bidor, to cover the southern approaches of the Kampar position against a wide outflanking movement from the coast.

The Battle of Kampar, was, by contrast, something of an anti-climax. The Japanese launched a frontal attack on 1 January 1942 and made little progress. The attacks were renewed the following day, with the heaviest weight falling on the British Battalion's positions East of the main road. Determined counter-attacks by the Jat/Punjabi Battalion helped shore up the British Battalion. Captain Graham's C Company, Sikhs and Gujars of the old 1/8th Punjab, put in a particularly determined counter-attack. One of the company sepoy's told the story:

I was Graham Sahib's runner during the attack. The position on which the counter-attack was to be launched was a very strong one. It consisted of three lines, the last one on the crest of a ridge. Before the attack the Sahib addressed the Company. he told us the situation, which he said was a very critical one. The British Battalion was in a most dangerous position. At all costs the attack had to succeed. The crest of the hill had to be taken. No one, he said, would witness the attack, but the honour of the regiment depended on it. He had every man served with two drams of rum. Then the attack started.

Graham's men took the first two lines and, by now reduced to only thirty, broke into the third. A mortar bomb blew off both Graham's legs below the knee, but although mortally wounded, he continued to shout encouragement and throw grenades. When the position was secured he was carried back. He recovered consciousness while passing the headquarters of the British Battalion, asked if the attack had been successful, and died.

Despite the stalwart resistance put up by the British Battalion and the Jat/Punjab Battalion, Lieutenant-Colonel Moorhead warned Paris that they could not hold out much longer. By this time, however, Paris' attention had already become attracted to another, more serious, threat to his division. On 1 December the Independent Company patrolling the mouth of the Perak River had reported the presence of tugs and landing craft, and that evening Colonel Watanabe's 1st Manoeuvres Unit, having landed unopposed at Utan Melintang, drove back the screen furnished by the 3rd Cavalry and advanced on Telok Anson. Paris ordered 12th Brigade to hold the approaches to Bidor and Tapah, but Watanabe's men made further progress on the 2nd, convincing Paris that he should evacuate the Kampar position to avoid encirclement.

11th Division successfully withdrew from the Kampar on the night of 2–3 January, and fell back through intermediate positions to the Slim River. The loss of Kampar was particularly damaging. It was by far the strongest position on the western side of Malaya, and the Japanese had paid dearly for the damage they had inflicted on 15th Brigade in their frontal assault. The flanking attacks up the Perak and Bernam Rivers were, as the Japanese were all too well aware, a decidedly risky operation, and one which even limited opposition from the navy or RAF would have rendered impossible. Percival commented sadly that 'neither the navy nor the air force was able to take advantage of this unique opportunuty.' Churchill was less forgiving, noting angrily that the episode was 'a blot on the past history of the British navy.' Tsuji regarded the manoeuvre with satisfaction.

In this operation the detachment of our men in the small boats had thrown common sense to the winds, but they caused consternation to the commander in charge of the units of the British army on the spot. In the face of the threat to his rear he retreated immediately and swiftly, leaving our men with their objective attained.

Percival had sanctioned the withdrawal from Kampar, but he ordered Heath to hold the Japanese North of Kuala Kubu until 15 January. This would, he hoped, permit him to retain control of Kuantan, on the eastern coast, till 10 January, thereafter concentrating 9th Division around Kuala Lipis and Jerantut, more or less parallel with the line held by 11th Division. If Paris was forced to fall back more quickly, it would, of course, imperil the left flank of 9th Division and compel the premature evacuation of Pahang.

Circumstances conspired to ruin Percival's plan. The regiment of the Japanese 18th Division which had landed at Kota Bharu in the north-east made slow progress down the coastal track towards its objective, Kuantan. On 30 December it came into contact with Brigadier Painter's 22nd Brigade, which was holding the airfield – long since evacuated by the RAF – and guarding against a seaborne assault. Painter's task was made more than usually difficult owing to the fact that both Heath and Percival had very different ideas as to his role. While Percival was anxious to deny the airfield for as long as possible, Heath was reluctant to risk the Brigade by ordering it to fight a full-scale battle for Kuantan. Heath suggested that Painter's troops should be concentrated West of the Kuantan River to minimise the chance of losing troops and equipment which might be cut off East of the river. Painter initially demurred, and by the time he was given the relevant formal order it was too late: half 2/18th Royal Garhwal Rifles were lost when the Japanese attacked on the night of 30–31 December.

After more high-level indecision, Painter was ordered to hold the airfield till 5 January, and deployed his troops accordingly. But late on the 2nd it became clear that the Japanese were preparing to launch a full-scale attack in which the Brigade would be likely to suffer heavily: moreover, 11th Division's impending withdrawal from Kampar made it even more likely that 9th Division would be required for action in the West. Painter was therefore ordered to withdraw to Jerantut immediately. The retirement was predictably messy: the Japanese cut off the rearguard, 2/12th Frontier Force Regiment, whose Commanding Officer, Lieutenant-Colonel A. E. Cumming, was awarded the Victoria Cross for his gallantry in leading his battalion through the road-blocks which separated it from the main body of the Brigade. 22nd Brigade reached Jerantut four days later, having lost one-third of its original strength.

Percival, anxious to retain the airfields of central Malaya until reinforcements had landed at Singapore, was as keen to hold the airfields at Kuala Lumpur and Port Swettenham as he had been to secure that at Kuantan. Heath seriously doubted his ability to carry out Percival's orders, fearing that Japanese landings behind 11th Division's left flank would force it to withdraw South of Kuala Lumpur by the middle of January. He attempted to counteract the amphibious threat by forming a scratch force of the 3rd Cavalry, three battalions and a field battery, under Brigadier Moir, commander of his lines of communication, and sending it to protect the Kuala Selangor area. Moir's force arrived just in time to thwart landings on 2–3 January, but Japanese troops, moving overland from Telok Anson, arrived there the following day. This increased threat induced Heath to send the whole of 6th/15th Brigade to the sector, ordering Moorhead to take over responsibility for the Pawang–Kuala Selangor area. Major-General Paris was thus left with only two brigades, one of them the exhausted 12th, to hold his main position on the Slim River.

On 5 January, while Moorhead's Brigade moved off to cover 11th Division's left rear, Percival met Heath and Gordon Bennett at Segamat in North Johore. Percival acknowledged that they were unlikely to retain Selangor, Negri Sembilan or Malacca for long, but hoped:

that we would be able to come back in our own time and that we would at least be able to impose a substantial delay upon the enemy. I did not contemplate giving up Kuala Lumpur until the middle of the month at the earliest, by which time our forces would, I hoped, be getting a bit stronger.

He intended 11th Division to fall back slowly to a position on the general line Segamat–Muar, while Bennett's force remained responsible for the defence of the East coast on the line Segamat–Mersing. He knew that Bennett would have liked to have taken over the West coast, but overruled this on the grounds that the administrative arrangements for such a change would prove too time-consuming. Finally, Percival recognised that III Corps stood in urgent need of reinforcement, and agreed to put 45th Indian Infantry Brigade at Heath's disposal as soon as it arrived in Malaya.

Events soon rendered these decisions nugatory. Paris took up what seemed, on paper at least, a sound position at the Slim River. 12th Brigade held a defended area at Trolak, well forward of the river, while 28th Brigade held the area of Slim River Station. This seemingly attractive concept of holding the main axis of Japanese advance with two brigades deployed in depth had, alas, serious flaws. 12th Brigade was bone-weary, yet, strengthened only with a troop of anti-tank guns and a few anti-tank mines, it was entrusted with the defence of the Trolak defile, the obvious target for any Japanese frontal attack. Moreover, the area was far less easy to defend than appeared at first sight, for the road had recently been straightened, and the old road, still perfectly usable, looped in and out of the jungle on the flanks of the new highway.

Things went wrong from the very start. The Japanese, who had as usual been pressing the rearguard closely, were in contact with 12th Brigade's outpost battalion, 4/19th Hyderabad, on the evening of the 5th. The 6th was ominously quiet, but Lieutenant-Colonel Stewart, hearing from a local Tamil that there were 'a hundred iron land-ships' on the trunk road, ordered the Hyderabads to withdraw by first light on the 7th. The Hyderabads had no chance to do so: a column of Japanese tanks and lorried infantry attacked straight down the road before dawn and, making good use of the loops of the old road, overran not only the Hyderabads but also the next battalion, 5/2nd Punjab. Stewart, reacting as best he could, for the telephone lines were all cut at about 5.00, ordered his reserve battalion to move up to Trolak and told the Argylls to block the road North of the village. The Japanese brushed these obstacles aside, and were in Trolak by 7.00.

The bad news reached Divisional headquarters at 6.30: 'There has

been some sort of break-through. Send Staff Officer immediately.'
Colonel Harrison, the GSO 1, drove off with his orderly, Ghulam
Mustapha, in 'the Pride of the G.S.,' a brand-new Ford V.8.

I felt good: it was a fine clear morning, and too early for the Jap air-boys. Just
before reaching the Slim bridge I passed the 350th Battery coming down the
road. This puzzled me a bit . . . I went on over the bridge. . . . Three miles on, I
rounded a sharp bend near the Cluny Estate, and thirty yards ahead of me I saw
what I took to be one of our armoured cars bearing down on me. The next thing
I knew was a deafening volley as machine-gun bullets shattered my windscreen.

Harrison took cover in the ditch, where he was joined by the
badly-wounded Ghulam Mustapha, who enquired, in an understanding-
ly pained tone, 'are those our armoured cars, Sahib?'

The Japanese armoured column, unbeknown to Harrison, had left
Trolak and continued its advance down the main road. It soon
encountered Stewart's reserve battalion, 5/14th Punjab, marching in
fours up the road on its way to reinforce Trolak. The two leading
companies were cut to pieces, though the two rear companies were
more fortunate and managed to find refuge in the rubber trees on either
side of the road. The tanks sped on, past a Gurkha battalion of ~~23rd~~ 28th
Brigade, in process of occupying its position near Kampong Slim.

Shortly after 8.00 the tanks caught up with 2/1st Gurkha Rifles,
marching eastwards to take up a position in the Cluny Estate. The
Gurkhas, attached from the rear while on the march, shared the fate of
5/14th Punjab. The battalion commander, Major Winkfield, described
how:

I was marching in the centre of the Battalion, which was in open file along both
sides of the road, leaving the roadway clear. We had marched about a mile when
I sensed a feeling of unease behind me. I couldn't understand it. True, the battle
sounded a bit close, but we were miles behind the front, and there was no air
about. The men behind were looking back and hurrying. They kept pressing
forward, so I sent [Captain] Wylie back to tell them to keep their distance. The
next thing I knew a gun and a machine-gun blazed in my ear; a bullet grazed my
leg, and I dived into the ditch as a tank bore down on me. It had passed through
half my battalion without my realising that anything was amiss.

Winkfield emerged from the ditch when the tanks had left, hoping to
order the battalion to resume its march, but, with the exception of the
dead and dying on and beside the road, 'It had vanished.'

Having scattered 2/1st Gurkhas, the tanks rolled on. Two batteries
of 137th Field Regiment were parked alongside the road in the Cluny
Estate, but the tanks were upon them before the guns could be brought
into action. Harrison arrived there not long after the tanks had left:

The ammunition trucks and limbers were burning hard, and shells were exploding and bullets crackling all round the place. I saw an ambulance bumping drunkenly over the broken ground until it hit a tree and overturned. There was a good deal of jitters about. A subaltern told me that they had been breakfasting in the rubber two hundred yards from the road when someone arrived and reported that the tanks had broken through. [Major] Drought had dashed off to order two guns into action on the road, but before anyone had connected, five tanks arrived, halted on the road, and strafed the hide.

The Slim River bridge was captured intact. The demolition party had not been warned to stand by, and in any case there were so many British troops on the far side of the bridge that it is unlikely that it would have been blown. The sappers had no anti-tank weapons, and the only vague prospect of stopping the tanks seemed to reside with Captain Newington's B Troop of 16th Light Anti-Aircraft Battery which hurriedly depressed the barrels of the two Bofors guns which would bear on the road and engaged the tanks at a range of 100 yards. The light shells simply bounced off the armour, and the tanks replied with devastating effect, causing heavy casualties amongst the gun detachments.

South of the bridge the tanks encountered the leading elements of 155th Field Regiment, moving up to deploy in support of 28th Brigade. The Regiment's guns were moving at quarter-mile intervals: the first gun-tractor was knocked out and the gun's detachment were killed as they tried to swing their weapon into action on the road. The second gun, Sergeant Keen's 4.5 howitzer of C Battery, was warned of the Japanese approach in time to come into action. Keen opened fire at a range of 120 yards, but his first two shots went wide as the tank clattered towards the gun, firing furiously. The gun's third shell, fired at a range of only 30 yards, stopped the tank, but it kept firing: Keen was killed, and Bombardier Skone took over, hitting the tank twice more and silencing it at last. 'The blitz,' commented the Divisional History, 'was ended.'

Those tanks had covered nineteen miles of road through our lines, heedless of danger and of their isolation. They had shattered the Division: they had captured the Slim bridge by their reckless and gallant determination.

It was no exaggeration to speak of 11th Division as being shattered. Lieutenant-Colonels Stewart and Selby held a perimeter around Kampong Slim until nightfall, collecting stranglers. They then ordered the destruction of the transport trapped North of the River, and fell back down the railway to Tanjong Malim. The railway bridge had been blown, and the retreat was made particularly difficult by the fact that the sappers only managed to bridge the gap with planks. By dawn on the 8th the survivors of the two brigades were assembled at Tanjong Malim. Only fourteen officers and four hundred men of 12th Brigade reached the rendezvous: 23rd Brigade was more fortunate, with about seven hundred and fifty of all ranks.

The scale of their victory astonished even the Japanese. Much of the credit went to two recently-commissioned second lieutenants, Sadanobu Watanabe, commanding the leading tank troop, and Moro-kuma of the leading infantry platoon. Watanabe had cut the wires leading to the demolition charges on the Slim bridge with his sword under a heavy fire, and the Japanese owed their success in great measure to this young officer's dash and bravery. Tsuji wrote happily that captures included thirteen heavy guns, fifteen anti-tank guns, and a large number of Bren-carriers and trucks. About twelve hundred prisoners were rounded up on the battlefield, and Tsuji estimated that more than two thousand stragglers surrendered over the next few days. Enough rations were captured to keep two Japanese brigades in the field for a month.

The Slim River battle wrecked British plans for a well-measured withdrawal. The Japanese advanced rapidly, and Tsuji gleefully recorded how:

On 11th January at 8pm our troops entered Kuala Lumpur, capital of the Malay Federation, without serious enemy resistance. The metropolis presented a dignified and imposing modern appearance. There were Chinese merchants' shops on practically all main streets, and from each of these hung the firm's name, written in *kanji* (Chinese ideographs). We felt as though we had entered the crossroads of the central provinces of China.

Kuala Lumpur had been the principle administrative base for the troops defending northern and central Malaya, and it was packed with stores which there had been no time to remove or destroy. No less than thirteen trains loaded with valuable equipment, including a large consignment of specially-printed maps of Johore and Singapore Island, fell into Japanese hands.

Some demolitions were successfully carried out. Group Captain Darley who in early December had been moved North to Ipoh, supervised the destruction of the airfield. Having blown up the fuel installations and hangars, he encountered a large steam roller.

We realised that this couldn't go all the way down to Singapore . . . And we had one or two cans of this detonite which we put in the thing in front, shoved it into the furnace box with all the ammunition we wanted to get rid of. And we had the car standing by. Lit the fuse and off we went . . . suddenly there was this enormous great bang . . . then out of the sky came whistle, whistle, whistle, and great hunks of metal came at me. . . .

The task was all but finished when three 'wild men' arrived, eager to booby-trap the facilities which remained undamaged.

I had a little loo of my own next to my office. And I said, 'Well, fix one there and when they pull the chain there'll be a bloody bang.' And he did that.

War correspondent Ian Morrison was in Kuala Lumpur shortly before its fall. "There was looting in progress," he wrote,

such as I have never seen before. Most of the big foreign department stores had already been whistled clean since the white personnel had gone. . . . The streets were knee-deep in boxes and cardboard cartons and paper. Looters could be seen carrying every imaginable prize away with them. Here was one man with a Singer sewing-machine over his shoulder, there a Chinese with a long roll of linoleum tied on to the back of his bicycle. . . . Radios, rolls of cloth, tins of preserved foods, furniture, telephones, carpets, golf-clubs, there was every conceivable object being fiercely fought for and taken away.

British troops were not averse to joining in. Gunner Topping visited a cinema in Ipoh just before the town was abandoned.

I noticed several men coming into the cinema armed with boxed of chocolates, tins of biscuits and minerals. Looting was taking place in the closed and shattered shops nearby.

Not wishing to be left out of the fun, Haines and I went outside to scout around. Several of the shops had already been broken into and stripped of everything worthwhile, but at last we found one with enough left to satisfy our requirements. Armed with an armful of loot we were just in time to slip back into the cinema before the MPs came on the scene and put an end to it.

WAVELL TAKES COMMAND

In late December 1941, as British commanders strove to shore up their creaking front in Central Malaya, with the disaster of Slim River yet to come, Churchill visited Roosevelt in Washington. In the course of the discussions the Americans floated the scheme of a unified American-British-Dutch-Australian (ABDA) command in the Far East, and it became clear that this was a price that Britain might have to pay in return for American agreement to a 'Germany first' strategy. On 27 December the Americans suggested that this new command should be entrusted to General Sir Archibald Wavell, Commander-in-Chief, India. Although the British Chiefs of Staff feared that this was largely an attempt to saddle a British commander with the opprobrium of being overrun by the Japanese, Churchill agreed to the proposal, and Wavell was offered the post on 30 December. He accepted immediately, though not without considerable misgivings.

Wavell received his directive as Supreme Commander of ABDA-CO 1 on 3 January. On the same day Pownall was told that his own command would be wound up, although he himself was to stay on in the Far East as Wavell's Chief of Staff. Three days later Churchill informed Duff Cooper that the new command arrangements rendered him redundant, and directed him to return to England at once. On 7 January, the day of the Slim River disaster, Wavell arrived in Singapore on his way to set up his headquarters in Java. Wavell was a capable and experienced commander, and initially approached his task with guarded optimism. He hoped that it would be possible to hold Johore until the arrival of British and Australian reinforcements, which could then be used to launch a counter-offensive. A trip up-country to visit Heath and Bennett soon persuaded him that III Corps was finished as a fighting formation. He gave verbal orders to both commanders and then returned to Singapore to brief Percival.

Percival spent a considerable time in Wavell's ante-room on the evening of the 8th, before entering to receive the Supreme Commander's orders. These were delivered without any discussion, and the plan they initiated differed sharply from Percival's own policy. III Corps was to withdraw by road and rail into Johore, leaving behind it only sufficient rearguards to cover various demolition schemes. 8th Australian Division, leaving one brigade group around Mersing, was to move to the West coast – as Gordon Bennett had advocated some days before – to hold the line Segamat–Muar. Barstow's 9th Division, strengthened by the newly-arrived 45th Indian Infantry Brigade, would assist Gordon Bennett, whose abilities Wavell rated highly, in this sector. Once III Corps, less 9th Division, had completed its withdrawal, it would take over responsibility for the defence of Southern Johore, taking the detached Australian Brigade at Mersing under its command.

The new plan differed from its predecessor in that Johore was now divided up laterally rather than vertically. Gordon Bennett, with one of his own brigades and the reinforced 9th Division, held the northern sector, while the southern sector was entrusted to the remnants of III Corps and the Mersing brigade. Percival felt that the plan had two weaknesses: formations would no longer be able to withdraw on their own lines of communication, as they had when the vertical division prevailed, and the AIF was split. Nevertheless, he admitted that he did not see how a better plan could have been evolved under the prevailing circumstances. Wavell acknowledged that he was taking a calculated risk by weakening the defences of the East coast to strengthen those of the West. It was, Wavell observed, largely 'a time problem between the rate of Japanese advance and the arrival of reinforcements.' As an indication that the ragged state of III Corps had dented even his robust optimism, Wavell gave orders for the construction of defences on the North side of Singapore Island in case of a retreat to the Island.

Wavell departed for Java on 11 January, taking Pownall with him. Percival had already set about implementing the new plan. He sent out written orders on the 9th, and on the following day he chaired a conference at Segamat at which the handover between III Corps and the Australians was arranged. Bennett's command was to be known as Westforce, and 9th Division came under its command on 13 January, the day after its arrival at Tampin. Once the withdrawal of III Corps through Westforce was complete, Heath asked Percival to appoint a new commander of 11th Division. While the defeats at Kampar and the Slim River could not be attributed to bad generalship on Paris's part, Heath believed that it was imperative for another officer to be appointed to restore the Division's morale. Brigadier Key, whose 8th Brigade had defended Kota Bharu at the opening of hostilities, assumed command of 11th Division on 14 January.

The fall of central Malaya also forced Air Vice-Marshall Pulford to re-examine his policy. With the loss of the airfields at Kuantan and Kuala Lumpur he was restricted to the four airfields on Singapore Island and one airfield and three landing-grounds in Johore. The overwhelming weight of Japanese air superiority meant that any of these bases might be attacked in great strength with little warning: there was a serious risk that the crated Hurricanes would be destroyed on the ground before they could be assembled and tested. In order to give Pulford more room to deploy his depleted squadrons, Percival granted him first call on all available labour for the construction and repair of airfields. But Percival could not have both the bun and the penny: the allocation of much of the work-force to Pulford meant that other important tasks could not be carried out. The RAF was in any case unable to provide effective defence for its own airfields: the Japanese habitually attacked in such strength that even if the Buffaloes took off in time to gain sufficient height to meet the attackers, they could rarely do more than tangle with the escorting fighters.

Even though the tide of war was flooding in Japanese favour, Yamashita and his staff faced numerous problems. Yamashita planned to take Singapore by 11 February, and was encouraged to believe in his ability to do this by reports of the sketchy nature of defences on the Island. But the resumption of the rapid southward advance would inevitably throw a heavy load on to Japanese communications. Tsuji's fellow staff officers criticised his estimates of artillery ammunition required for the operation, and Lieutenant-Colonel Hongo, staff officer responsible of transport, protested jokingly that 'you are breaking up the Railway Regiment and turning us into road coolies.' Tsuji recognised that Japanese sources could not furnish adequate rations and fuel: these, he wrote, would be 'completely dependent upon Churchill supplies.' He attributed the army's success in bringing up the required ammunition to the spirit of energy and co-operation which prevailed amongst the staff, and the fact that Yamashita himself, while paying close attention to detail, let his staff officers get on with their jobs.

By mid-January Yamashita had the 5th and Imperial Guards Divisions, five regiments in all, on the West coast, with two regiments of the 18th Division on the East coast. The remainder of this latter formation was initially scheduled to land at Endau, just North of Mersing, but Yamashita prevailed upon Field-Marshal Count Terauchi, commander of the Southern army, to send extra supplies to Endau while 18th Division's troops landed at Singora. Yamashita intended to use 18th Division for the assault on Singapore Island, and ordered one of its regiments to move from the recently-captured Kuantan to Kuala Lumpur by road, while the other, having taken Endau and Mersing, swung south-west to Kluang. The remainder of the Division would move southwards from Singora by railway. With 18th Division forming his reserve, Yamashita planned to send 5th Division along the main Kluang–Johore Bahru road, while the Imperial Guards operated along the West coast road, threatening Bennett's left flank amphibious landing.

Bennett had only four brigades on the West coast to oppose the advance of the 5th and Imperial Guards Divisions. Not only was he at a considerable numerical disadvantage, but one of his formations, the recently-arrived 45th Brigade, was woefully inexperienced. It had been formed in India in the summer of 1941 for service in the Middle East and about half its soldiers were raw recruits, still in their teens with only four or five months' training. The Brigade was in such poor condition in the autumn of 1941 that GHQ India had recognised that it required intensive training to enable it to cope with anything but a second-class enemy. The outbreak of war with Japan deprived 45th and its sister 44th Brigade of even this brief respite.

Given that the task facing Westforce was difficult, Bennett's initial dispositions made it no easier. The trunk road curled down from Tampin like a question mark, swinging away from the coast towards Segamat, forty-five miles from the sea, before running back to Yong Peng and Ayer Hitam, only seventeen miles from the coast. The Japanese had already demonstrated their ability to mount amphibious outflanking operations, and this knowledge might have induced Bennett to have made a reliable formation responsible for the defence of the Sungei Muar crossings and the defence of his left flank against assault from the sea. As it was, this task was entrusted to 45th Brigade, spread out along twenty-four miles of river line, with its reserve battalion at Bakri, watching the coast. The remainder of Bennett's formations were deployed in depth along the trunk road.

There can be no doubt that Bennett and his Australians enjoyed high morale, even at this desperate juncture. 'In the AIF,' wrote Sergeant Ken Harrison,

we had this sturdy confidence. We were young, we were fit, and even after the British and the Indians had copped it, we had absolutely no doubt that they wouldn't be able to deal with us. . . . At Gemas we went into action with a 2-pounder anti-tank gun we'd never fired. We were up against the crack Imperial Guards Division. Looking back I'm appalled at the innocence of it all. We were under-equipped. We had no experience. We were amateurs. A volunteer army of clerks, farmers and shopkeepers.

Driver Ian Wingfield recalled that:

Bennett was horrified at the constant retreat. He believed that the British weren't aggressive enough.

The battle started well. The advance of 5th Division was led by the Mukaide Detachment, a mixed force of a battalion of bicycle-mounted infantry, a tank regiment, artillery and engineers. On 14 January the leading elements of this force were successfully ambushed near Gemas by the Australians of the 2/30th Battalion, which, as Tsuji noted, 'fought with a bravery we had not previously seen.' The Australians held on in the face of fierce attacks throughout the 15th, and withdrew in good order that night.

But while the battle on the trunk road was going according to plan, Bennett's left flank was crumbling. On 15 January the Imperial Guards snapped up two companies of 45th Brigade North of the Sungei Muar, and on the 16th they crossed the River in strength, taking Muar itself in the evening despite the fierce resistance of a convoy of 7/6th Rajputana Rifles and an Australian field battery. The reserve battalion, 5/18th Royal Garwhal Rifles, moving up from Bakri in an attempt to clear the Muar road, was roughly handled, losing its commanding officer and a hundred men. By nightfall 45th Brigade's remaining battalion, 4/9th Jats, was cut off on the upper reaches of the Sungei Muar, and the few surviving Rajputs were moving round Japanese road-blocks to join the Garwhalis at Bakri. Bennett's flank was turned.

Bennett was reluctant to abandon the Gemas position, in which his Australians were giving such a good account of themselves and, moreover, he underestimated the strength of the Japanese force which had mauled 45th Brigade. He immediately sent 2/29th Battalion, reserve unit of 27th Australian Brigade, to Bakri, telling its commanding officer that he should be able to restore the situation there in order to return to Gemas within a few days. Percival took the threat more seriously. He ordered Heath to take responsibility for Westforce's communications, and sent two battalions of 53rd Brigade to Ayer Hitam, where they would come under the command of III Corps.

53rd Brigade was part of 18th Division, and was the first element of that formation to reach Singapore, arriving there on 13 January after an eleven-week journey. Divisional headquarters and its two other brigades, 54th and 55th, arrived in Singapore on 29 January, too late for the fighting on the mainland. The Division, containing a very high proportion of enthusiastic East Anglian Territorials, had orginally been destined for the Middle East, and its troops had received no jungle warfare training whatsoever. It is hard to assess which of its brigades was most unfortunate: 54th and 55th, which reached Singapore after the siege had begun, or 53rd, which was thrown into a savage battle in Johore within a few days of its arrival.

Bennett's position grew steadily worse. On the Gemas front, the Japanese soon began to feel their way round the flank of Bennett's leading formation, 27th Australian Brigade, and on 18 January were in action against 22nd Indian Brigade at Jementah in his left rear. On the coastal flank the situation was even worse. Although Percival had strengthened the threadbare 45th Brigade by sending it 1/19th Battalion from 22nd Australian Brigade at Mersing, replacing it with the remaining battalion of 53rd Brigade, a counter-attack on Muar failed and Japanese pressure increased. On the 18th Percival realised that he was faced by two Japanese divisions, 5th Division on the trunk road and the Imperial Guards along the coast. Under these circumstances the continued defence of the Gemas–Segamat area was likely to result in catastrophe as superior Japanese forces cut Bennett's communications. Percival accordingly ordered Bennett to withdraw to the general line Kluang–Ayer Hitam–Yong Peng.

In order to permit Westforce to break clear from the Gemas–Segamat area without worrying about its communications, Percival placed the coastal sector under Heath's command. Although the withdrawal of Westforce on Labis and Yong Peng was satisfactorily carried out, the unfortunate 45th Brigade was again savaged. Percival had intended that 45th Brigade would fall back through the defile at Bukit Pelandok, on the Bakri-Yong Peng road, which would be secured by 53rd Brigade. But the Japanese landed more troops at Batu Pahat, and rushed 53rd Brigade's leading battalion, 6th Norfolks, seizing Bukit Pelandok. The battle swayed to and fro around the key defile. 53rd Brigade counter-attacked before first light on the 20th, but was unable to hold its gains. Another attack was planned for the morning of the

22nd, but Japanese aircraft strafed the Brigade on its startline, causing heavy losses: Brigadier Duke cancelled the attack, a decision subsequently criticised by Bennett, who suggested that 53rd Brigade's failure led to the loss of 45th Brigade.

The plight of the encircled 45th Brigade grew increasingly desperate as it tried to fight its way past Japanese road-blocks, while strong enemy forces, supported by tanks, pressed hard upon the rearguard. Brigadier Duncan was killed leading a counter-attack in an effort to take some pressure off the rearguard, and command devolved upon Lieutenant-Colonel Anderson of 1/19th Australian Battalion, who eventually gave orders for the guns and transport to be destroyed, and for those who were still able to walk to make their way cross-country to Yong Peng.

Four of 4th Anti-Tank Regiment's guns had been sent down to help 45th Brigade. One was commanded by Sergeant Ken Harrison, who had already received his baptism of fire at Gemas. The guns did sterling service, one of them knocking out six Japanese tanks at point-blank range. But Harrison's detachment had to abandon their truck and their gun as the column disintegrated, and they struggled on through the Bakri swamps, accidentally shelled by their own artillery. Harrison told how:

The Japanese, too experienced to come after us, had seen our predicament and were dropping flare after flare over the swamp, and spraying the area repeatedly with machine-gun fire. We lay half submerged in the stinking water listening to the groans of our wounded, punctuated by the stutter of the guns, and the hiss of bullets. One young infantryman had been badly hurt when we had been shelled by our own artillery and was in agony. He kept crying out, begging a friend to shoot him. His sobs of 'Shoot me, Jim, kill me,' gave our position away to the Japanese. . . .

Eventually his friend did shoot him, but in the darkness he failed to hit a vital spot, and before the boy died he cried loudly in a shocked and bewildered voice, 'Oh, Jim, what did you do that for?'

Gunner Russell Braddon's 65th Battery, firing in support of 45th Brigade, had been heavily dive-bombed and mortared. The battery commander had been killed, and one of the guns put out of action by a direct hit. Hearing that the infantry to their front were under intense pressure, the remnants of the battery put down a heavy barrage under whose cover the infantry could withdraw. 'Eventually they did,' wrote Braddon,

whereupon we learnt that the situation . . . had so fluctuated . . . that most of our shells had fallen amongst Australians. They bore it with incredible equanimity. 'Ah', they shouted, as they beat in a steady line through the rubber towards us,

'The bloody drop-short boys!' And when we realised what had happened and tried to tell them what we felt, they just grinned and said: 'Don't matter, mate, gave us some encouragement to get back quicker. Would have been up there yet if youse hadn't hunted us out.' . . .Only the weary eyes told you what they really felt about this last unkind blow that had added to the already fearful toll of their numbers.

In all, some four hundred Indians and five hundred Australians, many of them wounded, managed to reach Yong Peng. The Official History describes the fate of the wounded who were left behind under the protection of the Red Cross when the remnants of the Brigade took to the jungle.

At Parit Sulong the triumphant Japanese troops, after treating the helpless wounded in the most inhuman manner, massacred all but the few who, by feigning death, managed to survive.

This savagery may have been provoked by the losses incurred by the Japanese. Tsuji recounted how:

The Gotanda Medium Tank Company came under heavy fire in a mined zone and lost its ten tanks one after the other – destroyed by a heavy concentration of shellfire and mines . . . the surviving officers and men of the company . . . attacked on foot, reaching the enemy artillery position and the Parit Sulong Bridge, where the last of them met a heroic death after holding up the enemy for some time.

A battalion of 5th Guards Regiment suffered severely in the fighting between Bakri and Bukit Pelandok, losing its commander, Major Ogaki, and over half its officers and NCOs in what Tsuji called 'the most violent battle of the campaign to date'.

Even before the destruction of 45th Brigade, Percival had come to the conclusion that he was unlikely to be able to retain Johore, and that a withdrawal on to Singapore Island was almost inevitable. On 20 January he told Heath, Bennett and Keith Simmons of these views in a secret and personal letter, outlining his intention of holding on to the line Jemalaung–Batu Pahat for as long as possible. He expounded his plans in more detail at a conference at Yong Peng on the afternoon of the 21st. They embodied a drastic revision of Wavell's policy of a defence conducted by formations operating in lateral areas of responsibility. Johore would once more be divided up vertically, On the right, 22nd Australian Brigade, now christened Eastforce, was to hold Jemalaung covering Kota Tinggi and its communications with Johore Bahru. Westforce was to be resposible for Kluang–Ayer Hitam area, while 11th Division, now with 53rd Brigade under its command, would hold Bata Pahat and the coast road. These three formations were to come under the centralised command of III Corps.

All three prongs of Percival's trident were soon in serious difficulties. On the left, Brigadier Challen's 15th Brigade was cut off in Batu Pahat. An attempt by 53rd Brigade to fight its way through to join Challen was frustrated, and 15th Brigade was soon forced to destroy its guns and transport and to split up in an effort to break out cross-country. One column of 1200 men reached the British lines, and another large party made its way to the coast, where it was rescued by a small flotilla of two gunboats and some small craft, and taken to Singapore. But Challen himself was captured, and the Brigade was so badly mauled as to be of no further use in the battle for Johore.

Indeed, the defeat of 15th Brigade convinced Heath that the battle for Johore was over. His left flank was now shored up only by the sorely-tried 53rd and 28th Brigades, and there was every chance that the Imperial Guards would sever Westforce's communications and render impossible its retreat onto Singapore Island. He therefore issued orders for the synchronised withdrawal of Eastforce and Westforce, while the remnants of 11th Division held the road-junction at Skudai through which Westforce would have to fall back. The retirement across the causeway linking Johore to Singapore Island was to be completed by the night of 31 January–1 February.

The final phase of the battle for Johore was marred by the confusion and calamity which had been recurrent features of the earlier stages of the fighting. Westforce, falling back down the railway and trunk road in close contact with the aggressive 5th Division, was soon in difficulties. Brigadier Painter's 22nd Brigade held a position near Layang while 8th Brigade passed through it and got clear. A railway bridge to Painter's rear was blown in error, severing the Brigade's communications. The Japanese soon worked their way round Painter's flanks, and when, on the morning of 28 January, he decided to fall back on his own initiative, it was too late. Having failed to break out down the railway line, the Brigade took to the jungle. Its four-day journey was nightmarish. There were no adequate maps, these having been lost in the fall of Kuala Lumpur, and the Brigade stumbled on through trackless jungle, its strength decreasing every mile. Eventually Painter and some 350 exhausted men surrendered to the Japanese on 1 February, only fifteen miles from Johore Bahru. Yet this was not the full measure of the disaster. On 28 January, Major-General Barstow, commander of 9th Indian Division, had walked up the railway line in a personal effort to re-establish communications with Painter. He was ambushed and killed.

Eastforce (22nd Australian Brigade) fought a more successful battle. On 25 January it was ordered to fall back to Jemalaung from its position on the Sungei Mersing. Its adversaries of the Japanese 55th

Regiment, part of 18th Division, followed up quickly, falling straight into an ambush which gave them a decidedly bloody nose. The Japanese appealed for reinforcements, but by the time Yamashita had sent a detachment of 5th Division from Kluang, the Australians were well on their way to Kota Tinggi. This time the Japanese did not pursue. 55th Regiment swung westwards to Kluang, and the Australians were able to make their way to Johore Bahru without further interruption.

On 26 January, while 22nd Brigade was on its way to Jemalaung, a Japanese convoy containing supplies and administrative troops appeared off Endau. Pulford organised three attacks on the transports and their escorting warships, but although the crews of his Vildebeestes and Hudsons pressed home their attacks with great gallantry in the face of fierce anti-aircraft fire and the determined opposition of Japanese fighters, little damage was done to the convoy. A naval attack proved equally fruitless: the old destroyers *Vampire* and *Thanet* were intercepted by the Japanese destroyer screen: *Thanet* was sunk, and *Vampire* was fortunate to escape undamaged.

Percival had considered attempting to hold a bridgehead in southern Johore, but had decided against it. There was no longer time to prepare proper defences, the bridgehead would be dependent on the Causeway for its communications, and its flanks would be open. On 28 January he held another conference, this time at III Corps headquarters in Johore Bahru. He agreed with Heath that the desperately over-stretched 11th Division was unlikely to be able to retain the Skudai junction for long: if it fell, Westforce wold be cut off. Percival therefore decided to bring forward the evacuation programme by twenty-four hours.

The withdrawal from Johore, a difficult manoeuvre at the best of times, went remarkably well. Gordon Bennett crossed the Causeway on the 30th, after a last glum look at Johore Bahru. 'Derelict cars and destroyed houses and bomb holes everywhere,' he wrote.

There was a deathly silence. There was not the usual crowd of busy Malays and chattering Chinese. The streets were deserted. It was a funeral march. I have never felt so sad and upset. Words fail me. This defeat should not have been. The whole thing is fantastic. There seems no justfication for it. I have always thought we would hold Johore. Its loss was never contemplated.

Shortly before the withdrawal from the mainland, Warrant Officer David Mason, of an Australian Mobile Workshop, was ordered to take twenty men to the Sultan of Johore's Palace to obtain weapons with which to re-equip his unit. Discipline had deteriorated so badly that the twenty had to be chosen by lot, after a great deal of 'vulgar scuffling.' Helped by two of the 'more or less restrained types,' Mason loaded his vehicle with literally armfulls of sub-machineguns, revolvers and binoculars, though he could find no ammunition. The remainder of his party eventually emerged into the courtyard with the fruits of their forage.

As twenty-seven Mitsubishi bombers droned overhead on their way to Singapore, our brave boys capered and danced, clothed in red evening dresses, each one sporting wigs of varying hue. Round their necks like Hawaiian wreaths were pearls and the missing ammunition belts, and our biggest member, suitably nicknamed 'Brown Bomber' hobbled uncomfortably in high heeled shoes.

The unit's second-in-command arrived the following day to conduct an inquiry into 'the affair of the Sultan's Palace,' but desisted after being threatened with an empty Webley .45 'by one of the miscreants suffering from a Johnny Walker hangover.'

Westforce kept the Japanese 5th Division at bay and fell back through 11th Division at Skudai, crossing the Causeway on the night of 30–31 January. 22nd Australian Brigade had already crossed safely, and 11th Division followed, passing through an inner bridgehead held by the Argylls.

Angus Rose, in temporary command of his battalion, described the scene.

I sent our pipers down to the causeway to play through the Australian battalions of the right and centre columns and the Gordon Highlanders, who formed the left rearguard, and at 0640 I received a message to say that we could withdraw at 7 o'clock. . . . It was a well-executed movement and, from my vantage point, I might have been watching a turn at the Aldershot Tattoo . . .
Down at the lock-gates the pipers had struck up and the troops swung across the causeway, still in open tactical formation, but to the accompaniment of 'Blue Bonnets over the Border.' I reported my last man to Colonel Stewart, who was standing on the mainland by the lock-gate demolition. He was determined to be the last man on the peninsula. Funnily enough he had been the first member of the BEF to land in France in 1914, so this completed a fairly unique double.

The Argylls were about half a mile clear of the Causeway when many of them were knocked off their feet by a huge explosion. British and Indian sappers, with the Navy's assistance, had prepared the Causeway for demolition. This was no easy task, and there were some technical difficulties in ensuring that sufficient of the structure was removed below water-level. At 8.15 a.m. on 31 January the demolition charges blew a seventy-yard gap in the Causeway. But in the Official History's sober words, this 'did not provide the expected obstacle since it was not more than four feet deep at low tide and therefore fordable.' This was a not inappropriate footnote to the loss of Malaya.

7

THE BITTER END
February 1942

SERIOUS preparations for a battle on Singapore Island did not begin until the third week in January. On the 19th Wavell, warned by his liaison officers that no orders seemed to have been issued for the defence of Singapore, ordered Percival to prepare suitable contingency plans. Wavell himself, however, had little confidence that Singapore could be held if the battle for Johore was lost, and cabled this opinion to the Prime Minister. He flew up to Singapore next day and, having visited Percival and Heath, concluded that there was little chance of stabilising the situation in Johore. A retreat on Singapore seemed to him to be not unlikely, although he ordered Percival to hold Johore for as long as possible in order to permit reinforcement convoys to reach Singapore. That evening, before flying back to Java, Wavell sent another telegram to Churchill, warning him Percival might soon have to fall back on to the Island, which was ill-prepared to resist an attack from the North.

The Prime Minister's reply was in the great tradition of Churchillian rhetoric:

I want to make it absolutely clear that I expect every inch of ground to be defended, every scrap of material or defences to be blown to pieces to prevent capture by the enemy, and no question of surrender to be entertained until after protracted fighting among the ruins of Singapore city.

These orders, were, as Woodburn Kirby pointed out, 'neither practical nor humane.' It was one thing for an army in the field, or a fortress from which all useless mouths had been expelled, to defend itself to the last extremity. But by mid-January 1942 the population of Singapore town, normally some 550,000, had been swollen to about a million by the influx of refugees from Malaya. John Burnham, an officer of the Sarawak Rangers, a Volunteer unit, described how:

Singapore was full of people who fled from Penang and the next week fled from Ipoh and the next week fled from Kuala Lumpur. You were constantly meeting friends who rushed in and said: 'Look, where can I stay, old boy, I've got my wife and two kids. . . .' All thoughts were to look after the safety of your friends and the contacts that you made with local people. . . .

Already the 'business as usual' mood had changed to one of uncertain anticipation, of shaken confidence interlarded with reassuring threads of normality. In early January Gerald Scott, a Shell employee who spent much of his spare time working for the Malayan Broadcasting Corporation, wrote that:

Singapore, somewhat belatedly, is in process of digging itself in-having presumably been taken in by the official bluff concerning the strength of the Malayan defences . . .

On the 17th he reported that:

with the front line 100 miles from Singapore it is confidently expected that the tide will turn somewhat in our favour . . . confidence in the ability to hold Singapore is now being felt on account of the arrival of much-wanted material assistance.

Many of the Island's inhabitants took the strength of the 'fortress' for granted. 'I think we were brainwashed, really,' remarked Dicky Durrant of the Post and Telegraph Department:

Till the *Repulse* and the *Prince of Wales* were sunk, and then we realised we were up against a formidable foe. But even then we were bullied up by a natural British optimism, which we know now was entirely misplaced. But that was our mental outlook at the time. It can't happen to us, we will survive: Singapore is a great fortress . . .

Even in mid-January the city's night-life sparkled on as if the war was a thousand miles away. Journalist George Hammonds visited the New World dance-hall, but could not get in because of crowds of waiting soldiers. The New World proudly advertised 'Non-stop dancing and cabaret and the usual tiffin dance on Sunday,' while the cinemas offered everything from romantic comedy to Greta Garbo and Ramon Navarro in *Mata Hari*.

The bombing struck a discordant note. The raid on the morning of 8 December had been followed by frequent attacks, usually carried out in daylight, in which large formations of Japanese aircraft bombed Singapore almost as they pleased. On 31 December Duff Cooper told the War Council that although the safety of Singapore depended upon the arrival of reinforcements, the collapse of civil defence might produce a crisis which would nullify the efforts of the armed forces. The civil population was, he suggested, far from confident that all possible steps were being taken to minimise the effects of air raids. He recommended that 'some drastic step' should be taken, and proposed that Brigadier Simson should be appointed Director-General of Civil Defence.

Simson was understandably reluctant to accept. He pointed out that Singapore was likely to be besieged, and, as the garrison's chief engineer, he would have a key role to play. Percival suggested a compromise: Simson would continue to hold the appointment of chief engineer, and would assume that of DGCD in addition. Simson protested that:

it was beyond the capacity of one person now, to carry out adequately the joint responsibilities for both organisations because of the shortage of time available and because military defences and civil defence had both been neglected for so long.

My plea was not accepted and General Percival instructed me to take over civil defence in addition to my duties as Chief Engineer.

Cooper bestowed wide powers on Simson in his capacity as DGCD. The Governor, however, sent for Simson the following day and restricted his authority by limiting it to Singapore Island, stressing that the Malayan Legal Department should be consulted if one of the DGCD's orders was challenged. The resourceful Simson was not unduly dismayed.

I carried Duff Cooper's plenary order in one pocket and Sir Shenton Thomas's more restrictive one in another. As seemed necessary, I exhibited whichever best suited my purpose at the moment.

Simson's was an uphill struggle. Accompanied by his deputy, Mr. F. D. Bisseker, he visited the Colonial Secretary on 1 January in an effort to obtain a suitable headquarters building and the appropriate staff. They were met, Simson wrote,

with a point blank refusal of help in any way. The refusal was couched in very rude terms.

Simson discovered that Bisseker was unpopular for having criticised the Singapore Government for its lack of preparation for war. Despite frequent suggestions that he should sack Bissecker, Simson refused to do so, and acknowledged the 'Trojan service' which Bisseker contributed to Civil Defence.

The lack of formal records makes it difficult to estimate accurately civilian deaths from bombing and, later, shelling. Simson thought that a figure of about 2,000 per day might be correct if it included wounded and missing as well as dead. From late December till mid-January an average of over 150 dead were buried daily, and scores more lay undiscovered beneath the rubble of their homes. There were few adequate underground air-raid shelters, for it had been erroneously assumed that Singapore's sandy soil rendered their construction impossible. Numerous slit trenches were dug, and large-diameter concrete pipes, 4–6 feet long, with their sides protected by earth and rubble, made useful improvised shelters.

Although Duff Cooper had feared that the Civil Defence agencies would prove unequal to the task, they coped remarkably well. Noel Barber described how:

the civil defence behaved magnificently, the Chinese volunteers in particular working under constant bombing with a fortitude many Europeans might have envied. Despite a shortage of hoses and helmets, the ARP and the AFS coped with hundreds of incidents and fires. Often there were no canteens, no food for hours on end as one raid was telescoped into another.

Simson paid particularly warm tribute to the work of Singapore's civil and military medical services which, he wrote, 'stood out like a beacon.'

Yet even the raids were not without their lighter side. One former resident wrote to Sir Shenton Thomas's daughter, telling her of the hard work done by the Governor and his wife, and of the bombs whose craters speckled the grounds of Government House. 'One day in the evening,' she wrote, 'we all met and measured our bomb craters to see who had the biggest.'

Although supplies of fresh food began to dwindle, the big stores continued to keep vast stocks of luxury goods. One shop offered gas stoves and electrical appliances at sale prices, while Robinson's, the well-known store and restaurant, displayed a stunning array of ladies' fashions. Some of the City's inhabitants were unimpressed. Many of the women evacuees from Malaya were reduced to living out of one suitcase, sometimes in spartan dormitory accommodation. They were often penniless, and had no idea of the fate of their menfolk. Used to servants, they were now forced to look after themselves and their children in the dripping misery of the monsoon. The elegant displays in Robinson's windows were not without more than a touch of irony. The plight of the evacuees was made harder by a sudden change in the long-established custom of doing business on credit. Noel Barber discribed the Chinese reaction to the defeats in Johore:

Every Chinese shopkeeper abruptly terminated the age-old chit system. Except in the clubs and some of the big stores, cash down was now the startling order of the day – and this could only mean one thing. As George Hammonds put it, 'It was the Chinese way of telling us we'd had it.'

Wavell was no more optimistic than the Chinese shopkeepers. His most recent visit to Singapore had left him in no doubt as to the ragged state of Percival's force. Moreover, he was well aware that the incoming reinforcements were unlikely to be much help. Neither 18th Division nor 44th Indian Infantry Brigade had been trained for the sort of fighting into which they would be thrown, and individual reinforcements from India and Australia would, in all probability, be no better. All the evidence suggested that Singapore would be unable to hold out, and that its defence would be measured in weeks, not months.

But Wavell's responsibilities extended far beyond the defence of Singapore. Continued resistance on the island would contain substantial Japanese forces, and prevent them from being used elsewhere: the longer Singapore held, the better Wavell's chances of bolstering up his crumbling front in other areas. If Singapore held out till March, something might be done to strengthen the Dutch East Indies or to reinforce Burma – invaded on 15 January –while Yamashita's men were still pinned down. Allowing the reinforcements to continue on their way to Singapore would make the successful continuation of the defence more likely, although Wavell must have doubted whether, even with the reinforcements, Percival would be able to hold on for long.

There was, then, a cogent military argument for diverting the reinforcements and ordering Percival to fight on as best he could with the forces at his disposal. In such a case, however, Singapore would probably fall quickly, releasing the Japanese 25th Army and its supporting air forces. There was also the burning political argument: failure to do everything possible to defend Singapore, its garrison and population, would have the worst possible effect on British prestige in the Far East, and might well be regarded, particularly by the Australians, as unforgivable.

Wavell was unfortunate in that he received no clear political directive. He had warned Churchill that the loss of Johore was imminent and the prolonged defence of Singapore unlikely, and the Prime Minister recognised that the question of whether to reinforce Singapore or to concentrate on Burma in an effort to keep open the Burma Road, the vital link with China, had to be faced urgently. Initially he seemed to favour diverting the reinforcements, warning the Chiefs of Staff on 21 January that:

We may, by muddling things and hesitating to take an ugly decision, lose both Singapore and the Burma Road. Obviously the decision depends on how long the defence of Singapore can be maintained. If it is only for a few weeks, it is certainly not worth losing all our reinforcements and aircraft.

When the news that Churchill was considering leaving Singapore to its fate reached Australia, the riposte from its Prime Minister was swift:

After all the assurances we have been given, the evacuation of Singapore would be regarded here and elsewhere as an inexcusable betrayal . . . the Australian people, having volunteered for service overseas in such large numbers, find it difficult to understand why they must wait so long for an improvement in the situation when irreparable damage may have been done to their power to resist, the prestige of Empire and the solidarity of the Allied cause.

There was also the question of American attitudes. The American garrison of the Philippines had withdrawn to the Bataan Peninsula and the island fortress of Corregidor, where it was holding on desperately with no better prospect of ultimate success than the garrison of Singapore. Churchill was uncomfortably aware that the reaction to 'a British "scuttle" while the Americans fought on so stubbornly at Corregidor was terrible to imagine.'

Churchill and his Chiefs of Staff failed to grasp the nettle. On 23 January the Prime Minister telegraphed Wavell, emphasising the importance of keeping open the Burma Road, but if this was a broad hint that Wavell should divert the reinforcements from Singapore, it did not produce the desired result. Wavell knew how the Australians felt, and realised that the continuing defence of Singapore would buy time. With no firm political instruction, he was unwilling to recall the reinforcements and leave Singapore to its fate: the convoys steamed on. It was not a decision Churchill was prepared to countermand, although he wrote later that: 'There is no doubt what a purely military decision should have been.'

PREPARATIONS FOR DEFENCE

'The battle of Malaya has come to an end,' announced Percival on 1 February,

and the battle of Singapore has started. For nearly two months our troops have fought an enemy on the mainland who has held the advantage of great air superiority and considerable freedom of movement by sea.

Our task has been both to impose losses on the enemy and to gain time to enable the forces of the Allies to be concentrated for this struggle in the Far East. To-day we stand beleagured in our island fortress. Our task is to hold this fortress until help can come – as assuredly it will come. This we are determined to do. . . . Our duty is clear. With firm resolve and fixed determination we shall win through.

There was little factual basis for the firm resolve of which Percival spoke with such warmth. It had long been presumed that any attack on the Island would come from the South, and that an attack from the North would be thwarted by the defence of Malaya. Not only were the fixed fortifications sited to engage a naval force attacking from the South, but the northern shore of the Island, upon which the Japanese assault would fall, was broken up by creeks and mangrove swamps which rendered conventional beach defence all but impossible. The usual tactical alternative to holding the beaches was to retain a strong counter-attack force for use against an enemy bridgehead: this option, however, was rendered unattractive by the Island's small size and limited communications.

Percival and his staff felt that the Janpanese would launch their attack on Singapore as soon as possible in order to free troops and aircraft for operations elsewhere. But while the main assualt was likely to come straight across the Johore Strait, Japanese command of the sea and the air meant that there was every possibility of simultaneous seaborne or airborne assault on some other part of the Island. Indeed, although Percival was to maintain in his book *The War in Malaya* that he expected the Japanese to attack in the North-West, he subsequently admitted to the Official Historian that this view was largely one of hindsight. The evidence suggests that he believed that the real threat lay to the North-East, though he concluded that 'we could not with safety neglect the defence of any part of Singapore.' The consequence of this assessment was that the defence of the Island was marred from the outset by an effort to hold too much territory with too few men.

There was no doubt where the vital ground on the Island really lay. The central area between the line Sungei Kranji–Bulim–Sungei Jurong on the West and the line Seletar–Paya–Lebar–Kallang on the East, held most of the important targets. Not only did the city and its docks, the ammunition dumps, oil storage tanks and reserve food stocks lie in this area, but it also contained the three main reservoirs, situated on the high ground between the Nee Soon–Mandai road and the city itself. Much of the Island's peacetime water supply came from Johore in pipes running along the Causeway, and these had been destroyed when the Causeway was gapped. Water rationing enabled the Island's increased population to survive on the water stored in its reservoirs, but their destruction or capture would force Percival either to capitulate or to fight on in the certain knowledge that casualties amongst the garrison and civilian population would be astronomic. British commanders had long been aware of the importance of this central area, and two defensive lines – known as switch lines – had been sited to cover it. In the West, the Jurong line ran between the Sungei Jurong and Sungei Kranji, while the Serangoon line, in the East, ran between the headwaters of the Sungei Serangoon and the Kallang–Changi Road.

Percival discussed the problem of defending Singapore Island with Wavell when the Supreme Commander paid his 20 January visit. Wavell suggested that the 18th Division, the most robust of Percival's formations, should be posted in the North-West, where he thought attack was most likely. The North-East, the next most dangerous area, would be held by 8th Australian Division, while the reconsituted Indian formations formed a general reserve. Percival had already ordered Keith Simmons to study the Northern coast and to plan its defence by three brigades. Because the coast-line was so heavily broken up by creeks and marshes, Percival recommended that the defence should be based on a fabric of defended posts covering likely approaches, backed by mobile reserves.

On 23rd January Percival promulgated his defence scheme. The Island was divided into three sectors. The Northern sector, its boundary running South from the Causeway to just East of Bukit Panjang village, and thence jinking eastwards to a point South-West of Changi, where it swung North to the coast, was the responsibility of III Corps. The Western sector, covering the coastline from the Causeway in the North to the mouth of the Sungei Jurong, was entrusted to 8th Australian Division, while the Southern sector, running all the way along the South coast from the Sungei Jurong to Changi, was to be held by the troops of Singapore garrison – two Malaya Brigades, and the Straits Settlements Volunteer Force Brigade. When 18th Division arrived, it was to move into a Reserve Area North of Singapore City: Percival intended that it would later change places with III Corps, allowing the tired Indian formations to be pulled back into reserve.

The losses incurred in the fighting in Johore forced Percival to make major alterations to his plan. The bruised Australian Division retained the Western Sector, but it was reinforced with the green 44th Indian Infantry Brigade. III Corps was subjected to a far-reaching reorganisation, after which 11th Division comprised two Indian brigades, 8th and 28th, and the 53rd British Brigade. 8th Division was broken up, and the Corps was given 18th Division to compensate for its loss. Two brigades, 12th and 6th/15th, formed the reserve, but the former was reduced to only one and half battalions, and the latter had left all its equipment in Johore. Percival estimated his total force to be:

somewhere in the region of 85,000 men. This is not to say that there were 85,000 fighting men, for this included the non-combatants, i.e. the Royal Army Medical Corps, the Pioneer and Labour Units, etc. It also included a large number of base and administrative personnel, who had little training in the use of weapons, and for whom no arms were available. It would probably be not far wrong to say that about 70,000 of the total number were armed and equipped . . . not a large number to defend a coastline of about eighty miles.

Part of Percival's problem stemmed from the fact that he was attempting to hold too wide an area. Major-General Woodburn Kirby has pointed out that:

By trying to defend the whole coast when it was obvious the Japanese would concentrate on one carefully selected point, Percival was weak everywhere, no formation had any reserve for immediate counter-attack, the command reserve was too small to be of any value. . . . Once they had effected a landing the Japanese were thus given the opportunity of driving deep into the vital central area of the island before a reserve could be collected to check them.

Moreover, Percival had shifted the emphasis of defence since his conversation with Wavell on 20 January. His greatest weight now lay East of the Causeway, suggesting that it was there that he expected the assault to come.

Not all his commanders agreed. Gordon Bennett, whose Australians, now reinforced by an Indian Brigade, were holding the North-West sector, repeatedly suggested to Percival that his was the most vulnerable area. It is clear from Percival's dispositions that he thought otherwise. The strained relations between Percival and Bennett did not make rational discussion of the matter any easier. Bennett also disagreed with Percival's tactical doctrine, which was based on preventing the Japanese from landing or, if they succeeded in landing, stopping and destroying them near the beaches. Bennett argued that:

there were not enough fighting troops to cover the front effectively all round the coast. As it was, many units were spread out along the whole coastline of the island, even on the southern beaches which were never attacked.

He nevertheless admitted that the alternative, concentrating behind the beaches and counter-attacking Japanese bridgeheads, was rendered difficult by the mangrove swamps behind the shoreline.

Bennett's men were unenthusiastic diggers in at least one sense. Charles 'Morrie' March of 2/10th Field Company, Royal Australian Engineers, remembered how:

Before the Japs landed on the Island we were stationed out at Ama Keng, on the coast there. We had a lorry and an armchair strapped to the top for observation. They were supposed to be landing on the other side of the Island, round Changi, but we could see thousands of the buggers. Our job was to prepare slit trenches but our blokes wouldn't dig. They said it was too bloody hot. Stuff the trench. Then a shell would come over and there'd be four of us in a one-foot deep slit trench.

Percival took two other steps whose value even Bennett did not question. He organised the self-defence of all combatant administrative units, to reduce the drain on his fighting manpower, and expanded a force of Chinese irregulars. The latter had already been operating on the mainland with some success, under the command of Lieutenant-Colonel John Dalley of the Federated Malay States Police Force. As early as 1940 Dalley had suggested that a network of guerrilla parties should be set up in Malaya, for activation in the event of a Japanese invasion. His report was pigeon-holed, and it was not until mid-December 1941 that Dalley was asked to implement his scheme. 'It's a bit late,' he complained,

six months ago, even three months, I could have net-worked the country. We shan't be properly organised. We haven't selected our men. We haven't got our food and munitions cached. They should all be in position. Still, I'll do what I can.

Dalforce was perhaps 4,000 strong by the time the siege of Singapore began. Some of Dalley's men had been left behind on the mainland to form the nucleus of what became a substantial and effective anti-Japanese force, assisted by British instructors. Many of his recruits were members of the Malayan Communist Party, illegal in the pre-war years, and he had been responsible for the arrest and imprisonment of some of them. Now they rallied to "Dalley Sin Sang" in surprising numbers, as Percival acknowledged:

This force was recruited from all classes of Chinese – college boys and rickshaw pullers, loyalists and communists, young and old.

Dalley had to be something of a diplomat to keep his heterogeneous band in order. 'To keep everybody happy,' he said,

we got some red cloth and made a red triangle on the shoulder for the Communist half. . . . One chap thought he ought to be a general. I made him a sergeant, so that was all right.

Dalforce was desperately short of both weapons and trained officers. Percival admitted that Dalley's recruits 'would have made excellent fighters had we been able to arm and equip them properly.' It was nearly two years since Dalley had first suggested the formation of a guerrilla force: a golden opportunity had been lost.

Bennett might have gained a sense of ironic satisfaction had he known what was in Yamashita's mind. Pre-war Japanese plans envisaged the attack being launched against the North-West coast of Singapore Island, and Yamashita's intelligence reports confirmed that this area seemed more lightly held than the North-East. He had also made his own assessment of the vital ground on the Island, recognising, as Tsuji put it, that 'The last line of resistance of the city would be the heights of Bukit Timah. Loss of the reservoir would be fatal.'

Yamashita briefed his senior commanders at Kluang on the

morning of 1 February.

Reading in a clear voice his face was flushed, and on the cheeks of the men listening tears could be seen. The spirits of the seventeen hundred men killed in action since the landing at Singora were believed by all to be present at this meeting.

Yamashita planned to assault the North-West shore of the Island with the 5th and 18th Divisions, using landing-craft and rafts which would be concentrated, in great secrecy, in the upper reaches of the Sungei Skudai, Sungei Malayu and Sungei Perpat. The Imperial Guards Division was to create a diversion East of the Causeway. The assault would be preceded by a heavy bombardment, in which the Japanese gunners would initially shell both East and West of the Causeway, switching their fire to concentrate on the attack sector at the last moment.

Once ashore, the main assalt force was to seize Tengah airfield as its initial objective and then press on to Bukit Panjang village. The Imperial Guards, meanwhile, were to capture Mandai village, and then to move Eastwards to Nee Soon, cutting off any British troops in the area of the naval base. Once the general line of the high ground of the Bukit Mandai was secured, an attack would be made on the Bukit Timah heights, leading to the capture of the reservoirs. If the British did not surrender at that stage, operations would be launched against Singapore City itself.

Japanese commanders and their staffs had few illusions about the task confronting them. Tsuji philosophised that 'the sword we had so hurriedly polished would fall upon the head of the fortress which had been prepared for a hundred years.' There was barely enough artillery ammunition for the attack and the subsequent fighting: supplies landed at Endau in late January made the operation feasible, but, with a reserve of only 250 rounds per field gun and 125 per heavy gun, Yamashita would be in difficulties if the battle dragged on. He was, however, convinced that a swift attack, with Bukit Timah and the reservoirs as its objective, offered him the best prospect of success. His initial orders specified that 7 February would be the day of the attack – X-Day, in Japanese terms – but he later postponed it till the 8th.

Army Headquarters were established in the Sultan of Johore's palace, overlooking the Straits. This was yet another calculated risk, for the five-story observation tower, in which the operations room was situated, was a likely target for British guns. Once more the gamble paid off: British artillery, on orders from Malaya Command, was not allowed to engage the palace. Tsuji believed that it was a first-rate location for

Army Headquarters: not only did it give Yamashita and his staff an excellent view over the Straits and the North shore of the Island, but is was so close to the front line that it discouraged most of the casual visitors who usually descended upon headquarters.

While the Japanese prepared for the attack, Percival's men steeled themselves to meet it. Their situation was anything but encouraging. In order to preserve secrecy, Percival had forbidden the construction of the defences planned by Keith Simmons and his staff until the positions were occupied, and once more tired troops were faced with the back-breaking task of digging and wiring. Most of the reinforcements which reached Indian and Australian units were of particularly poor quality. Many of the Australians had been in the army for only a few weeks – 'corner boys of Sydney swept up and put into khaki and sent immediately to Singapore.' Some Australian troops were to be involved in ugly incidents in the final stages of the battle for Singapore: before judging them too harshly, we should recall that their training and discipline were sketchy in the extreme. Most of them were simply not in the same league as the splendid AIF battalions which had been in Malaya when the Japanese attacked. Lance-Corporal Jack Simmons of 2/9th Australian Field Ambulance summed up the feelings of many of his countrymen.

We had great confidence in 'They'. 'They' would come to our aid. 'They' would send air cover. 'They' would stop the Japs. But we never discovered who 'They' were. Were they the Brits? The Yanks? The Good Lord?

There were portents of disaster everywhere. Colonel Harrison, GSO 1 of 11th Indian Division, was surprised to find that 18th Division had only just disembarked. 'I felt,' he wrote, 'that they had merely re-embarked on "a sinking ship".'

On 29 January he attended a conference chaired by Brigadier Paris, temporarily charged with siting defences, and asked some questions.

'Was there any plan regarding withdrawal to a smaller perimeter in the event of the enemy breaking through on some sector of the coast?' I was told that there was no such plan.

'Might I have a map?' I was given a one-inch map on which the area of the Naval Base was a pure white blank. No details had been committed to it for reasons of security.

'Could I have a plan of the Base?' There was none available at Fort Canning.

Could I have a map showing the run of defences in our area?' There were no defences in our area.

After the conference Paris drew him aside. 'I'm sorry, old boy,' he said. 'I quite understand what you expected to find, but it just doesn't exist.'

The destruction of the Naval Base struck a heavy blow at morale, both civilian and military. The task was entrusted to 11th Division's sappers, who carried out some demolitions, and prepared others as discreetly as possible. The news that the base had been evacuated by the Navy depressed many who heard it. 'Never throughout all the fighting,' wrote George Hammonds,

did I ever feel such a sense of utter dismay. It seemed impossible that this naval fortress which had cost £60 million and taken seventeen years to build could have been thrown away like this – without even a fight for it.

'The worst part,' said Signalman Fred Mutton,

was that we heard the Navy had gone and they had started blowing up the naval base. The floating dock had been sunk in Johore Strait. My mate said, 'What the hell? Time we were getting weaving. We're supposed to protect the naval base; now they've blown it up and ratted, so what are we waiting for?'

Gordon Bennett shared the general dismay at the fate of the Naval Base. 'We were here to defend the Naval Base rather than the city of Singapore,' he wrote.

This demolition of the docks even before we withdrew from the mainland reflects the lack of confidence in our cause. The morale of the men is undoubtedly affected when they find demolitions going on behind them. It is an admission of defeat.

Ian Morrison wandered round the almost deserted base, marvelling at the equipment which had been left behind amid scenes of a hasty evacuation.

Here were the great furnaces where huge blocks of iron and steel could be forged and rolled, enormous hydraulic presses, vast troughs into which the molten metal was poured. Here were lathes of many types. . . . Here was the huge boiler-shop, with the great boilers still there. . . . Towering up into the sky over the store-rooms and machine-shops was the great crane which could lift an entire gun-turret out of a battleship. . . . At the petty officers' mess there were three dartboards stacked just inside the entrance. In one of the rooms there was an unfinished meal on the table.

The withdrawal from the Base had indeed been confused. A programme of demolitions, known as Scheme Q, was to have been carried out by the dockyard staff. Rear-Admiral E. J. Spooner who, as Rear-Admiral Malaya was responsible for the Base, had been ordered by the Admiralty to ensure that key personnel were sent away from the Island in time. On 31 January he dispatched most of his dockyard staff to Ceylon. 'No doubt,' commented the Official History, the Admiral wished to seize the opportunity of evacuating valuable technicians while shipping was still available but the hurried evacuation of the Base left an unfortunate impression in the minds of many soldiers who did not know that the Admiral, although perhaps precipitately, was acting under instructions.

Neither Malaya Command nor III Corps was officially informed that responsiblity for carrying out Scheme Q had now developed upon the army, and this made the demolitions less effective than they might have been.

Percival was, in any case, in something of a quandary over demolitions. He had been ordered to hold Singapore to the last, but to ensure, if it fell, the destruction of everything of military use to the Japanese. On 2 February he pointed out to the Chiefs of Staff that these missions were mutually exclusive: the programme of destruction would have a catastrophic effect upon the will to fight, and the demolition of certain essential stocks would fatally prejudice the defensive battle. The Chiefs to Staff replied four days later, ordering Percival to give priority to the Naval Base, and also to destroy all the fortress guns, making a start on these demolitions immediately. It was fortunate that a good deal of destruction had already been done in the Naval Base, for from 3 February onwards Yamashita's gunners were able to interfere with work carried out in daylight along the North shore.

Japanese shellfire also increased the burden borne by the RAF. Pulford had already sent his surving bombers and flying boats to Sumatra, leaving only fighters on Singapore Island. Although the arrival of the Hurricanes, the first of which was flown on 15 January, made the battle minimally less one-sided, the new aircraft performed far less well than had been expected, and their pilots, unused to the climate, always fought against heavy odds. Despite their mounting losses, Pulford's men managed to intercept every incoming raid, but they did relatively little damage to the numerous bombers and their powerful fighter escorts.

On 4–5 February the airfields at Seletar, Sembawang and Tengah all came under artillery fire, and were abandoned. Brigadier T. H. Massy-Beresford, commander of the newly-arrived 55th Infantry Brigade, visited Seletar aerodrome shortly after its evacuation. 'It was,' he said,

the most magnificent one I had ever seen. There were swimming pools, tennis courts, an enormous officers' mess block. . . . It was like going into Herculaneum or Pompeii when they dug it up. I went into the Officers' Mess and there was a table laid . . . for thirty people, and all the plates and spoons and knives out there. I went into the offices at the back and there were half-empty cups of tea and note books open and files, and not a soul. Absolutely deserted. . . . It was a most devastating sight, and it had been evacuated, pretty hurriedly, a few days before on the grounds that it was not servicable, and there wasn't a hole in the landing strip. I had to send gunners and sappers to make holes so that the Japs couldn't land. . . .

The withdrawl from the three northernmost aerodomes restricted Pulford's surviving fighters to Kallang airfield, which soon became the target of concentrated bombing raids: by 6 February it was barely usable.

In addition to intercepting air-raids, Pulford's hard-pressed fighters also met approaching convoys, providing them with close escort on the last stage of their journey. Convoys arrived successfully on 22, 24 and 29 January, but the last convoy, carrying elements of 18th Division, came under heavy air attack as it approached the Island on 5 February. The old, coal-fired *Empress of Asia*, with a semi-mutinous crew, lagged behind the other three vessels in the convoy, and was singled out by Japanese pilots. She was soon ablaze from stem to stern and, although most of her troops were rescued, all the equipment she carried was lost. Once again bad luck wagged its bony finger at the British, for the *Empress* contained the small arms which were to have equipped Dalforce and the guns of 125th Anti-Tank Regiment.

THE BATTLE FOR THE ISLAND

On 8 February Japanese air and artillery activity increased in intensity, and from 1.30 pm onwards the North shore of the Island was heavily shelled. Neither Percival nor Bennett attached undue significance to this, believing it to be part of the familiar daily softening-up. Percival's intelligence branch was by now fairly sure that the Japanese were concentrating opposite the North-Western shore, and 8th Division's patrols confirmed this on the 8th. But the news came too late to enable Percival to alter his development or to do more than shell the areas in which the Japanese were forming up. Moreover, since he was hoping to fight a lenghty battle for the Island, Percival was reluctant to allow his gunners to fire an extensive barrage against what might prove to be a feint.

Angus Rose, his battalion now merged with marine survivors from *Prince of Wales* and *Repulse* to form a four-company force nicknamed the Plymouth Argylls, felt certain that the bombardment heralded an attack. 'It was obvious,' he wrote,

that the Japs were going to attack that night. Apart from the barrage, the conditions of moon and tide conformed to those under which the Japanese invariably undertook amphibious operations. . . . The Colonel looked grave. . . . I knew neither of us had confidence in the beach defences. I had seen quite a bit of the western perimeter in the last week. The troops were very thin on the ground. Posts were not mutually supporting; there was very little depth; there were inadequate reserves; the field works were flimsy as digging was impracticable on account of the high water level. The earth stockades that I had seen would not stand up to the barrage which I was now hearing.

Rose checked his equipment and put fresh water in his water bottle before going to bed. He was not surprised to be awoken at 4.00 am. 'I suppose,' he said, 'that the little bleeders have landed.'

Rose was only too right. At about 10.30 pm on the 8th the barrage had increased in intensity as Japanese landing-craft began to cross the Straits, the sound of their engines drowned by the crash and roar of shellfire. Yamashita and his staff watched from the palace. 'From the glass door of the palace tower,' wrote Tsuji,

as one looked down on the Johore Strait and on the blaze of fire on both sides, one gained but little idea of the progress of the battle. There was no difference in the sound of our own shells and the enemy's. The boom of artillery, the crash of explosives, the flashes of the guns and the red lotus flames of fires enveloped the whole of Singapore Island.

At ten minutes past midnight on the morning of 9th February first of all on the 5th Division front and shortly after on that of the 18th Division, blue flares were fired high in the sky, signifying that the landing had been accomplished as planned. At the Army Command Post, not one man, Army Commander or staff officers, could speak. The moonlight shone dimly on tears flowing down all our cheeks.

The assault fell squarely on Brigadier Tayalor's 22nd Australian Brigade between Tanjong Buloh, just West of the Causeway, and Tanjong Murai, north-west of Tengah airfield. Taylor had brought a number of searchlights with him from Mersing, and these had been sited to illuminate the Straits. He had, however, given orders that they should not be switched on without specific orders. The effectiveness of the bombardment made it difficult for such orders to be transmitted. In mid-evening Gordon Bennett, who believed that the 22nd Brigade's sector was the most vulnerable part of the Island and was by then certain that the growing weight of fire heralded an attack, ordered the lights to be switched on. It was then discovered that all telephone cables had been cut by shellfire, and by the time the order went out by runner it was too late, and the lights were never switched on. The breakdown in communications also limited the value of defensive artillery fire. When the gunners reacted to the SOS lights sent up by the infantry, many Japanese were already ashore, and the opportunity of shelling the first wave before it hit the beach had been lost.

Two Australian battalions, 2/18th and 2/20th, sustained the first impact of the two Japanese divisions. Their machine-guns took a heavy toll, but the sheer weight of numbers proved too much for them. Both battalions were badly mauled, 2/20th losing no less than 334 killed and 214 wounded, rather more than half its strength. Some forward posts held on while the Japanese pushed past them, and fought until they were overrun by the follow-up troops: one of 2/20th's companies was destroyed to a man.

At about midnight, Taylor gave Bennett a report of the situation emphasising that he urgently required reserves in order to counter-attack at dawn. Bennett did what he could, placing first the weak 2/29th Battalion and later his special Reserve Battalion and a machine-gun company at Taylor's disposal. He also ordered his gunners to shell likely Japanese concentration areas in Johore, and asked Percival to provide maximum air support at first light.

None of these counter-measures had any decisive effect. Taylor salvaged elements of his two forward battalions and, with the aid of the reinforcements sent him by Bennett, strung together a defensive line from Choa Chu Kang village to north-west of Tengah airfield. He had little hope of holding this for long in the face of persistent Japanese infiltration, and a counter-attack was quite out of the question. Pulford sent ten Hurricanes and four elderly Swordfish to support the Australians at dawn, but although this small force managed to intercept a Japanese raid and destroy some aircraft, it was unable to accomplish anything of lasting value.

'I had learnt in exercises we held in England,' Percival wrote, 'not to commit your reserve until you are quite certain you are dealing with the real thing.' At 8.30 on the morning of the 9th he decided to move his command reserves 12th Brigade, to the Bukit Panjong area, where it would come under Bennett's command. Two and a half hours later he ordered Heath to put 6th/15th Brigade, III Corps reserve, at one hour's notice to move. There was little chance of these measures achieving success. 12th Brigade contained only the weak Plymouth Argylls and the slightly larger 4/19th Hyderabad, and 6th/15th Brigade had not recovered from its tribulations on the mainland. Nothing short of a major redeployment would have sufficed. Percival knew by now that a large Japanese convoy anchored off the Anamba Islands was intended to invade Sumatra: he could therefore have weakened the garrison of the Southern area to strengthen the North-West. Woodburn Kirby has suggested that Percival could have concentrated 18th Division in the Bukit Timah area, having first manned the Serangoon switch line to cover the Eastern approach to Singapore City.

Percival went forward to discuss the situation with Bennett at about midday. They met at Bennett's headquarters, a group of estate buildings near Bukit Timah village: there was frequent bombing and shelling, and

Percival recalled it as being 'not a very healthy spot.' It was decided that 27th Australian Brigade should continue to hold the Causeway sector, and that 22nd Brigade, with the assistance of 12th Brigade, would occupy the Jurong switch line. Bennett's left flanking formation, 44th Indian Brigade, was still holding its forward defences between the Sungei Berih and the Sungei Jurong: Percival decided, after some discussion, that this brigade would fall back onto the left of the Jurong line. While Bennett issued orders to his formations, Percival made arrangements to bring 6th/15th Brigade up to the race-course on the Bukit Timah road, where it would come under Gordon Bennett's orders. Percival then returned to his headquarters and drafted an instruction to Heath, Bennett and Simmons. In this secret and personal document Percival told his senior commanders that, if the Japanese reached the Bukit Timah road, he would fall back to hold a tight perimeter round Singapore City. Bennett passed on the information contained in this document to his brigadiers.

Even as the senior commanders tried to establish a cohesive front, the situation deteriorated still further. Taylor had some initial success in reorganising his battered Brigade. But Angus Rose found some of the Australians badly shaken by the time the Argylls arrived. 'As soon as the troops had debussed,' he wrote,

we started to dig slit trenches. . . . Hardly was the top soil off than a high-level attack developed. Down came the bombs, chiefly on rear battalion HQ and the two marine companies. There were quite a few casualties.

Mike Blackwood, who commanded the armoured car platoon came up and asked me if I'd go and help at an Australian gunner command post where there were a number of casualties. The Major's arm had been blown off. Two or three men were dead and there were several wounded. . . . The Australians asked me what they should do with the dead and I suggested that they should bury them where they were. This was their first blooding and I could see they were appalled by the sight of the dead men with their glassy eye-balls and their swollen tongues lolling idly in their gaping mouths.

Taylor asked Brigadier Paris of 12th Brigade to hold the Northern end of the Jurong line, with the Special Reserve Battalion on his left. The remnants of 22nd Brigade moved into an outpost line covering the main position. During the night of 9–10 February Bennett ordered Taylor to concentrate on the Jurong line, and placed 6th/15th Brigade at his disposal. Taylor pulled 22nd Brigade back from its outpost position, and by 9.00 on the morning of the 10th the line was held from North to South by 12th Brigade, 22nd Brigade, the Special Reserve Battalion, 6th/15th Brigade and 44th Brigade. Most of these formations were already well below strength, and their cohesion was strained by a night move into an area with which they were unfamiliar.

Japanese patrols were already in contact with the Jurong line when Bennett's order, based on Percival's secret and personal instruction to senior commanders, reached his brigadiers. Taylor misunderstod the order and, thinking that it called for an immediate withdrawal onto the reduced perimeter covering Singapore City, at once went back to reconnoitre his new position, ordering his brigade to fall back. This retirement exposed the flank of 12th Brigade, and Paris, who had already made the alarming discovery that his right flank was also open, decided to retire to the Bukit Panjang cross roads. The commanders of 6th/15th and 44th Brigades also misread Bennett's order, and began to fall back, around late morning, to the new perimeter. By nightfall on the 10th the Jurong line had been abandoned.

Things were every bit as bad on Bennett's right flank. Gordon Bennett's protégé, Brigadier Maxwell of 27th Australian Brigade, became increasingly preoccupied with the threat to his left flank during the 9th. He asked Bennett for permission to withdraw towards the Woodlands Road. Bennett denied his request, but allowed him to send his reserves forward to strengthen his left flank. While briefing his two battalion commanders for this move, Maxwell added that a withdrawal from the coast might soon become necessary, and outlined his future plans.

Yamashita, meanwhile, had command problems of his own. General Nishimura of the Imperial Guards was far from pleased at the secondary role allocated to his division, and his staff kept pressing Yamashita, his forward command post now established in a rubber plantation near Tengah airfield, for permission to cross West of the Causeway. Yamashita gave way, and the sector chosen for attack was that held by 27th Brigade. Japanese artillery softened up Maxwell's positions during the afternoon of the 9th, and at 8.30 that evening Nishimura's division began its crossing. The first reports to reach Army Headquarters at Johore Bahru were depressing. Nishimura arrived, accompanied by his Chief of Staff, and shouted:

The Konoye Division, just as they commenced to cross the strait near the Causeway, became caught in petroleum to which the enemy set fire. The front-line regiment was enveloped in fire while on the water and almost annihilated. The leader of the Kobayashi Infantry Regiment was seen swimming in a sea of fire and his fate in unknown! This disaster is the Army's responsibility.

It soon transpired, however, that this report was unduly alarmist. Some casualties had indeed been caused by burning oil, which had drifted with the tide from the ruptured tanks in the Naval Base area. Ironically, some preparations had been made to float petrol over the water and then to ignite it, but Command Headquarters had ordered that the drums prepared by the Engineers for this purpose should be moved East of the Causeway. They were never used. Despite the losses caused by the burning oil and the fire of Maxwell's Australians, the Imperial Guards established a bridgehead, driving the defenders back to Kranji village. The defence was still holding firm there when, at about midnight, Maxwell ordered his battalion commanders to implement the plan discussed that afternoon, withdrawing to the area of Mandai. The retirement of 27th Brigade opened up Paris's right flank, contributing to his withdrawal on the 10th: it also laid bare the left rear of 11th Division.

News of 27th Brigade's withdrawal seeped along the chain of command only gradually. 11th Division heard of it by way of a scrap of paper given to the Gurkha officer commanding the left-hand platoon of 2/2nd Gurkhas on the Division's extreme left. 'Position on Mandai Road,' it announced, 'near Bukit Mandai and 195 feature near 13 M[ile] P[ost].' 'This was serious news,' commented the Divisional History: the Japanese were now free to cross the Strait West of the Causeway undisturbed by small-arms fire, and the Division's left flank was overlooked by the high ground vacated by the Australians. Local counter-attacks by 11th Division temporarily stabilised the situation, but the Woodlands Road lay open to a Japanese advance into the key central area.

Wavell visited Singapore for the last time on the morning of the 10th, flying up from Java to do so. He drove with Percival to Gordon Bennett's headquarters, now in Holland Road, South-East of Bukit Timah. Their arrival coincided with a bombing raid, and Percival recorded:

the unedifying spectacle . . . of three general officers going to ground under tables or any other cover that was available. There was a good deal of debris and a few casualties outside, but the party of VIPs escaped untouched, though I lost both my car and my field-glasses.

Information at Bennett's headquarters was somewhat sketchy: it was not until Wavell and Percival reached 11th Division that they heard of the retirement of 27th Brigade.

This withdrawal made the establishment of a central reserve in the Bukit Timah area even more necessary than ever. Wavell and Percival drove on to Heath's headquarters, where Percival ordered Heath to form a three-battalion force and send it to the Race Course without delay. Heath combined the reserve battalions of 54th and 55th Brigades and with the 18th Reconnaissance Battalion to form Tomforce, named after its commander, Lieutenant-Colonel L. C. Thomas. Percival also put 27th Brigade under Heath's command for the time being, ordering

Maxwell to occupy and hold Mandai village.

Wavell and Percival then returned to Bennett's headquarters, arriving there at about 2.30 pm. They heard the discouraging news of the abandonment of the Jurong line, and Percival, recognising the threat to the Bukit Timah area which was, as he put it, 'vital to the defence', ordered Bennett to counter-attack and re-establish this line. The operation was to be in three phases, and was to commence that evening and end on the afternoon of the 11th.

'General Wavell was not giving much away,' observed the staff of 11th Division, 'except the confidence with which he invariably inspired those who were fortunate enough to meet him.' The Supreme Commander was undoubtedly radiating a good deal more confidence than he actually felt. He paid a farewell visit to Sir Shenton Thomas that evening, and sat in the Governor's sitting room, thumping his knees with his fists and repeating 'It shouldn't have happened.' Wavell later acknowledged that: 'I left Singapore on the morning of 11 February without much confidence in its continued resistance.'

Wavell was in no doubt as to the Prime Minister's view. On 10 February Churchill sent a signal which reached him in Singapore. 'There must be no thought,' snapped the Prime Minister,

of saving the troops or sparing the population. The battle must be fought to the bitter end at all costs. . . . Commanders and senior officers should die with their troops. The honour of the British Empire and the British Army is at stake. I rely on you to show no mercy on weakness in any form. With the Russians fighting as they are and the Americans so stubborn at Luzon the whole reputation of our country and our race is involved.

Wavell left Percival a note urging him to fight on to the end, 'to prove that the fighting spirit that won our Empire still exists to defend it.' But he was determined to save something from the collapse, and before he left Singapore Wavell ordered the last of the RAF fighters to leave the Island.

Percival's position deteriorated still further on the night of the 10th–11th. The Japanese 5th Division advanced up the Choa Chu Kang Road, while the 18th Division pressed along Jurong Road. This thrust met Gordon Bennett's counter-attack force on the way to its start line. 12th Brigade was swamped by Japanese armour and infantry. Most of the Argylls were cut off, and split up into small parties in an effort to break through to a rallying point on the Singapore–Causeway pipeline. A journalist described how three Argylls passed through a British position on their way to the rendezvous.

An officer advised them to get some sleep instead of making for the pipeline, which could only be approached by crossing positions held by the Japanese. 'My orders were to join the battalion there, sir,' replied the Corporal in charge. 'If we're the last of the battalion I'm the senior NCO. My last order was to hold the pipe line. If the CO's alive he'll be expecting us. If he isn't he'll expect us to be at the pipeline. So we'll be moving off, sir.'

If life was harsh for men in the front line, the plight of the wounded was even less enviable. 2/10th Australian General Hospital had been established in a Chinese School on Bukit Timah Road. Sister Betty Jeffrey recalled how:

There were casualties everywhere . . . so many we hadn't the room to nurse them, so the male staff erected a marquee on the lawn tennis courts belonging to the Guest House we had converted to a hospital. The Japs came over regularly and bombed and strafed and there were huge tears and holes in the canvas. Then it started raining and from then on we nursed our men in beds sinking into the wet grass. It was chaos, we had to nurse on our knees . . . in gumboots.

As the tide of battle rolled closer to the hospital, patients became involved in the fighting. 'I remember one particular soldier,' said Sister Jeffrey.

He had not taken his boots and socks off for many days in that heat so he had tinea very badly. I had difficulty separating his leg from his sock – it took a very long time and it must have hurt like hell, but he didn't say a word. When I had finished there was renewed fighting on the road outside our hospital and this soldier got off the bed, grabbed his rifle and raced out to help the defence. He was back about half an hour later, on a stretcher, and had one leg missing. As he was carried past me, he looked at me and said 'after all your hard work!'

By dawn on the 11th the leading elements of 5th Division were at Bukit Timah, while 18th Dvision, after a confused night's fighting against 22nd and 44th Brigades, had reached Reformatory Road between Bukit Timah and Pasir Panjang. Gordon Bennett ordered Tomforce to counter-attack to retake Bukit Timah and Bukit Panjang, but the attack soon ground to a halt after a promising start. Percival sent Bennett 2nd Gordons from 2nd Malaya Brigade at Changi, and adjusted the inter-formation boundaries so as to make Bennett responsible for the ground East of the Race Course.

On hearing news of the change in boundaries, Heath held a conference to review the situation. The fall of Bukit Timah left 11th Division's flank exposed, and there was danger of the Japanese infiltrating between the reservoirs. He therefore ordered Major-General M. B. Beckworth-Smith, commander of 18th Division, to form another three-battalion composite force, which would come directly under Corps Headquarters and could be used in the area of Thomson Village or the reservoirs.

Brigadier Massy-Beresford, an able and energetic officer, was given command of Massy Force, and his account gives clear evidence of the confusion now prevailing. His force was to consist of 1st Cambridgeshires from his own brigade, 4th Suffolks from 54th Brigade, and 5/11th Sikhs from Southern Area. 'I was to meet them at a map reference,' recalled Massy-Beresford,

to stop the enemy. . . . What enemy or where, I didn't know. So I got in my car, gave the necessary orders for the Cambridgeshires to pack up . . . no tools, no wire, no sandbags, no reserves, just men and rifles, and I directed them to this reference point. . . . I went to that map reference that he gave me and began setting up my headquarters, and I got in the car and went motoring around . . . and I made a bit of a plan. . . . Got back to my rendezvous and met General Percival. And he said, 'Look here, I'm afraid I've got to alter your plan and there's got to be a different sector.'

Massy-Beresford promptly made another plan, but his chances of successfully carrying it out were small. He managed to get his own Cambridgeshires in position, but the Sikhs were 'under 200 strong and completely exhausted,' and he lost contact with the Suffolks while bringing them forward under air attack.

While Massy-Beresford was trying to pull his force together, Major-General Key of 11th Division was contending with difficulties which were almost as great. At 7.30 on the morning of the 11th he received a message from Maxwell to the effect that 27th Brigade had been restored to Gordon Bennett's command. Just over two hours later Maxwell appeared at Divisional Headquarters, and announced that he had been directed to occupy Bukit Panjang village. He had accordingly sent off his two battalions, although he had no news of their progress. Well might the Divisional History call this a 'bombshell'. Key had launched a series of local counter-attacks to bolster up his left flank: with the Australian withdrawal, however, his flank and left rear were dangerously exposed. Only a company of Australians, which Maxwell had been unable to extricate, and 2nd Buluchis now secured Nee Soon against a Japanese thrust down the Mandai. Road. It is more than usually difficult to disentangle the conflicting evidence surrounding this episode. There is no proof that either Bennett or Percival ordered Maxwell to return to the former's command, and it seems not unreasonable to assume that Maxwell took the step on his own initiative.

Whatever the reasons for Maxwell's move, its consequences were serious. Heath decided that he must now pull his entire corps back from the coast, and warning orders to this effect went out towards midday. Key's sappers completed their final demolitions in the area of the Naval

Base, and 11th Division withdrew to a line covering Sembawang airfield and Nee Soon. By nightfall on the 11th something like a continuous front had been established. On the extreme right, 53rd Brigade had swung back from the coast, and now held the sector between the Sungei Simpang and Sembawang airfield, where it met 11th Division. Key's line ran parallel with Nee Soon road, almost as far as Thomson Village. Massy Force held a line curling around the base of the hills North of Singapore City, its left flank joining Tomforce in the area of the Race Course. South of Race Course Village the front bulged Westwards, before running South, parallel with Reformatory Road, to the coast at Pasir Panjang.

But already the new line was cracking ominously. As part of 11th Division occupied its final position,

a company of the immature boys who formed the reconstituted 1/8th Punjabis was heavily mortared and streamed back into DHQ (Divisional Headquarters). The situation was restored by the personal intervention of the Divisional Commander.

The ill-fated 27th Brigade had split up. Both its battalions had failed in their attacks on Bukit Panjang: one returned to 11th Division, and the other joined Gordon Bennett. Bombardier C. W. L. Prime of 18th Division's 118th Field Regiment described his withdrawal from Seletar:

There was obvious chaos going on. Going along these roads there were Indian troops and other troops coming, and transport all over the place. At one place there was a junction where five roads met. There was a Japanese plane sitting over the five road junction just machine-gunning everything as it came along and there was absolute chaos. . . . Nevertheless, I found a battery command post. We redeployed the guns of our battery – 483 Battery – and we became immediately operational.

Morale was now decidely patchy. Perhaps surprisingly, many British soldiers continued to hope for the best. 'We were actually still optimistic,' said Prime.

No-one was in fear, we were waiting for them to come. We'd never seen an enemy in our lives before, but we did know what to expect. . . . In our little enclosure in this English School we seemed to be quite together and OK. This is it: that is what war's about. We suddenly found out. In a fortnight.

Reactions to Wavell's last message differed. Gunner Topping recalled how:

Colonel Napier said to the men of his Advanced HQ 'There is no thought of a further withdrawal. With the passing of each hour the land left at our disposal diminishes. Here we shall make our stand. If need be we will fight to the last man!' So it had come to this at last. Deep down inside me I had known for days that there was to be no evacuation of Singapore by the army. . . . The situation looked hopeless, only putting off a little longer that fateful moment when, with our backs to the sea, we would go down fighting for this land that, before the war, was only a place in the geography book, of her people and her ways I knew nothing.

Brigadier Massy-Beresford admitted that Wavell's message brought him close to tears,

because every word he said was true. He practically said 'Your morale is down to zero, for Christ's sake do something about it: what about the Americans on Bataan? We have got to do something. This is disgraceful.' It was all true. It was quite frightening . . . we had had no chance to do anything at all, good or bad, and here was this raspberry . . .

Massy-Beresford responded by organising a counter-attack by his own force and by Tomforce, which had now come under his command: Heath, however, refused to sanction the attempt.

By this time Singapore City was an apocalyptic jumble of normality and horror. Several days after the landing, George Hammonds walked into Raffles Place.

The famous square – the real heart of white Singapore – had hardly been touched. Even the noises of war were muffled by the high buildings, and the square was filled with people of all colours – some in white ducks, some shorts, others in sarongs – either busy or unconcerned, going in and out of the shops, talking at the corners. An Indian street trader squatting on the pathway dozed over his tray of cheap trinkets; a Malay driver was fast asleep at the wheel of a tuan's parked car; a food hawker bobbed along, two containers dangling from the bamboo across his shoulders . . .

Yet Orchard Road, not far away, was heavily shelled by Japanese guns. 'All day long,' wrote Noel Barber,

the military traffic tore along it, running the gauntlet of the shells that whined and crashed. Half the buildings seemed to have been hit by now. Abandoned or burnt-out cars littered every corner. Water gushed along deep gullies from unmended pipes. Here and there bodies lay waiting to be collected . . .

A giddy night-life lurched on with the war only a few miles away. Warrant Officer David Mason entered the Raffles Hotel with some companions who had been sharing a trench in the *padang*. They

found the bar area packed with officers, mostly in khaki, but some older field officers still wore full mess kit. There were few women, but those that we saw wore evening dresses, and seemed to be having quite a time with a ratio of ten to one male attendance. We headed for the bar naturally, but were stopped on the way by a trio of British Staff Officers: 'I say, you men, what the devil do you think you're at, you scruffy devils? Get the dickens out of here before you're thrown out.' The music had started playing again and we strategically withdrew to the strains of 'We'll meet again.'

Not all the party were prepared to leave quietly. One, Titch from Rochdale, who had attached himself to Mason's group a few days before, ran back to the ballroom and screamed: 'You right lot of bluudy moonky barstids, . . . ye can get fooked, that's wut.' Looters and deserters, some of them drunk on stolen spirits, roamed the streets. One British deserter, bearded, filthy and unarmed, entered the Chartered Bank in Raffles Place, and produced bundles of banknotes of various currencies, saying that he wished to deposit them. The incident was a grim omen.

Fears that the Japanese would get drunk on stocks of captured liquor and commit atrocities prompted Sir Shenton Thomas to promulgate a total ban on liquor. This was to come into force on Friday 13th, but big firms started smashing up their stocks immediately. L.C. Hutchings, general manager of Robinsons, noted that it took a team of men a day and a half to destroy all his stock. 'The place smelt like sixteen breweries,' he recalled.

It might have been the fumes or it might have been emotion, but tears rolled down my face when we came to twelve cases of Napoleon brandy. I decided to pop one bottle away to celebrate the completion of the job. I looked forward to that last nip. But when I'd finished all the smashing, and went for the bottle I had hidden . . . it was gone.

For others the experience was something of a personal tragedy. Jimmy Glover, managing director and editor of the *Malaya Tribune*, had been collecting fine French wines against the time when he would retire up-country. He and George Hammonds spent an evening 'smashing bottles of precious liquid from some of the finest vineyards in France.'

Large stocks of money were also destroyed. Eric Pretty, the acting Federal Secretary, burned some five million Straits dollars in the Treasury. 'I never imagined,' he observed ruefully, 'that I'd have so much money to burn.' John Burnham was asked by a friend to assist with the destruction of a quarter of a million Straits dollars. After much discussion, during which they fed a large fire in the middle of the room with 100 dollar bills, they decided to keep a thousand dollars each: who can blame them?

The Singapore waterfront had been the target of repeated air attacks ever since the outbreak of war, and by the second week in February it was heavily damaged. Offices and godowns had been burnt, harbour installations ruined, and a number of small craft sunk. The Harbour Board's labour force was hopelessly overstretched; Simpson's Civil Defence organisation supplied the docks with some 2,000 labourers daily, and civil defence assistance when required. Even so, there was no time to disperse the vast food stocks housed in sixty-four large warehouses: forty-six of these were destroyed by air attacks, and all the others were damaged. Simson observed that the reserve food stocks should never have been concentrated in a single area in the first place: had the siege been prolonged, he suggested, food shortages would have proved another limiting factor in holding out.

A growing number of evacuees made their way through the ravaged docks. The lack of a clear official policy over who was and who was not a 'useless mouth' made the question of evacuation a difficult one. Wives were often reluctant to leave husbands whose duties compelled them to remain in Singapore. Husbands, alarmed by rumours of Japanese atrocities in Hong Kong and Malaya, pressed their wives to leave, feeling that it would be easier to face an uncertain future without the added anguish of worrying about the fate of the families. Some women, like Edith Rattray, already driven from her home, the Green Cow Tavern in Cameron Highlands, refused to leave. 'I've been turned out of my home,' she said,

but I'll not be turned out of my country. Whatever the Japs may do, I'll stay put.

Passenger bookings had been centralised at the P & O offices, where clerks took down particulars and handed out embarkation slips. Receiving an embarkation slip was often only the start of the nightmare. Evacuees could take little luggage, and it was agonisingly difficult to decide which possessions should be salvaged. Ann Scott was collected by her father. 'He came and collected me from my office,' she said,

And told me to pack a suitcase, take a bedding roll and within a quarter of an hour we were on our way like a lot of families were. . . . Being eighteen I couldn't bear to leave some of my things, so I packed my suitcase full of evening dresses, because I couldn't bear the thought of leaving them.

Nearly forty years later she still regretted the loss of her collection of Fats Waller records.

On arrival at the docks, evacuees discovered that:

all the Asiatic labour had completely deserted the dockside area. European civilians who had come down to see them off and say good-bye, and naval ratings, helped them to carry such luggage as they had for the journey. Later, at the shipside, there was the wildest confusion and, regardless of embarkation slips, passports and inventories the women and children poured on board.

One evacuee recalled:

one most amusing incident in all this turmoil there. There was one of the stewards, and a good looking British woman. And she was tearing up and down, absolutely almost demented, and she said, 'I've lost my baby, someone has taken my baby, have you seen it?' And a bystander looked up and said to her, Pardon me, ma'am, but was it a naval baby?' She looked absolute daggers at him and said 'Are you inferring that I've been sleeping with a sailor?' And he got the message . . . and said 'I'm sorry, madam, I didn't mean that at all. But a young naval officer has just gone up the gangway carrying a cradle with a baby in, and I thought you were looking for a naval baby.'

The last convoy to escape sailed on 12 February, with the cruiser *Durban* and the three other naval vessels still remaining at Singapore escorting the last of the large transports. The ships carried RAF ground crews, naval personnel, and a number of selected army technicians and specialists: Angus Rose was amongst them. 'I went up on deck,' he wrote,

to take a last look at Singapore. The 9.2 inch guns from Blakang Mati were firing over our heads. Away to the west there was a continuous thunder of fire from the battle front. I could vaguely discern that part of the line for which we had been destined. The moon should just about be rising, but the whole sky was blotted out by the smoke from the oil fires. The only illumination was from the countless conflagrations and the muzzle-flash of guns.

Flight-Lieutenant Arthur Donahue, an American serving with the RAF, had a similar view of the doomed city as he flew his Hurricane from Kalleng on his way to Java.

My final memory of Singapore, as it appeared to me looking back for the last time, is of a bright green little country, resting on the edge of the bluest sea I'd ever seen, lovely . . . except where the dark tragic mantle of smoke ran across its middle and beyond, covering and darkening the city on the seashores.

The city itself, with huge red leaping fires in its north and south parts, appeared to rest on the floor of a vast cavern formed by the sinister curtains of black smoke which rose from beyond and towered over it, prophetically, like a great over-hanging cloak of doom.

THE LAST ACT

On the evening of Wednesday 11 February a Japanese reconnaissance aircraft dropped a signalling tube trailing red and white streamers on the outskirts of Singapore City. It contained a message from Yamashita to Percival. 'In the spirit of chivalry,' urged the Japanese commander, 'we have the honour of advising your surrender.' Yamashita warned Percival that further resistance was futile, and could only increase loss of life. He concluded with instructions for the British surrender emissary, who was to advance down the Bukit Timah Road with an escort bearing the Union Jack and a white flag.

Percival sent no reply to Yamashita's invitation, but he was convinced that the end was not far off. On Thursday 12 February he went up the Bukit Timah Road as the Japanese 5th Division attacked the area of the Race Course. He concluded that these was a very real danger of the Japanese achieving a clean break-through, for there was little to stop them once they penetrated the crumbling front. After consulting Heath, he decided that it was essential to abandon Changi and the North-East coast to concentrate on a tight perimeter round the city. He then went on to see the Governor, and discussed the destruction of money and vehicles.

Percival's orders for the demolition and abandonment of the Changi defences went out at 8.30 that night. Although the coastal defence guns had not been faced with the attack they had been designed to meet, they had not proved entirely useless. Many of the coastal batteries could traverse their guns to fire inland, although in doing so they lost the benefit of their sophisticated fire-control equipment. Lieutenant-Colonel C. C. M. Macloed-Carey, second-in-command of 7th Coastal Artillery Regiment, wrote that his guns produced:

mostly harassing fire, sometimes at the request of the Army, and sometimes at targets picked out at random.

Macleod-Carey rarely saw a Japanese soldier. On one spectacular occasion, however, he spotted a Japanese observer atop a factory chimney. He turned the three 9.2 inch guns of Connaught Battery onto the Japanese, and had the satisfaction of seeing him disappear in a cloud of smoke and debris.

Gunner Marshall, whose battery arrived at Changi on the 10th, saw the 15-inch guns of the Johore battery engaging targets inland.

This gun was firing armour-piercing ammo. They had no HE. They hit the Johore Railway and made a considerable mess of it. I got that from a Jap later, who said that there were very heavy Jap casualties among troop concentrations at the railway.

Tsuji seems to have owed his life to the fact that the fortress gunners had little high explosive. Shelling forced him to abandon his car near Tengah aerodrome, and he continued his journey on foot, accompanied by his driver,

Just at that moment there was a shellburst which shocked our eardrums, while the blast jarred our spines. The flash seared my eyes, and I was thrown into the roadside ditch. In my agitation I thrust myself into an earthware drainage pipe. . . . Up to this moment I had no experience of such heavy projectiles, which tore holes in the ground fifteen or sixteen metres in diameter and four or five metres deep. They were probably fifteen- or sixteen-inch fortress guns which had been swung round 180 degrees to fire over the land instead of over the water out to sea . . .

Tsuji was probably on the receiving end of the Johore or Connaught Batteries. The armour-piercing shells, the batteries' main ammunition, buried themselves deeply in the ground before exploding: had they had more high explosive, historians might have been deprived of the pleasure of reading Tsuji's flowery prose.

By dawn on the 13th Percival's force was in its new position. On the extreme right, 2nd Malaya Brigade, withdrawn from Changi, covered Kallang airfield. 11th Division, on its left, held a line swinging North of Woodleigh and back to Braddell Road. Major-General Key was installed in a house belonging to a Scandinavian consul: 'it was,' commented his Divisional History,

tastefully furnished and decorated in the modern style; it boasted a piano; it was very comfortable and extremely incongruous.

18th Division, fighting as an integrated formation at last, held a long sector from Braddell Road to Bukit Timah Road. But it never recovered from the dislocation of the last few days. 'We were very . . . well trained,' commented Massy-Beresford,

but what we lacked was any blooding. You see, no-one had heard shots fired in anger, no-one had seen a chap killed, nobody had seen anything. . . . You have got to begin gently, you know. If we had gone to Africa we would have been put into strict training, then into a reserve position, and then into a quiet position, and then into a non-quiet position. It would all have been worked up. But to plunge them into that place was hopeless. One couldn't have expected anything better. But to break up that division all to brigades like that was a terrible thing to do. . . .

Gordon Bennett's Australians were responsible for the Farrar Road – Tanglin Halt sector, and 44th Indian Brigade and 1st Malaya Brigade continued the line to the coast.

Over the next two days the situation deteriorated steadily, both at the front and in the city. On Friday 13th, an appropriate enough date, the Japanese 5th Division punched a salient into 18th Division's line near the Bukit Timah Road. Things were even worse the following day: a determined attack dislodged 1st Malaya and 44th Indian Brigades from the line Tanglin Halt – Pasir Panjang, driving them back into the outskirts of the city.

The Alexandra Hospital was overrun by Japanese infantry. Captain Walter Salmon of the Royal Signals had been wounded by a mortar bomb and taken to the hospital. He was moved down from a ward on the top floor to a canteen on the ground floor because of shelling, which may have saved his life, for:

the Japanese . . . just went through the mass of people right, left and centre, staff, patients, everyone. And they went systematically through the wards, bayoneting, especially if they could find anybody who hadn't got a wound. . . . I think there must have been about 250 patients and staff who were literally assaulted in a very short space of time, including the surgical team in one of the operating theatres. . . . We in this little place, the canteen, could see the Japs running up and down the corridors, because we could see their feet (under the door), but they never came in all the time this was going on.

The Japanese had attacked on the pretext that some Indian troops had set up machineguns in the hospital grounds. The incident undoubtedly occurred without Yamashita's knowledge or consent. Captain Salmon remembered that on the following day Yamashita and his staff toured the hospital.

Yamashita saluted us, he went round all the beds and saluted everybody and apologised very profusely. . . . He brought up some crates of tinned fruit, and he took a bayonet and opened these tins of fruit and came round himself doling the peaches out of the tin. . . .

There was a burst of fire outside the hospital shortly afterwards, and Salmon was told that Yamashita had ordered the summary execution of some Japanese looters.

In the city itself, meanwhile, matters were nothing short of desperate. Large numbers of armed deserters were prowling the street, looting or hiding from the bombing. Some commandeered small boats in which to make their escape, and others forced their way aboard larger vessels. David Mason met a British officer on the beach three days before the surrender.

He was alone and dressed in Malay costume, wearing a sarong, sandals, and skin stained brown. He was carrying two satchels, weighing him down a little. . . . After some conversation he said that he had 'adequate money and gold watches' if any of our party were interested in helping him get off the island. . . .

The staff of the Harbour Board had been withdrawn on the 10th, leaving the army to struggle with the chaos of the docks. As the perimeter had narrowed, so the weight of shellfire falling on the city had increased. The Civil Defence was no longer able to cope, and the damage to the water-mains meant that there was no water for drinking or fire-fighting in all except the lower areas of the town.

At 2.00 p.m. on the 13th Percival presided over a conference of senior commanders and staff officers at Fort Canning. Various possibilities were discussed, including that of organising a counter-attack to recapture the vital ground around Bukit-Timah. None of the formation commanders had any confidence in such an operation, and maintained that their troops were too exhausted. Heath and Gordon Bennett advocated surrender, warning that Yamashita's troops might

171

easily run amok if surrender was delayed too long.

Percival decided to continue the struggle. He did, however, agree to Rear-Admiral Spooner's request that all the remaining sea-going vessels in the harbour should sail that night. These craft were filled with military and civilian evacuees, and armed deserters forced their way aboard some of them. Few of them escaped. The Japanese navy had now blocked the Southern approach to Singapore, and most of the vessels were either sunk or forced ashore. The launch carrying Pulford and Spooner, for example, was pursued by a Japanese destroyer and was beached on a barren island, where most of its passengers, including Pulford and Spooner, died of starvation or sickness.

Despite his decision to fight on, Percival recognised that the end was very near, and told Wavell that there would soon come a time when continued resistance would no longer serve any useful purpose. 'You must continue to inflict maximum damage on the enemy for as long as possible,' replied the Supreme Commander,

by house-to-house fighting if necessary. Your action in tying down enemy and inflicting casualties may have vital influence in other theatres. Fully appreciate your situation but continued action essential.

Early on 14 February Simson warned Percival that a complete failure of the water supply was believed to be imminent. Percival attended a meeting at the Municipal Officers to discuss this, and then went on to the Singapore Club to meet the Governor. Sir Shenton was also worried about the provision of water, and feared the outbreak of an epidemic. The Japanese had in fact taken the last of the reservoirs on the 13th, but the British engineer at Woodleigh Pumping Station remained at his post, and the Japanese, probably out of reluctance to cause the epidemic which Thomas feared, did not destroy the pipe-line or close the valve. Percival paid Simson another visit in the afternoon, and discovered that the water situation seemed to have improved slightly. 'I went home feeling rather hopeful,' he wrote.

I thought that with any luck we might be able to master the water difficulty, while at the front, in spite of one or two danger spots, the enemy's rate of advance was slowing down.

The Japanese were certainly encountering stiff resistance. Tsuji witnessed a counter-attack which he believed took place on the 12th, though it is more likely to have been Tomforce's exploit on the previous day.

As noon approached the enemy bombardment increased and a large force of enemy soldiers surged up the heights like a tidal wave under cover of the barrage. They were supported by armoured cars. It appeared as if the British were staking everything on a counter-attack. 'This is gallantry, is it not?' I said to myself, and involuntarily I was lost in admiration.

British artillery fire had an increasingly damaging effect. Tsuji admitted that, by the morning of the 15th, the ammunition accumulated for the assault on Singapore Island was nearly exhausted.

We had barely a hundred rounds per gun left for our field guns, and less for our heavy guns. With this small ammunition supply it was impossible to keep down enemy fire by counter-battery operations.

Bad news started to reach Percival immediately he had attended a communion service at Fort Canning on the morning of Sunday 15th. At 9.30 that morning he held a conference with all his commanders, and the deteriorating water supply and worsening administrative situation were discussed. The water was unlikely to last for more than twenty-four hours, and there were serious shortages of 25-pounder and Bofors ammunition. Percival put forward two alternatives. Either a counter-attack should be launched with the aim of recovering the reservoirs and the food depots in the Bukit Timah area, or the army should capitulate. The commanders were unanimous in opposing a counter-attack, and some argued that they would be unable to resist another determined attack. 'It was in these circumstances,' said Percival 'that I decided to capitulate.'

A telegram arrived from Wavell that morning. 'So long as you are in a position to inflict losses and damage to the enemy and your troops are physically capable of doing so,' it read,

you must fight on. Time gained and damage to the enemy are of vital importance at this juncture. When you are fully satisfied that this is no longer possible I give you discretion to cease resistance. . . . Whatever happens I thank you and all your troops for your gallant efforts of the last few days.

At 11.30 a small deputation left Fort Canning and drove out along the Bukit Timah Road towards the Japanese lines in a car displaying a white flag. After being disarmed and taken to Japanese headquarters, they were met by Lieutenant-Colonel Sugita, and discussed the procedure for arranging a cease-fire. It was agreed that British forces would cease fire at 4.00, and that a large Japanese flag would be flown briefly from the top of the Cathay Building to indicate that Percival accepted the cease-fire and was on his way to meet Yamashita at Bukit Timah. The deputation then made its way back to Fort Canning, arriving there at the height of an air raid.

There was some confusion over the cease-fire arrangements. Guy Hutchinson of the Johore Volunteer Engineers recalled being told to stand-to, but not to fire at any Japanese unless they fired first. One survivor, a dispatch rider in 18th Division, took round an order stating: 'Every available round to be fired from every available gun.' Captain Kemmis Betty's Gurkhas were horrified by news of the armistice. They were planning a counter-attack.

when at about 4 o'clock we were suddenly told to stop in our tracks. . . . They could not believe that the British Raj could do this sort of thing, and particularly some of the Gurkha officers and NCOs . . . were quite overcome by this and were openly in tears about the situation.

Gunner Topping heard of the cease-fire early in the afternoon from an officer whose voice trembled with emotion. 'Many of the men,' he recalled,

also resented having to surrender. It would be better, they said, to fight on until the last man fell than to be taken prisoner by these yellow devils. . . .

The news came as a cruel blow to 'Pinkie' Evans, now a sergeant in the Manchesters. 'Somehow everything went quiet,' he wrote.

Two soldiers went to pass by and I ordered them to stop, and asked what they were doing. They told me we had surrendered. I could have cried. What a bloody waste of lives.

Major-General Key broke the news to his commanders and staff officers at a divisional orders group some time after 1.00 p.m. 'The General told us the decision,' recorded his GSO 1.

It had been decided to capitulate. The provisional hour for the 'Cease Fire' was 4 p.m. . . . All equipment and guns were to be handed over intact.
    A gasp greeted this last remark. I asked to be excused and left the conference. Toosey (Commander, Royal Artillery) followed me: 'I can take a lot, but I can't take this,' he said. I told him to cheer up; that the first seven years were always the worst; and that even 25-pdrs sometimes blew up by accident. He brightened a bit at this. . . .
    Later, thank God, General Wavell wirelessed his orders that all Field Guns were to be destroyed. Our two Field Regiments made a grand mess of theirs, and a hell of a lot of noise doing it.

But for some the news came as a relief. To the demoralised refugees and deserters in the city, it offered an end to the air attacks and shelling. Two Chinese residents remembered how:

Every concrete building was crammed with refugees. . . . Amongst us were many soldiers. They had thrown away their arms. We showed no resentment. Far from looking askance at them, we shared what we had with them. . . . They were no heroes. Neither were we. They had done their poor best. That was enough for us. We accepted them as companions in misfortune.

Lance-Bombardier Alan Toze of 122nd Field Regiment met a

soldier near the Supreme Court Building.

'A man can stand so much,' said he in a broad Scots accent. 'The Argylls have done their bit: we were too few against too many.'

Percival, accompanied by three other officers, arrived at the Bukit Timah cross-roads at 5.00 in a civilian car flying a Union Jack and a white flag. The party was met by Sugita, and led into the damaged Ford factory, which Yamashita had deliberately chosen as being the largest covered area available: he was eager that the surrender ceremony should be witnessed by as many spectators as possible. A long table had been set up in the middle of the floor, and chalk-marks indicated the positions to be taken up by Japanese observers.

Yamashita kept Percival waiting for some time and the two commanders exchanged formal handshakes before sitting down. The negotiations were blunt and to the point. After enquiring if any Japanese soldiers had been captured, and asking what had become of Japanese residents, Yamashita asked Percival whether he surrendered unconditionally. Percival tried to play for time, asking for a few hours in which to consider his reply. 'I want to hear a decisive answer,' snapped Yamashita, 'and I insist on an unconditional surrender.' 'Yes', replied Percival. Yamashita announced that the surrender would take place with effect from 8.30 Singapore time, and warned that if the terms were violated he would immediately launch a general offensive. Percival asked Yamashita to guarantee the safety of the lives of the English and Australians remaining in the city. 'You may be sure of that,' answered Yamashita. 'Please rest assured. I shall positively guarantee it.' Percival signed the surrender terms at 6.10 p.m.: the two commanders exchanged another handshake before parting.

Yamashita's brusqueness reflected something more than a cruel desire to hector his adversary. He believed that Percival over-estimated the strength of the Japanese forces, and was afraid that he would learn the truth. He therefore pressed for an immediate and unconditional capitulation, telling his interpreter that he wanted to hear nothing from Percival except 'yes' or 'no'. Yamashita also felt some sympathy for Percival, who looked more gaunt than ever, with pale face and bloodshot eyes. He told his ADC afterwards that he wanted to say a few kind words to the British commander:

But he could not say anything because he does not speak English and he realised how difficult it is to convey heartfelt sympathy when the words are being interpreted by a third person.

Percival returned to Fort Canning to issue the requisite orders. He sent a last message to Wavell.

175

Owing to losses from enemy action, water, petrol, food and ammunition practically finished. Unable therefore to continue the fight any longer. All ranks have done their best and grateful for your help.

'Thereafter,' records the Official History, 'all communication with Singapore ceased.'

8

THE ROAD TO CHANGI

THE GUNS FALL SILENT

WHAT follows is a strange story of the triumph of human willpower over conditions that are impossible to imagine in terms of a civilised country today. The media in Britain have long been obsessed with life in the P.o.W. camps in Germany and the activities of the S.S., and we have been surfeited with such sagas as *Colditz*. If you speak to a FEPOW (Far East Prisoner of War), however, you will not hear tales of jolly japes and pranks perpetrated against bewildered comic-opera guards. Instead, the captives were herded together, beaten, starved, deprived of medical supplies, and sometimes literally worked to death in the Japanese camps.

What annoys the FEPOWs is that their sacrifice has received scant publicity, apart from the film *Bridge on the River Kwai* which fills many of them with scorn. There have been a number of books on the subject, but none of them, except perhaps for Russell Braddon's *The Naked Island,* has been a 'best seller'. Even today there is still great bitterness towards their captors, which is understandable, although protest is more or less limited to a refusal to buy Japanese cars.

The guns fell silent at 8.30 p.m. on 15 February 1942, and it was the very silence that seems to have made the most impression on the weary troops as they relaxed in their positions and tried to take stock of their situation. The odd fact is that nothing happened immediately, and there was a strange form of hiatus. Under the terms of the surrender, Percival was permitted to keep selected bodies of men under arms to preserve order, for Yamashita had no intention of letting his tired troops loose in the fleshpots of the city. The transition of power was amazingly smooth in most cases, although difficulties in communication meant that many units were never officially informed of the surrender.

Sergeant Charles McCormack, an RAF technician who had joined up with some soldiers, was sitting under a tree on the evening of 15 February, when suddenly one of them noticed the silence:

None of us moved. The gunfire had stopped. There was no sound but the soft slithering of the leaves in the undergrowth, a couple of dogs barking in the distance.

Lieutenant-Colonel Macleod-Carey, second-in-command of 7th Coast Artillery Regiment was in his headquarters on Mount Faber:

At about sunset we distinctly heard Japanese soldiers farther up the road shouting *Banzai, Banzai, Banzai.* Shortly afterwards orders were received from Fort Canning that we were to cease fire and we were informed that the great fortress of Singapore had fallen.

Brigadier Simson's impressions were very vivid:

That last night of 'freedom' in Singapore seemed very eerie. There was complete silence after weeks of violent explosions and other noises. The gloom that darkened the shattered buildings and deserted streets was not entirely due to the pall of smoke and soot from petrol, oil and burning buildings, some of which had raged for several days. It was partly in the mind, the bitterness of defeat and failure.

John Burnham had spent the morning helping a colleague to burn a quarter of a million dollars and had then paid off his Chinese staff:

I was left alone in the office, and I thought, what the hell am I going to do now? I went to the club on the shore where I had my car, and I thought, well, I'm not going to hand this over. So I got in and drove it down to the docks. When I came to the jetty wall, I got into the driving seat, started her up and then jumped out ten feet away – in she went into the water. I walked back to the office and went into Raffles Hotel. There were a few people looking around completely lost, wondering what to do. I went and had a drink – there were still some Chinese serving, quite cheerful. . . . One asked if there was anything he could do for me. 'Would you like to take a bottle of whisky with you?' I said, 'Thank you very much, I'll do that', so I packed a bottle in my pocket and walked back to the office.

Brigadier Massey-Beresford remembered how

we just sat there for 24 hours, and I stamped my field glasses and pistol into the ground. Everybody smashed their weapons and then an awkward thing happened. You see, in this comic war we were fighting, we had occupied a villa. There was furniture, there were children's toys and things, and while we were waiting for orders from the Japs, the owner appeared. Everyone felt sort of ashamed that we had to apologise for being in his house.

Another survivor recalled that:

the Australian units I called on wouldn't accept the order that they had to lay down their arms and surrender. . . . But twenty minutes later they had to pack up. I remember going back to Clooney Hill and all the men were dejected. We were told we had to stay put in our positions until the next morning. . . . We piled all our arms, and the next thing I remember was just getting down on the ground and sleeping under the stars.

For most, this eerie period was an opportunity to catch up with lost sleep or to obtain a last decent meal. The British talent for making the best of a bad job was well to the fore. Those who could wandered at will in Singapore and simply helped themselves to anything that was going. Cars were just left with the keys in the ignition and the shops threw open their doors. Most units maintained strict discipline, but the city was crowded with a mob of undisciplined troops who had slunk away or had become separated from their units. In spite of the wholesale destruction of liquor, there was enough to drink.

One dispenser of human comforts was Robinsons department store. A small select group who had found their way there, lounged in cozy chairs in the furniture department and drank the welcome tea provided by the manager's wife. The management had thoughtfully filled all the available baths when it was thought that the water supply would be cut off, and these were put to good use. The ladies' hairdressing salon provided talcum powder and eau de cologne in plenty.

Others ate a 'surrender dinner' of the tinned food that was available in vast quantities. In the cathedral, the Bishop of Singapore conducted a well-attended service and the congregation lustily sang 'Oh God, our help in ages past'. They had to squeeze into the choir as the nave was a casualty station and the hymn singing was punctuated by the groans of the wounded.

That evening the official communiques were issued and passed around. Percival's was short and to the point, but can have provided little in the way of consolation:

It has been necessary to give up the struggle but I want the reason explained to all ranks. The forward troops continue to hold their ground but the essentials of war have run short. In a few days we shall have neither food or petrol. Many types of ammunition are short and the water supply, upon which the vast civil population and many of the fighting troops are dependent, threatens to fail. This situation has been brought about partly by being driven off our dumps and partly by hostile air and artillery action. Without these sinews of war we cannot fight on. I thank all ranks for their efforts throughout the campaign.

Signed: A. E. Percival,
Lieutenant General,
General Officer Commanding Malaya.

179

Major-General Keith Simmons, the fortress commander, also issued a message to the troops in the Southern sector, part of which ran: 'You have had little support from the air, you have been outnumbered and outgunned.' This reflects the belief held by senior commanders at the time that the Japanese were far more numerous than they actually were. How else could the defeat be explained?

The victors too were relaxing, although modestly. At Yamashita's headquarters, a party was laid on for the staff. On the menu were dried cuttlefish, chestnuts and saki. Those present turned towards the north-east (the direction of the Imperial Palace) and drank a solemn toast, but the occasion was not a cheerful one for all. Colonel Tsuji wrote:

Since my appointment to the 25th Army as Staff Officer in charge of operations, I had vowed to the Gods to abstain from wine and tobacco until my cherished wish was accomplished. We had expected that on this day we would drink until our glasses were 'bottoms up'. But what actually happened was that we could not enjoy our wine or eat our delicacies. They tasted bitter and seemed to choke one's throat because of the three thousand several hundred seniors, colleagues and soldiers with whom we could not share this day's joy. Thinking of the feelings of the families of the dead men caused the wine to be bitter indeed.

Congratulations were received from the Emperor, but a vast problem remained. The city was in ruins, the water supply was severely damaged, fires raged unchecked and the streets were littered with unburied corpses. The limited Japanese forces had to contend with a prisoner population that greatly outnumbered them, as well with the hordes of Asians.

The actual occupation started on the morning of 16 February when Tsuji, accompanied by two staff officers, drove down the Bukit Timah Road – to Fort Canning.

Passing shell craters, burnt-out cars and trucks, and other traces of the recent severe fighting, we entered Singapore city, which was a whirlpool of chaos. . . . The first thing in the city to strike the eye was the waves of men in khaki uniforms. Many of them still carried their rifles, walking about and nibbling bread. Groups of them were squatting on the road smoking, talking and shouting in rather loud voices. Strangely enough, however, there was no sign of hostility in their faces. Rather there was an expression of resignation as is shown by the losers in fierce sporting contests.

Tsuji went on to report that headquarters had been cleaned up and that an orderly hand-over took place. This was all very 'correct' and there seems, at least on the part of Yamashita, to have been no sense of ill will. Much of the Japanese conduct, good and bad, was simply capricious, and a pre-conceived plan of ill-treatment is difficult to prove.

But dreadful atrocities were committed, both in battle and after the surrender, and these cannot simply be ignored. Some Japanese, it is true, were horrified after the war when the full enormity of their crimes was brought home to them, and the British executed some 200 Japanese for crimes committed against British subjects.

The tendency has been to regard the fighting troops in a better light than those who followed on afterwards, but it is difficult to differentiate between the two. As a survivor has testified:

. . . the Manchester Regiment were holding [on] until they became overwhelmed and had to retreat out of it. They got reinforcements and went back in again at the first light of day the next morning, only to find that the Japanese had executed every Malayan civilian, man, woman and child, in that kampong, by the sword. They'd cut their heads off and impaled them on the spikes of the railings . . . there were 40 heads and they remained there three or four months after we were captured. There had been four or five British troops who had not got out in time – they were found nailed to the trees.

'Special' Japanese treatment was almost immediately meted out to the Chinese population who had been active for years in collecting money for the war against Japan in their homeland. The China Relief Fund had collected millions of dollars and had acted as the rallying point for expatriate Chinese all over the East. While most Malays were more or less apathetic to the change of power, the Chinese knew well what was in store for them. Just how many disappeared without trace will probably never be known, and quite a few Malays used the golden opportunity to pay off old scores by informing. In a small book published in Singapore just after the war, N. I. Low and H. M. Cheng recorded:

The raping varied in intensity. Some localities suffered more and some less. . . . Barricades had gone up all over Singapore, at which all were searched before they were allowed to proceed, or refused passage, as the whims of the sentry dictated. At one barricade a Chinese pedalling a loaded tricycle was told to stop. He did so, but the moment the sentry turned away to deal with someone else, he made off as fast as he could. He was overtaken and manhandled, made to kneel down and was clouted on the head until he fainted. When he came to he was thrashed until he fainted again.

The first period of robbery, rape and humiliation was followed by an organised round-up of the Chinese community. The handful of desperadoes of Dalforce were the excuse, and the Chinese were handed over to the mercies of the Second Field *Kempetai* (military police) for suitable chastisement. Orders were issued by Lieutenant-Colonel Satoru Dishi, and on the afternoon of 17 February, the Chinese were told to congregate at specified points. The Reverend James Song was a boy of ten at the time, but he remembers what happened:

We were living in Singapore and from there we were all driven and made to walk about six or seven miles to a place in the country where we just had to find accommodation. Fortunately we had an uncle who lived there, and we sort of camped in his house. Then all the men above the age of fourteen were called up and paraded in front of the Japanese. Anyone who had what they thought were rather rough palms indicating that they had been soldiers or something . . . were taken away. Something like 20,000 of them were shot. We were near the sea and for days afterwards we saw bodies floating up on the seashore. . . . Because human beings are very funny, you may have neighbours, trusted neighbours, but when you are driven away into a temporary concentration camp, the neighbours come and plunder your houses.

While the Chinese suffered, the day after the surrender was almost like a holiday for the British, both civilian and military, as initially the Japanese were little in evidence. In accordance with orders, the key people stayed at their posts and struggled to keep the essential services going. Some soldiers, however, saw their conquerors at uncomfortably close quarters. One soldier had been on an errand and was then told to return to his unit:

I was going back along the Bukit Timah Road . . . and a half drunken Japanese motorcyclist who had this enormous 'Indian' motorcycle and side-car, stopped me and told me to leave my machine where it was in the gutter and to get into his side-car. . . . He kept saying 'you my prisoner'. So, I had to sit in this side-car which had no seat in it. There were grenades rolling about and bottles of the rice wine they call saki and also rounds of ammunition rolling about. . . . He was going along this main road, revving and roaring along. He was looking at me most of the time, instead of where he was going. Every now and again there was a telegraph pole, and I could see myself getting wrapped around it if he didn't look what he was doing. Anyway, very fortunately, when we got to the next crossroads, there was this Japanese policeman with white gloves on. He put his hand up and stopped him. . . . I lost my friend and was very glad to get out of his clutches.

Senior officers had more direct contact with their conquerors. Major-General Key was sent for and escorted to the headquarters of the Imperial Guards Division where he was received by the Chief of Staff: 'They sat me down at a table,' recalled Key, 'and gave me a glass of milk and a cigarette.' Then the two men started to discuss the war.

'Well,' I said, 'we didn't make this war.'
And he said, 'well, who did?'
'Start with Germany,'
'yes,'
'and Italy,'
'yes',
'then you came into it.'
He said, 'you attacked us.' I said that I was under the impression that you

did all the attacking. We were merely on the defensive.

Brigadier Simson was given a guided tour of the city, including a ringside view of Japanese instant justice.

Between two young Japanese officers in the back seat of a car, I was driven around the streets of Singapore for two hours. It was here that I had an early demonstration of Japanese culture. Some shops were being looted. The car halted, and without an order the two guards in the front seat stood up and fired one shot each into the crowd. The crowd dispersed, and we drove on without a word having been spoken. Near the docks we stopped again to see some fifteen coolies with their arms trussed behind their backs with barbed wire. . . . There were eight Chinese among them. These were separated from the rest and they were then beheaded in front of the crowd by an executioner using a two-handed Samurai sword.

Dennis Russell-Roberts joined the select few at Robinsons and spent a comfortable night on an expensive sofa in the furnishing department. His account of the events of 16 February expresses perfectly the sense of unreality:

some of the officers were playing billiards in the games department, some were selecting suitable footware in the shoe department, but most of them were sitting in silence, a confused and rather sad expression on their faces. . . .

Outside the building not a single Japanese soldier appeared on the streets. . . . Our situation seemed quite unreal.

Then a fellow officer entered the building.

'What about the Japs', I enquired?
'I never ran into one,' he answered. 'There's hardly a Jap on the streets anywhere. It's incredible'.

The prudent ones spent their time amassing the necessities of life to face an unknown future in internment or as prisoners of war. Others were busy doing what they could for the wounded. The Japanese gave orders that the General Hospital had to be evacuated within twenty-four hours. Over a thousand civilians who could walk were simply sent home while the others were transferred to the mental asylum. The military wounded were sent off to a variety of places including the Cathedral, the Singapore Club, the Cricket Club and the Raffles Institute – soon to become the Japanese headquarters.

Like many others without jobs, Vincent Beck, a civilian railway engineer, was working in the Fullerton building:

No news early on, later a communication read to say that the administration would continue as at present. The Japs arrived about 10 a.m. but our flag was still flying after noon. Worked most of the day in hospital on the third floor of our building, stretcher bearing and assisting Matron with dressings.

183

During the course of the morning a Japanese officer visited the Governor at his headquarters at the Singapore Club, and told him that all civilians would have to assemble on the Cricket Club *padang* the following morning (17 February). The military authorities were separately informed that they had to get their men to Changi Camp where they would be imprisoned. The distance from the centre of Singapore to Changi is approximately 15 miles.

Under the name of Sir Shenton Thomas, a communique was issued stating that:

The existing administrative and economic systems continue to exist. . . .

No communication with the outside world is permitted. No person may leave Singapore Island without permission from the Japanese High Command. . . . The Japanese Army will afford protection to the civilian population. . . . It is the duty of every man and woman in Singapore to co-operate in the task of restoring order and cleanliness in the town. . . .

THE MARCH TO CHANGI

Incredible as it may seem, some 85,000 military prisoners tramped off to Changi under the command of their own officers and with hardly a Japanese to be seen. 'Pinkie' Evans remembered:

Lieutenant-Colonel Holmes marched his battalion of the Manchesters to Changi, wearing around his neck His Majesty's portrait. Everywhere on the way to Changi the Malays, Chinese, Tamil and Indians would wave the Rising Sun. We, the white soldiers who they thought would save them, had let them down.

Captain Peter Kemmis-Betty:

and then we started the long trek, all day, into Changi Camp – about a 17 mile walk which a major physical ordeal for the elderly who were already exhausted. The Japanese made the occasion quite dramatic by making clear that they were in command. The occasional Chinese and Malay chap beside the road minding his own business was shot dead just to impress us. . . .

Major-General Key was faced with the problem of moving his whole division. He went back to the Imperial Guards Headquarters where he had earlier been interviewed and succeeded in getting passes for 80 lorries, although the Japanese staff officer 'went red in the face'. He managed to transport a vast amount of supplies into the camp which kept a lot of the men going during the early weeks of captivity.

Captain Russell-Roberts attached himself to one of the columns:

[it] presented a pathetic sight. It was led by at least four files of Brigadiers and full Colonels, each of them laden with kit and carrying attaché cases and all manner of small baggage. Behind them followed a full company of officers and

finally a long line of weary looking soldiers who came from all parts of England. As we passed Raffles Hotel we could see a group of English women in the upstairs windows who signalled to us the V for Victory sign. This encouraged the troops to burst into song. They sang all the old favourites, and how sad they made one feel. When they sang 'There will always be an England' it was too much. Many a pair of eyes grew dim.

Gunner Topping was also in the long trek:

The column grew in size as thousands of British Tommies joined the ranks of marching men, who until yesterday had been free but were now marching into captivity which would stretch over three and a half years of toil and slavery. . . .

The sun beat down on the ever-growing column of prisoners as they wound out from the city suburbs. . . . The march had not taken many miles before the evidence of the 'mess' to be cleaned up was observed all around. The column at one point was compelled to make a detour in the road to pass all that remained of a burnt-out vehicle and its occupants. Two burned and blackened bodies lay among the wreckage, so charred that to tell whether these unidentifiable objects had been friends or foes was impossible. . . .

Further along the road ran close to a row of spiked railings, and adorning the points were the severed heads of several newly executed Malays and Chinese – patriots who had remained faithful to the British crown, their sightless eyes turned in the direction of the silent, dirty and perspiring column as they marched slowly by.

While the bulk of the prisoners were herded into the Changi area, some were not so fortunate. Sergeant McCormack found himself in a special camp reserved for those who had fallen foul of the Japanese. He had been involved with others in the killing of three Japanese on 16 February, not knowing that the surrender had taken effect and was taken off to a camp at Pasir Panjang. En route his party was guarded by Sikhs, who in his words, seemed to have gone over to the enemy 'lock, stock and barrel'. Indeed, it soon became obvious to the prisoners of war that Indians were to be their guards, and British officers were forced to salute Indian privates.

Brigadier Massy-Beresford remembered:

Going from my perimeter to the hospital to see the wounded, I had to go through a series of Indian sentries who had gone over to the Japs. They had their rifles loaded, cocked, and bayonets fixed. They would point them at you. 'Salute properly or we will fire'. . . . In fact those visits to the hospital were a thing that remained in my memory. To have that from the Indian troops, and those who resisted, poor devils, had the most appalling time.

Right from the beginning, the Indians had been destined to play a part in the Japanese dreams of co-prosperity in Asia. On 17 February, all Indian units, without their British officers, were segregated at Farrar Park in Singapore, and subjected to massive pressure to join the Indian

National Army. This had been set up by the Japanese and was led by renegade Indian officers. It was to take part in the liberation of India from British rule, and it was not surprising that many joined. After all, they had been fighting Britain's battles in a country that was not their own. Japanese propaganda offered them a chance to join in the liberation of their country and to shake off the humiliation of being treated as second-class beings. Accused by the British of 'disloyalty' after the war, how could they be expected to be loyal to concepts such as Britain or the British Empire? The Japanese cry of 'Asia for the Asians' had an emotive appeal.

Many, however, remained loyal. The Gurkhas, to a man, displayed courage of the highest order in spite of terrible sufferings in imprisonment. The Indians who refused to join the INA were subjected to inhuman treatment and many were tortured to death or beheaded.

Meanwhile, it was the turn of the civilians, who assembled on the *padang* on the morning of 17 February, headed by the Governor. Lady Thomas, who although ill, had refused to be evacuated, was still in hospital. Some two thousand men who were not required to stay at their posts and about three hundred women and children stood there on the sports ground in the blistering heat. They had been told to bring clothes for ten days and that food would be provided, but then a Japanese official arrived and said that they would have to fend for themselves.

Some of the government officials were allowed to use their cars, but the Governor had been selected for special humiliation and was told that he had to walk. Dressed simply in slacks and a shirt, Sir Shenton stood with the rest on the *padang*, accompanied by his personal assistant, Lesley Davies.

John Burnham was with three friends all from the Sarawak civil service:

We had a stretcher, one person to each end, with our stuff in the middle. Then we were given orders after hanging about for around three hours, to start walking, though nobody knew where. . . . Ever since, whenever I've seen anybody carring a stretcher I've always had the greatest sympathy. My golly, we didn't have much on that stretcher but after two miles it was hell carrying that damn thing. We were all arguing about whose suitcase should be lightened.

Vincent Beck was also one of the internees.

When we arrived at the *padang*, women were separated from the men, boys of nine and over went with the men. We were then lined up and counted . . . and told we would have to walk to a place near the Seaview Hotel. We set out at 1 p.m. having had nothing but a drink of water. We arrived at Nuger flats near the Seaview where we thought we were going, but after a long wait they told us to move again. So we set off and found three places, the women were alone in one big house, the men had the Police Station at Joo Clast and the residences of the late Sutan Kader called Karekal. . . . There was hardly any water at any of the houses, it just dribbled from the taps, and despite promises re. food we had nothing at all that day.

The civilians were concentrated in that area until 5 March, gradually getting themselves organised and managing to forage for some supplies. Then they were moved into the civilian prison at Changi where they were to spend the first period of captivity.

ATTEMPTS AT ESCAPE

Not all those left behind in Singapore went into the bag, and it is necessary to leave the prisoners for a while and to consider the escapees, many of whom made dramatic bids for freedom. A few even managed to get away after being cut off during the fighting up-country, and dodging the Japanese, often hostile natives and the jungle environment, managed to reach the coast. There, they obtained small boats for the hazardous voyage to Sumatra or Java.

One of these was Signalman William Ball who got away after the Slim River battle where he was cut off. He and a small party of British troops wandered in the jungle for a month before they reached the coast, where a Chinese schoolmaster organised a boat to take them to Sumatra.

Most of the escapes, however, were from Singapore Island. In official terms, anyone who left before the surrender without permission was a deserter, but afterwards, it was the duty of all military personnel to escape. At the time Singapore fell, Java and Sumatra were still in Allied hands, but not for long. Once the Dutch East Indies had been lost, there was nowhere much to go. In addition, the Japanese did not understand the escaping urge. For those who were caught, it was not a case of a period in solitary confinement as in the German camps. It meant immediate execution.

Eight men escaped from Pudu Gaol at Kuala Lumpur where Russell Braddon was imprisoned, but were soon betrayed by natives – the Japanese offered money for such information. They were brought back and two days later they were seen at the gaol entrance:

All their gear had been dumped near them – haversacks and clothing – but they themselves were still fiercely shackled and were filthy dirty. They looked very weak.

The Japanese motioned them towards the gaol gate. Inquiringly, Van Rennan (one of the escapees) gestured with his foot towards the pile of kit bags. The Japanese nodded negatively, emphatically. It could mean only one thing. They knew it: and we knew it.

The bulk of the European women and children had been evacuated from Singapore during January, as well as a number of non-essential military personnel who were sent away to fight elsewhere. Most of the RAF personnel were taken off to Sumatra and Java, although a few who were left behind, joined up with army units or helped in civil defence.

When it seemed that Singapore was bound to fall, it was decided to evacuate the remaining women and children as well as some male civilians and military technicians. For this purpose a motley collection of small vessels was assembled in the harbour area. It is impossible to give an exact figure, but around seventy 'little ships' left between 10 and 16 February – most of them being either captured or sunk by naval gunfire or bombing.

On the evening of Wednesday, 11 February, a large group of civilians and military nurses left on four small ships that had been serving as naval auxiliaries. Included in the party were the technicians and broadcasters from the Malayan Broadcasting Service, Cable and Wireless Staff, the Ministry of Information officials, engineers and other specialists who had been permitted to leave. The ships were the *Giang Bee*, the *Vyner Brooke*, the *Mata Hari* and the *Kung Wo* and they were accompanied by a number of smaller craft.

Giles Playfair, who was on the staff of the MBC, wrote about the departure from Singapore:

In the twilight we stood around in mournful little groups and watched Singapore burning. It was a terrible awe-inspiring sight and I would like to have photographed it, although I knew that in any case it would never fade from my memory. It really did seem as if the whole island was alight, but at times great new sheets of flame would leap into the sky, and we would know that yet another store of incalculable wealth had been set ablaze and would soon be worthless.

The scenes at the harbour entrance during these last few days were pretty hair-raising. Many accounts speak of armed parties of deserters storming boats that were leaving. Sentries were placed on the dock gates and attempts were made to keep order. Gerald Scott, an employee of the Shell Company had stayed behind to help in the distribution of petroleum products to the essential users. He had to take a lorry into the docks on the evening of 13 February with supplies for a launch which he and some others from the company were to use to make their escape – with full authorisation. In his diary he described the scene while waiting for a permit to enter the docks:

I had driven the lorry to within a few yards of the gates but now I decided to back her away a bit as we were now surrounded by several thousand soldiers. The guard commander was getting apprehensive lest any trouble should break out. He ordered the British troops to give way and clear a space in front of his gates and the Australians had to do the same on the other side. The soldiers quietly moved back but some Australians lingered. The guard commander was getting a bit rattled. 'If you blighters don't get back I'll let you have it,' he shouted. In the silence that followed a rifle was cocked. The situation looked nasty. Suddenly one of our party stepped forward and said 'look here you chaps – this won't get us anywhere – we're all trying to get through these gates – where's your sense of humour?' It did the trick – the Australians moved back.

Unknown to those who were planning to escape, a Japanese naval task force was moving into the Banka Strait between Sumatra and Java, and a landing was made at Palembang on 14 February. Thus they were leaping from the frying pan into the fire.

On the morning of 12 February, the cruiser *Durban* and three other naval vessels left Singapore, escorting two merchant ships carrying the remainder of the RAF ground crews and men from the Naval Base. On board the *Empire Star* was RAF Corporal William Lee, en route for Batavia:

A character, Ginger by name, and I, agreed to man the only old Hotchkiss gun on the for'ard deck. Late morning and the now familiar three Japanese aircraft appeared from the direction of Singapore. There was no apparent panic. Ginger and I to the Hotchkiss gun. Other RAF men grabbed rifles and machine guns and lined the ship's rails. The Japanese were overhead. The destroyers' anti-aircraft guns opened fire. . . . Everyone armed opened fire. Bullets and shrapnel seemed to be everywhere.

After the larger ships had all left, there were still many launches and other small craft left in the harbour. As Noel Barber wrote:

More than war, more than bombs and shells, more than the shadow of defeat, Friday the 13th left a lasting legacy of bitterness which persists to this day, because of another extraordinary 'secret' evacuation.

This particular day became known as Black Friday. Early in the morning a meeting was called at Fort Canning to plan the evacuation of 'key military personnel' in some forty small boats which were still available. Brigadier Simson was at the meeting and was allotted 300 places for 'young technical civilians who would be needed to continue the war elsewhere'. Of these places he distributed 75 to the Public Works Department which was headed by a Mr. Nunn. In spite of the Governor's order that heads of departments were to remain until the last, Nunn gave passes to himself and his wife who had apparently refused to be evacuated without him. They left that evening along with a large number of others, most of whom were either captured or died at sea – including the Nunns.

The ships which had left during the night of 11–12 February had in the meanwhile met their fate. After creeping through the minefields which guarded the approaches to Singapore, they headed south towards Sumatra or Java, sitting targets for the swarms of Japanese bombers. Frank Brewer was on board the *Grasshopper*, an aged gunboat.

The next morning at daylight (12 February) there were three of our small ships in line ahead steaming down the channel on the Sumatra side of the Lingaa Archipelago. At about 0800 hours a Jap seaplane circled around and let go one bomb which missed. I thought this was not a good omen for the day, and it was not, for about 1100 hours there were two squadrons of Jap bombers over us. They first got the *Dragonfly* with eleven hits simultaneously and she went down in three minutes. It was a ghastly sight as she was only half a mile ahead of us and I had a full view . . . there were only about six survivors. Our gunboat had been very cleverly handled by the commander, and by quick use of the helm he had missed the first two sticks aimed at us. . . . By the time the third stick hit us we were only six hundred yards off the nearest island. Luckily not one of the three bombs which hit us disabled either the engine or the helm. . . . As soon as we were hit the commander made straight for the shore and put the gunboat aground as we were on fire. . . . We got all the wounded and unwounded ashore that afternoon and slept that night in the jungle.

After further adventures, Mr. Brewer managed to reach safety at Colombo.

The *Vyner Brooke* had about 200 people on board, including a contingent of Army Nurses and civilian men, women and children. While heading for the Banka Strait she was hit by two bombs, one of which burst in the main saloon. Sister Betty Jeffrey gave a graphic description of the end of the *Vyner Brooke* in her book *White Coolies*:

I had been so busy helping people over the side that I had to go in a very big hurry myself. Couldn't find a rope ladder so tried to be a Tarzan and slip down a rope. Result, terribly burnt fingers, all skin missing from six fingers and both palms of my hands; they seemed quite raw. I landed with an awful thud and my tin hat landed on top of me. . . . We all swam well away from her and grabbed anything that floated and hung onto it in small groups. We hopelessly watched the *Vyner Brooke* take her last roll and disappear under the waves.

After hours spent in the water or in the two lifeboats that got away, the survivors made the shore, only to be captured by the Japanese. Some of those in the water were picked up by two young RAF officers in an outboard motor boat and ferried to the shore. This act of mercy cost the officers their lives, as a Japanese naval vessel arrived on the scene and machine-gunned them.

The *Giang Bee* managed to steam 160 miles from Singapore when she ran into a group of Japanese warships. The captain tried to surrender but could not understand the Japanese signals. Finally he ordered his passengers to abandon ship, but when they tried to row to the destroyers, the latter refused to have anything to do with them. Finally, at about 10.30 in the evening of 13 February, the *Giang Bee* was sunk by gunfire and the warships simply made off. The castaways managed to reach land on Sumatra but were soon rounded up and interned.

The *Mata Hari* met a similar fate to the others in the convoy. On Sunday, 15 February, she met the flotillas that had sunk the *Giang Bee* while off the port of Palembang. She was forced to surrender, but while waiting to be boarded, those on board witnessed a most gallant action. On the scene came HM Motor Launch 311 which was commanded by Lieutenant Christmas of the RNZVR, bound for Java. The Japanese warships opened fire and the ML sped into the attack with her ensign flying. Armed with a three-pounder pop-gun and two machine guns, she engaged the enemy at close quarters but was simply blown out of the water.

One could continue on this theme for many pages and the escapes from Singapore are worth a whole book on their own. So far we have managed just a sketch of some of the official escapes, but there were numerous private enterprise efforts, the most famous of which was the departure of Major-General Gordon Bennett about which there is still controversy. On the night of 15–16 February, together with a small party, he slipped away without informing Percival that he was going and without appointing a successor. His own justification was that it was his duty to survive in order to be able to offer the benefit of his experience of fighting the Japanese. Nobody would deny his personal bravery, but his conduct was made the subject of an official enquiry in Australia. He never again commanded troops in the field.

Cecil Prime was one of a group of nine NCOs and officers, all of whom were artillery specialists, who late in the evening of 13 February were detailed for evacuation. They went to the docks, only to be told that there was no ship for them. They hung around all through the Saturday bombarded with orders and counter-orders, until finally they were told to arrange their own escape. One of the officers found a lifeboat and they launched this early on the Sunday morning. While rowing away from the shore they came across a steam launch and transferred onto it. By then the group had been expanded by stragglers to 25, and incredible as it may seem, they managed to get up steam. Two hours before the city surrendered they put to sea and in spite of frequent groundings and the absence of a chart, they reached safety in Java.

'Gabby' Gavin of the East Surreys found that his Jungle Warfare unit had disintegrated, and on the afternoon of 15 February, he made his way to the docks with a few friends.

I despatched Len and the orderlies in search of supplies while I took Joe with me to get a boat, by fair means or foul. I got one too, a sampan broad in the beam and sound, even if it was only nine feet long. I planted Joe in it with my Tommy gun while I went after oars which were missing from the boat.

I eventually had to get into the harbour and swim after oars, going from one craft to another until I had, not oars, but six paddles, short and stumpy, but better than nothing.

He lost his own friends on the docks but collected substitutes in the form of three very drunken soldiers. The four of them left on the morning of 16 February, simply paddling out into the Malacca Strait.

I put Little Jock . . . in the prow of the sampan to look for mines which probably never existed although Little Jock saw several. He would have seen the Loch Ness Monster if he'd thought about it, but anyway, despite his mines we crept safely forward to the headland.

This venture was one of the lucky ones, and Gavin managed to follow the chain of islands towards the South, although he was later captured. Most of the others who set out in frail craft never made it.

The prisoners of war and the internees were, meanwhile, settling down to what was to be three and a half years of bitter captivity, although they did not know this at the time. The civilians especially were bouyed up by constant rumours that they would be exchanged for Japanese nationals in Allied hands. Once in Changi camp, the military found themselves left largely to their own devices. The British sense of order soon asserted itself. Officers' messes were set up and privilege caused deep resentment. On the other hand, without the bonds of discipline, the plight of the men could have been far worse. With certain exceptions, the officers set a fine example, and once the working parties had been sent off up into Siam, rank ceased to have any meaning at all – all were equally starved and wore only loin cloths. Throughout the period of captivity, hunger was to be the constant companion.

Captain Walter Salmon, who survived the massacre at the Alexandra Military Hospital, was transferred to Changi where he went into the hospital:

the beds, such as they were, were absolutely touching, no way round them at all. But I take my hat off to the medical staff there, they did absolute wonders with nothing and under the most appalling conditions. I'll never forget the rations, because our chaps couldn't cook rice for love nor money in those days. It just used to come out like bill posters' glue on big plates and stuck on the top was one cube of pineapple. That was your meal at about 8 o'clock in the morning and you had the same thing at lunch time and the same thing in the evening, with a mug of tea, no milk and no sugar. . . . There were a certain amount of rations available, tinned rations, but I'm sorry to say that such rations weren't distributed fairly. I know of two men who boasted that they never tasted rice for two years.

The first few weeks witnessed terrible overcrowding, but gradually the various units sorted themselves out. Later, the Japanese organised a series of perimeters which separated the larger formations, and one had to obtain permission to move from one to the other. G. K. Topping wrote:

A new life was opening up before every man at Changi, a life totally alien from that which was experienced by even the poorest of poor living in the meanest hovel in England, but as the months dragged slowly by, conditions began slowly to adjust themselves. The Japanese called for parties to work in Singapore, unloading ships in the docks.

For many, these working parties were a welcome release from boredom and a golden opportunity to steal rations or other items. They worked under the command of British officers and were guarded by the Japanese.

The tribulations of the prisoners belong to another book. Over the years they were split up, many being sent to work on the infamous railway in Siam. The 'lucky' ones were those who stayed behind in Changi who later had to work on the construction of an airfield for the Japanese. When the internees were moved out of the prison at Changi, the soldiers were moved in.

After about three weeks billeted in houses under guard, the civilians were collected together at the gaol, and as they marched inside its grim doors, they struck up 'There'll always be an England'. Vincent Beck wrote in his diary:

Clayton, Hossack and myself fixed ourselves in a cell BIII 29, and was it hard. The cells in our block were intended for one Asiatic prisoner and had a big concrete slab in the middle for the bed and an Asiatic lavatory in one corner. We had to sleep one on the slab and one on each side. Others slept in workshops on the ground floor, in the exercise yards etc. There was no water when we arrived. . . . The prison was built for 650 prisoners and you can imagine that with nearly 2,800 in it, every facility is overstrained.

The wives and children were rigorously separated, and no communication was allowed. The internees were not made to work, and spent their time in thinking about the next meal, in trying to grow vegetables and in amateur theatricals. Radios were soon in action, but these were subsequently discovered, and some of their owners were executed.

Every FEPOW and internee has his or her story to tell, albeit a grim one. Those who came home survived an ordeal almost too terrible to describe in prose – an ordeal that brought out the very best in them, and in some cases the very worst. Sergeant Bill Homfrey wrote the following while in hospital in March 1945 at a time when Europe was getting ready to celebrate the end of its war:

There are some mean, greedy, thieving, selfish people about whose deeds make one despair for the future of the British race. It is well to believe that these people are only a small minority, but at times it seems to be the policy of the majority. When we drew into the quayside in India there were many who laughed at the natives rushing for and squabbling over the cigarettes we were gracious enough to throw them. I am glad to remember, now, that that pastime didn't attract me at the time. I have since seen the same 'gracious ones' – now prisoners – scrambling for cigarettes themselves. There are some who will even go to the swill tubs of the IJA or pick up 'dog ends' around the Nippon billets, first making sure that they are seen, so as to gain the sympathy of the IJA. Taking extra rations from our own cookhouses is only too common; uneven distribution being one method of favouring the few. Stealing clothes, and other things, and selling them was very prevalent; but now there is not much left to get hold of. Selling drugs, marmite and other medical comforts for personal gain was another and more wicked vice which, I am glad to say, has now been almost entirely stamped out.

I have, however, met quite a number of honest men – men who have thought things out a bit for themselves and realised how selfish they used to be. How we used to take the comforts of home for granted. How angry we used to get if the dinner wasn't on the table just when we wanted it. How often have we been rude and disgruntled for no real reason. It is so difficult to some of us to make 'small talk' and so easy to laze in a chair when we might be helping in the house or garden. In future, we now, we will be unselfish and pleasant at home. I hope this resolution will last, but am afraid that after a few months at home we may forget this lesson.

9

AFTERTHOUGHTS

Singapore, mighty fortress.
Guardian of the East.
The Japanese didn't think so.
They took it in a week.

'Pinkie' Evans,
The Manchester Regiment

THE prisoners and internees had three and a half years to mull over the fate which had befallen them, and much of their time was spent in discussion – and recrimination. In the mass of literature which has appeared since, blame has been apportioned in thick slices – to the civilians in Malaya, the army, the high command, and the Government in England. It is not our purpose to point the finger in any particular direction, and the reader, having studied the evidence, can make up his or her own mind. It is, however, worth looking briefly at some of the verdicts on the tragedy of Singapore.

It must be recognised from the outset that the historian writing forty years after the close of the campaign has the benefit of working under the bright light of hindsight, and is far better informed than those on the spot at the time, who had to stake their reputations and frequently their lives on the basis of judgement which was often little more than a gamble. All the actors in the tragedy – even the Japanese – became familiar with what the Prussian military theorist Clausewitz termed 'friction'. We recognise the same phenomenon as 'grit in the works', and speak of 'Sod's Law' or 'Murphy's Law': if something can possibly go wrong, it will inevitably do so. The more complicated a command structure is, the more likely it is that it will fail to work satisfactorily under pressure. In Malaya and Singapore there were far too many cooks tinkering with the broth.

195

Two major issues merit our consideration. Firstly, given the balance of forces at the start of the campaign, was the fall of Singapore inevitable, and secondly, even if disaster was bound to occur eventually, could more capable commanders have postponed the evil day? There is no doubt that the garrison of Singapore and Malaya was, in December 1941, well below the level that all competent authorities deemed essential for successful defence against a major attack. There were, as we have seen, weighty reasons for this: British and Commonwealth forces were desperately overstretched, and Singapore came, as Percival recognised, 'a poor third' in terms of strategic priorities.

The root cause of this overstretch lay in the general attitude of the democracies and the actions of a series of British governments in the inter-war years. The holocaust of the First World War caused a general revulsion for things military, and a widely-held belief in the 1920s that an age of universal peace and general disarmament had dawned contributed to a reluctance to take the problems of defence seriously. Britain, her centuries of parliamentary democracy overlaid with bitter folk-memories of Cromwell's major-generals and a lingering suspicion of standing armies, has traditionally neglected her defences in times of peace.

In his book *The Hunting of Force Z*, Richard Hough probes at the heart of the matter.

It is the people themselves, subject to the hopeful, fumbling, imperfect workings of democracy, who are fully responsible for their own defence. They, understandably, and invariably, demand security at the lowest possible cost.

It is notoriously difficult to evaluate the cost-effectiveness of defence. Politicians, for perfectly understandable reasons, tend to look upon defence expenditure as the premium paid for insurance against an improbable and distant natural disaster. It is only when the storm seems imminent that they are prepared to pay an adequate premium, but at this stage, almost by definition, they cannot obtain the cover they so urgently require. There has also been a well-established tendency for British governments to accept a mis-match between commitments and capabilities: nowhere was this better illustrated than in the case of Malaya and Singapore.

Louis Allen made a well-balanced assessment of the reasons for Singapore's fall. 'Singapore could have been saved,' he wrote,

by better pre-war planning, by a timely truce to internecine warfare between the services, by adequate wartime reinforcements in planes and tanks, by more decisive leadership on the spot and a true historical perspective at the centre of power, in London, in the two decades before.

Inadequate pre-war planning and lack of a proper historical perspective were both crucial. They prevented those responsible for the defence of Britain and her colonies from taking realistic steps to bridge the gulf that yawned between Britain's world-wide commitments and her ability to match them with the men and machinery of defence.

Given the substantial disadvantages under which the defenders of the Far East laboured on the outbreak of war with Japan, what steps could have been taken to ensure that resistance, even if ultimately unsuccessful, was as prolonged as possible? Churchill was not alone in comparing Percival's performance with that of the American Lieutenant-General Jonathan Wainwright, who held the old island fortress of Corregidor until 6 May.

A more rational command structure would undoubtedly have helped. In a leading article in the *Daily Telegraph* on 15 February 1972, the 30th anniversary of the surrender, Sir Robert Scott – who as Rob Scott had represented the Ministry of Information in Singapore – described the advent of Duff Cooper as 'a classic case of power without responsibility.' He went on to illustrate Cooper's lack of familiarity with the situation.

Locally he failed to grasp the implications of a multi-racial society and he did not take into account our treaty relations with the Malayan Sultans. Evacuation of Penang was one example. To Duff Cooper this meant Europeans. Thomas (the Governor) was adamant that there should be no discrimination on racial grounds. . . . This episode, early in the campaign, did more than any single event to shake public confidence in Britain and to affect relations between the military and civilian administrators for the remainder of the campaign.

. . . A few days after war broke out, Duff Cooper set up a War Council with himself in the chair. It was a stormy meeting. Brooke-Popham pointed out that he took his instructions from the Chiefs of Staff, Thomas that he took his from the Colonial Secretary, the Admiral that his were from the Admiralty. . . .

The Singapore War Council was an ineffectual committee debating issues sometimes difficult but relatively secondary. . . . The decisions rested not collectively but with individual members.

One idea that was floated at the time, and has been much discussed subsequently, was for the appointment of a 'supremo' with overriding authority in both civil and military spheres. In early January 1942, Duff Cooper wrote to Lord Moyne, Secretary of State for the Colonies, proposing that Sir Shenton Thomas should be removed, and replaced by a military governor for the duration of the war. The man he proposed was Major-General Keith Simmons, the Fortress Commander – and, incidentally, one of the few senior officers whose reputation had not been tarnished by the defeats up-country. Duff Cooper also discussed his idea with Brigadier Simson, but by then it was, in any case, far too late.

Brigadier Massy-Beresford still has strong feelings on this issue. When he landed with his brigade of 18th Division, he was amazed by the lack of a feeling of urgency. He believes that the appointment of a 'Monty' type of personality, as he puts it, could have done wonders in promoting the spirit of resistance, and that improvisation could have solved a lot of problems. The rear echelons could have been ruthlessly combed to put men with rifles in the front line. A commander prepared to fight to the bitter end would have:

removed the bulk of the population – pushed them over the causeway or out to the islands, and cut it down to a few thousand. And then . . . abandoned nine-tenths of the vehicles, taken the tarpaulins off them and collected water. After all, at intervals it poured buckets. . . .

A 'Monty' given full powers six weeks ahead (of the Japanese invasion of Singapore Island) could have done something, but nobody could have hung out for three years. It would have gone in the end.

This sort of argument cannot be dimissed merely as wishful thinking. If one resolute man had been given overall powers in good time, an abject surrender could have been turned into an epic defence that would rank with Malta or Leningrad. But at what a cost. A last-ditch defence of Singapore after the expulsion of the population would have done more damage to Britain's status in the Far East than the surrender itself. It would have been seen as ample evidence of Britain's lack of concern for her colonial population and her willingness to turn a thriving Asian city into a battlefield. The end would have been bitter indeed, and might not have justified the means.

There was some talk of appointing Wavell as supremo in Singapore, rather than giving him the somewhat vague ABDA command. He seems to have believed at the time that resistance could be usefully prolonged, 'if the troops can be made to act with sufficient vigour and determination.' There was more than a little truth in his assertions that:

The trouble goes a long way back; climate, the atmosphere of the country (the whole of Malaya has been asleep for at least two hundred years), lack of vigour in our peacetime training. . . . But the real trouble is that for the time being we have lost a good deal of our hardness and fighting spirit.

Percival resented this harsh judgement. He pointed out that, at the time, Wavell was 'a disappointed man', having been sacked from his command in the Middle East. 'He therefore,' complained Percival, 'resorted as commanders have frequently done, to blaming his subordinates.' But Wavell undoubtedly had considerable ability. Sir Robert Scott noted that:

Field-Marshal Wavell . . . made a great impact on the tired and beaten troops as I saw when, the day after the disaster at Slim River, he arrived unexpectedly in the forward area knowing nothing of the events of the night. Had a leader of his standard been in command, the Japanese estimate of 100 days to capture Singapore – against the 70 days it took – might have proved too short. On his last sad visit he told Thomas that he bitterly regretted not having taken personal charge.

Wavell's criticisms were directed as much against Percival himself as they were against his troops. Percival has undoubtedly had a raw deal from posterity. His personal bravery, ability as a staff officer and genuine concern for the welfare of his troops are all beyond dispute. He found himself fighting a battle whose framework had been pre-ordained long before he took command. The disposition of his forces in the early stage of the campaign was dictated by the need to defend the scattered airfields, a natural consequence of the pre-war policy of basing the defence of Malaya upon air power.

Major-General Woodburn Kirby, in *Singapore: The Chain of Disaster*, suggested that Percival made two major mistakes. He failed:

First, to concentrate in the vital area west of the central range his forces which were at the outbreak of war scattered all over Malaya to defend the airfields, . . . second, to make every effort to construct field and anti-tank defences at bottlenecks on the north–south communications and to ensure that the three approaches to Johore Bahru were covered by permanent defences on which to retire.

Such a policy of concentration would certainly not have commended itself to Brooke-Popham, to whom it would have looked like the abandonment of the airfields. Moreover, once the Japanese were firmly established in Malaya, the fall of Singapore would have been only a matter of time. Percival was saddled with an impossible plan: by making such modifications to it as lay within his power he could have delayed, but not averted, the fall of Singapore.

Percival's qualities were not such as to suit him for the task of inspiring in his subordinates the determination to fight on to the last ditch. Morrison was close to the truth when he wrote:

He did not know how to deal with any group of men. He was a competely negative person.

He undoubtedly lacked charisma, and that vital but intangible essence which enables a commander to inspire men to the highest pitch of heroism and determination. Percival's humanity showed itself in both his decision to surrender and in his post-war devotion to the welfare of ex-servicemen. In his book on the campaign he refrained from off-loading blame onto the shoulders of others, and avoided levelling accusations at either his superiors or his subordinates. Few defeated generals have shown such equanimity. Percival's tragedy was that he had responsibilities far beyond his capabilities thrust upon him, and that he lacked the ability to inspire and lead.

The appointment of a military supremo, who may well have taken Massy-Beresford's line over the expulsion of at least part of the civilian population, would doubtless have thrown into sharp perspective the differences in attitude between the military and civil authorities. Sir Shenton Thomas regarded his position as one of trust, and felt responsible for all the people – brown, yellow and white – in the colony that had been entrusted to his care. We have seen how furious he was at the evacuation of Europeans only from Penang. The expulsion from Singapore of the native population would have cut clearly across the principles for which Sir Shenton and his subordinates stood.

If the evacuation of Singapore was not a practical possibility, could better use not have been made of locally-raised troops? Frequent accusations were made at the time of the campaign about Fifth Column activities indulged in by the Malays, but these suspicions have never been properly substantiated. Many soldiers who fought in Malaya recall the kindness and sympathy shown towards them during the long retreat. The Malays were described in somewhat patronising tones in the Official History as:

a gentle, dignified but somewhat easy-going race, content to lead a simple life and accept the edicts of their rulers with a good grace.

If, however, we look back to our examination of Nineteenth-Century Malayan history, it will be seen that the Malays were anything but peaceful before the arrival of the British. The concept of the Malay as a quiet and pacific individual owed not a little to the efforts of generations of British colonial administrators.

Pacifying the Malays was one thing, but militarising them was quite another. Victor Purcell took the view that:

If the British government had made it its policy to militarise the people of Malaya before the war, such action would certainly have provoked an international outcry. The pacifists would have declared that we were turning a peaceful people into soldiers in the pursuit of our own imperialistic ambitions.

Lord Strabolgi, writing in 1942, had other ideas on the subject.

To have raised Asiatic armies in Malaya something like a revolution in the outlook and policy of the British Colonial Office was required. In December 1942 the officials . . . still clung to the ideas of the nineteenth century where native populations were concerned. They were treated as immature wards to be defended by a small garrison of European or other alien troops. If the Chinese, for example, were trained to arms, or were armed, the theory of these antediluvians was that they might be in a position to demand political concessions. There was also the ridiculous idea that the white man's prestige demanded that only he should be the armed defender. Yet if the white man could not defend his Asiatic fellow subjects against another Asian power, what became of his prestige?

That the Chinese could fight was forcefully demonstrated by the desperadoes of Dalforce. Ian Morrison pointed out that:

There were over half a million Chinese in Singapore. They had made Singapore quite as much as the British had made it. They emerged, in my opinion, from the two months of warfare in Malaya with flying colours.

After a visit to Dalforce, with which he was favourably impressed, Morrison lamented that the arming of Chinese volunteers had taken place two years too late. 'They had what the Indian and Malay troops lacked,' he wrote,

a personal venom against the Japanese. . . .They were inspired by something which nearly all the other fighting forces lacked. If they had been better trained and better equipped, they might have played a vital role in the fighting on the mainland.

It is often asserted that there were insufficient weapons available to arm a proportion of the native population. There certainly was a shortfall of modern small-arms when the decision to raise Dalforce was eventually taken. The under-employed workshops of the Naval Base could have been used to produce improvised weapons, but there were few other facilities for the production of war materials in Singapore or Malaya. Britain tended to regard her colonies as a source of raw materials and a market for manufactured goods. The establishment of manufacturing industries in the colonies was actively discouraged, as this would have given rise to competition for British industry. This policy meant that, when faced with war on their own doorsteps, the colonies had to rely on the import of all war materials.

Louis Allen suggested that the real impact of the loss of Singapore was:

not a strategic one, but a moral one. The British relationship with those races of Asia they protected began to crumble, as the Japanese moved down the Peninsula. The Europeans moved out, the Asians were left in the path of the invader.

After the surrender the Japanese had a propaganda field-day. Although they soon lost their credibility in the eyes of most of the native inhabitants, some of the anti-British vitriol burned deep. A guerrilla movement grew up, largely Communist-inspired, which was to a great extent armed and equipped by British agents. But the 'Malayan People's Anti-Japanese Army' transmuted itself after the war into the 'Malayan People's Anti-British Army', and during the Malayan Emergency the British found themselves fighting some of the very people they helped to arm and train.

The Reverend James Song, in Singapore during the Japanese occupation, pointed to this link between resistance to the Japanese and subsequent opposition to the British.

Those who hated the Japanese got involved in the guerrilla fighting. And they brought back with them a lot of propaganda about the shortcomings of the British. And virtually overnight when the war was over, the word got around that the British were wonderful masters in the past, but it would be much nicer if we were masters of our own fate. When the war was over, it was virtually at the same time that British influence in Singapore had come to an end.

Britain's post-war decision to relinquish Malaya and Singapore had a variety of motives. It was one element of a widespread retreat from Empire, a withdrawal dictated by a mixture of local and international pressure, ideological and economic trends, and the belated realisation of the unrealistically wide spread of Britain's commitments. The roots of this decision stretch back at least as far as the fall of Singapore, and there is ample evidence that few British soldiers felt the same way about the Empire in 1940 as their grandfathers had. The crusading zeal, the will to win at all costs, to keep the flag flying, had gone for ever.

We have, wherever possible, let the participants in the campaign, great and humble, tell their own stories. A poem by an anonymous but humble member of the RAF, vividly expresses the ennui and resentment of those garrisoning the outposts of an Empire upon which the sun was rapidly setting. It is a fitting end to our story.

The Malayan Malady

The tropic moonlight leaves me cold,
With all its myriad stars untold,
The Black Sumatra's sudden rain,
The tom-tom's maddening refain,
The rubber trees, unlovely whores,
With obscene scars and running sores,
The whining mossies round my net,
Have failed to fascinate me yet.

I hate the morning's blinding light,
I hate the all-suffocating night,
I hate the listless afternoon,
I hate the dark that comes too soon,
The frangipane's cloying smell,
And all the other smells as well.

The futile trek from flick to hop,
The floor shows at the Cathay top,
The naval blokes in portly rig,
Who execute a stately jig,
The Army subs with weak moustache,
The RAF so short of cash,
The shrivelled dames, the men of cheese,
From all of these, I crave release.

The Tuan Besars from Hull and Kent,
The Towkays, Datos, Tenghus too,
The curry tiffins, the evening pahits,
The blaring bands, the shaded lights,
The Colonels' and the Majors' wives,
The smug intrigues, the double lives,
The lovelies at the Bomber Ball,
By Jesus Christ, I hate them all.

I hate the all-pervading stink,
Of squalid crowded Chinatown,
With it bodies yellow, black and brown,
Its salted fish and sundry slops,
The petty spite, the stupid brag,
The social tripe in the local rag,
The vapid bleat
From the girls of the local fishing fleet.

Yes – how I hate this tragic land,
This ceaseless waste of precious time,
The apathetic boredom grim,
In all its aspects fair and bland,
God – how I hate this tragic land.

BIBLIOGRAPHY

1. Despatches

Brooke-Popham, Air Chief Marshal Sir Robert. *Despatch on operations in the Far East from 17 October 1940 to 27 December 1941* (Supplement to the *London Gazette*, 20 January 1948).

Percival, Lieutenant-General A. E. *Despatch on operations of Malaya Command from 8 December 1941 to 15 February 1942* (Supplement to the *London Gazette*, 20 February 1948).

Maltby, Air Vice Marshal Sir Paul. *Despatch on air operations during the campaign in Malaya . . . from 8 December 1941 to 12 March 1942* (Supplement to the *London Gazette*, 20 February 1948).

2. Books

Allen, Louis. *Singapore 1941–1942* (London 1977).

Attiwill, Kenneth. *The Singapore Story* (London 1959).

Barber, Noel. *Sinister Twilight* (London 1968).

Bennett, Lieutenant-General H. Gordon *Why Singapore Fell* (Sydney 1944).

Braddon, Russell. *The Naked Island* (London 1952).

Bryant, Sir Arthur. *The Turn of the Tide* (London 1965).

Caffrey, Kate. *Out in the Midday Sun* (London 1974).

Callahan, Raymond. *The Worst Disaster: The Fall of Singapore* (London 1977).

Churchill, W. S. *The Second World War* (Six volumes: London 1948–54).

Harrison, Kenneth. *The Brave Japanese* (Sydney 1966).

Hough, Richard. *The Hunting of Force Z* (London 1963).

Jeffrey, Betty. *White Coolies* (Sydney 1954).

Leasor, James. *Singapore: The Battle that changed the World.* (London 1968).

Legg, Frank. *The Gordon Bennett Story* (London 1965).

Morrison, Ian. *Malayan Postscript* (London 1942).

Percival, Lieutenant-General A. E. *The War in Malaya* (London 1949).

Rose, Angus. *Who Dies Fighting* (London 1944).

Roskill, Captain S. W. *The War at Sea*, Volume I, *The Defensive* (London 1954).

Russell-Roberts, Denis. *Spotlight on Singapore* (London 1965).

Simson, Brigadier Ivan. *Singapore: too little, too late* (London 1970).

Spencer Chapman, Lieutenant-Colonel F. *The Jungle is Neutral* (London 1963).

Strabolgi, Lord. *Singapore and After* (London 1942).

Swinson, Arthur. *Four Samurai* (London 1968).

Tsuji, Colonel Masanobu. *Singapore: The Japanese Version* (London 1962).

Weller, George. *Singapore is Silent* (New York 1943).

Woodburn Kirby, Major-General S. *Singapore: The Chain of Disaster* (London 1971).

et al. *The War Against Japan*. Volume I, *The Loss of Singapore (Official History)* (London 1957).

3. Unpublished Sources

The authors were fortunate in being granted access to a number of unpublished sources, notably diaries and memoirs. The following were particularly useful:

Beck, Vincent. (Civilian) *Diary.*

Gavin, 'Gabby', (The East Surrey Regiment) *Memoirs.*

Harrison, Colonel A. M. L. (HQ 11th Indian Division) *History of 11th Indian Division.*

Hutchinson, Guy, (Johore Volunteer Engineers) *Memoirs.*

Key, Major-General B. W. (HQ 11th Indian Division) *Notes on the Indian Army and the defence of Kota Bharu.*

Lee, William, (RAF) *Notes.*

Prime, C. W. L. (Royal Artillery) *Notes and Diary.*

Scott, Anne, (Civilian) *Unpublished manuscript.*

Scott, Gerald, (Civilian) *Diary and personal letters.*

Topping, G. K. (Royal Artillery) *Memoirs.*

Toze, Alan, (Royal Artillery) *Notes and sketches.*

Many of the above also granted interviews: a full list of acknowledgements follows. It should, however, be emphasised that our use of unpublished or interview material does not presume that our conclusions and judgements are necessarily those of the survivors who so kindly furnished the material.

ACKNOWLEDGEMENTS

Our gratitude for their very kind permission to include in this volume passages from the undermentioned work is due to the following authors (or their executors, trustees or representatives) and publishers:–

Mr W. David Mason, for quotations from his forthcoming *The Blind Mice*.

Mr Louis Allen, for quotations from *Singapore 1941–42* (Davis-Poynter).

The Macmillan Press Ltd, for quotations from A. G. Donahue's *Last Flight From Singapore*.

Mr Richard Hough, for quotations from *The Hunting of Force Z* (Collins).

Leo Cooper, for quotations from Brigadier Ivan Simson's *Singapore: too little, too late*.

The literary estate of F. Spencer Chapman and Chatto and Windus Ltd, for quotations from *The Jungle is Neutral*.

Mr Russell Braddon, for quotations from *The Naked Island* (Bodley Head).

Jonathan Cape Ltd, for quotations from Angus Rose's *Who Dies Fighting*.

Mr James Leasor, for quotations from *Singapore: The Battle that changed the World* (Hodder & Stoughton).

Associated University Presses for quotations from Raymond Callahan's *The Worst Disaster*.

Faber and Faber for quotations from Ian Morrison's *Malayan Postscript*.

The Controller of Her Majesty's Stationery Office for quotations from Major-General S. Woodburn Kirby *et al.*, *The War against Japan*, Vol. I, *The Loss of Singapore*.

Alec Harrison and Associates on behalf of Ken Attiwill, for quotations from *Singapore Story* (Frederick Muller Ltd).

Angus and Robertson for quotations from Lieutenant-General H. Gordon Bennett's *Why Singapore Fell*.

Ure Smith Pty. Ltd for quotations from Colonel Masonobu Tsuji's *Singapore: The Japanese Version* (Constable).

Mr Noel Barber for quotations from *Sinister Twilight* (Collins).

George Philip & Son Ltd for quotations from Dennis Russell-Roberts' *Spotlight on Singapore*.

Cassell Ltd for quotations from Winston S. Churchill's *The Second World War* and Major-General S. Woodburn Kirby's *Singapore: The Chain of Disaster*.

Angus and Robertson (UK) Ltd for quotations from Betty Jeffrey's *White Coolies*.

Mr Ken Harrison for quotations from *The Brave Japanese*.

Many people involved in the campaign were good enough to discuss their experiences with us. We are particularly grateful to:–

Mrs Betty Jeffrey, Mr M. C. March, Mr Ken Harrison, Mr Jack Sammons, Mr Ian Wingfield, Mr W. David Mason, Mr Harold Burn, Lt. Col. P. Kemmis-Betty, Mr William Lee, Mr M. L. Durrant, Mrs Vera Magnay, Mr and Mrs T. Morris, Mr and Mrs Gerald Scott, Mr J. Burnham, Wg. Cdr. T. Vigors, Maj. Gen. W. Key, Mr M. Selfe, Brig. T. H. Massey-Beresford, Rev. James Song, Capt. W. Salmon, Mr. C. Prime, Sir Robert Scott, Mr W. Homfrey, Mr G. P. Adams, Mrs K. Clarke, Gp. Capt. F. Griffiths. Mr J. Notley, Mr A. Toze, Mr L. Davis, The Countess of St. Germans, Gp. Capt. H. S. Darley, Capt. Eric Strong.

Mr Patrick Mahoney kindly allowed us to make use of his research material for his book *Battleship* (with Martin Middlebrook).

SELECT INDEX
of the More Important Places and Persons
Mentioned or Quoted in the text

March, Charles; 58, 149.
Massy-Beresford, Brig. T.; 154, 163, 165, 170, 178, 185, 198, 200.
'Matador'; 70, 77 et seq, 84, 98.
Matsuoka, Yosuke; 49.
Maxwell, Lt-Col.; 58, 159, 163.
Mersing; 23, 68, 72, 126, 131.
Moir, Brig.; 68, 125.
Moorhead, Lt-Col. H.D.; 85, 123, 125.
Morris, Terry; 22, 28.
Morrison, Ian; 4, 8, 130, 153, 210.
Muar; 134.
Murray-Lyon, Maj-Gen.; 68, 87, 97 et seq, 116.
Mutaguchi. Lt-Gen. R.; 65.

Napier, Lt-Col.; 112.
Nagasaki; 32.
Nishimura, Lt-Gen. T.; 64, 159.
Noble, Adm. Sir P.; 38, 47.

Paget, Lt-Gen. Sir B.; 74.
Pahang; 68, 124.
Painter, Brig.; 68, 124, 138.
Palliser, Rear-Adm. A.F.E.; 77, 91 et seq.
Paris, Brig.; 68, 122, 132, 152, 158.
Patani; 22, 63, 69, 81, 116.
Pearl Harbor; 62, 95.
Penang; 10, 44, 56, 65, 68–9, 109 et seq, 116, 142, 200.
Perak; 11, 60, 70.
Perak River; 115–7, 122, 124.
Percival, Lt-Gen. A.E.; 5, 22, 55 et seq, 64 et seq, 73, 77, 83, 97, 102, 104, 110, 114 et seq, 118, 120, 124 et seq, 131 et seq, 137–9, 141, 143, 146 et seq, 155 et seq, 168 et seq, 177–9, 198.
Peringat; 79.
Perlis; 63, 68, 73.
Perry, Commodore; 32.
Phillips, Adm. Sir T.; 75, 90 et seq.
Port Arthur; 17, 33.
Port Dickson; 56, 72.
Port Swettenham; 125.

Pownall, Lt-Gen. Sir H.; 74, 118–9, 130.
Prime, C.W.M.; 164, 191.
Prince of Wales; 75, 77, 90 et seq, 110–11, 142.
Province Wellesley; 12, 71.
Pulford, A.V.M. C.W.; 55, 59, 77, 83, 80, 117, 132, 139, 154, 157.

Raffles, Sir Thomas Stanford; 10.
Raffles Hotel; 13, 165, 178, 185.
Repulse; 75, 77, 91 et seq, 110–11, 142.
Rich, Flt.Sgt. C.; 90.
Rose, Angus; 65, 67, 77, 140, 155, 158, 168.
Russell-Roberts, Lt.Col. D.; 6, 26, 183–4.

Saeki, Lt-Col.; 101, 105.
Salmon, Cpt. W.; 170, 192.
Sansom, Sir G.; 96.
Scarf, Sq.Ldr. A.K.S.; 89–90.
Scott, Gerald; 142, 188.
Scott, Sir Robert; 96, 197–8.
Seletar; 18, 83, 154.
Selfe, Montague; 7, 110.
Sembawang; 154, 164.
Shanghai; 19.
Shogunate; 31 et seq.
Simmons, Maj-Gen. K.; 56, 68–9, 72, 121, 137, 148, 152, 158, 180, 197.
Simpson, Brig. Ivan; 59, 73, 120, 143 et seq, 167, 178, 182, 189, 197.
Singora; 22, 53, 63, 69, 80, 88 et seq, 132.
Slim River; 121 et seq, 199.
Song, Rev. James; 181, 202.
Spencer-Chapman, F.; 117.
Stewart, Lt-Col. Ian; 69, 122, 126, 140.
Strabolgi, Lord; 1, 9, 200.
Stungei Muar; 134.
Sungei Bata; 105.
Sungei Patani; 60, 68, 88–9, 98, 100, 117.
Sydney; 16.